Realistic Visionary

Realistic Visionary

A PORTRAIT OF
George Washington

PETER R. HENRIQUES

UNIVERSITY OF VIRGINIA PRESS
CHARLOTTESVILLE AND LONDON

University of Virginia Press
© 2006 by the Rector and Visitors of the University of Virginia
All rights reserved
Printed in the United States of America on acid-free paper

First published 2006

9 8 7 6 5 4 3 2 1

LIBRARY OF CONGRESS CATALOGING-IN-PUBLICATION DATA

Henriques, Peter R.
   Realistic visionary : a portrait of George Washington / Peter R. Henriques.
      p.   cm.
   Includes bibliographical references and index.
   ISBN 0-8139-2547-9 (cloth : alk paper)
 1. Washington, George, 1732–1799. 2. Presidents—United States—Biography.
 3. Generals—United States—Biography. I. Title.
   E312.H54 2006
   973.4′1092—dc22

                                                                    2005028801

Frontispiece: Houdon bust of George Washington. (Photo by Nina Leen, courtesy of Time and Life Pictures/Getty Images)

For my wife, Marlene,
And my four sons, Mark, Tom, Gregg, and Tim

There is nothing like a family
and a love that is always there.

Contents

Preface

> I fancy the skill of this Gentleman's Pencil, will be
> put to it, in describing to the World what manner
> of Man I am.—*George Washington*

OBJECTIVE EVIDENCE FOR ASSERTING THAT GEORGE WASHING-
ton deserves the premier position among all American statesmen is
overwhelming. Americans in the eighteenth century were a divided
and fractious people, but somehow George Washington—and he
alone—was the one man who united all hearts. His popularity among
his contemporaries and his record of accomplishment remain unchal-
lenged. He was unanimously elected commander in chief of the Continental Army, unanimously elected president of the Constitutional
Convention, unanimously elected the first president of the United
States, and unanimously reelected president of the United States.
George Washington was truly America's "Indispensable Man," the
essential man not only in winning our independence from Great Britain but also the essential man in the successful effort to write and
ratify our constitution and the essential man in successfully keeping
the country united and at peace during its early vulnerable years, as he
guided a disparate group of states toward genuine nationhood. People
today forget how close the American experiment came to irrevocable
failure and extinction. George Washington was critical in preventing
the collapse of the whole endeavor. Without his great skill as a unifier
and without his charisma and national vision, the United States of

America would not exist today as a single independent nation. It is a record of leadership without parallel in American history.

George Washington's fame has remained relatively intact since his death over two hundred years ago, although current historians rank him only third on their list of great presidents. (He ranks significantly lower among the general population.) Yet, while he may still occupy a prominent place in the pantheon of American heroes, most Americans view him as cold and remote and, frankly, something of a bore. In the words of one biographer, "No great man in history has a name so lifeless or a monument so featureless and blank. Jefferson and Lincoln, adoptive saints of democracy, dominate their own memorials; Andrew Jackson's very horse breathes fire; Washington's tribute alone reveals no warming touch of flesh."

But in fact, the force of George Washington's personality is the most striking and most commonly overlooked aspect of the historical man. The widely accepted view of Washington as a man of limited ability who was little more than a figurehead and effective symbol is simply incorrect. Joseph Ellis, in his brilliant study of Washington appropriately entitled *His Excellency*, expressed it perfectly. Washington was "the most ambitious, determined, and potent personality of an age not lacking for worthy rivals."

By focusing on compelling and revealing aspects of Washington's life and character, I attempt to make this remarkable man accessible to a wider readership. The flesh-and-blood George Washington is not the priggishly perfect George Washington as portrayed by hagiographers like Parson Weems (the creator of the cherry tree myth). Washington can be justifiably criticized for his role as a slaveholder, his views on Native Americans, his land dealings, and his tactics as a general. He made mistakes, committed indiscretions, and occasionally engaged in deceit; he was excessively ambitious, extremely sensitive to criticism, and prone to greed and vindictiveness.

Nevertheless, like most George Washington scholars, the more I have studied the man, the more I have come to admire him. Despite an intensely passionate personality with the capacity for violent outbursts, he came amazingly close to living up to the very difficult role he had chosen for himself: to be a complete gentleman and, ultimately, to be the embodiment of revolutionary virtue. As Richard Brookhiser notes, "that is the striking thing about this man: the consistency of his behavior with his ideals, and his efforts over twenty-four years to make the two line up." Washington was not only a great man; he was a good man as well.

His greatness is confirmed by his record of achievement. Few men have ever set higher goals or come closer to reaching them. As Don Higginbotham has effectively argued, Washington, with a clarity matched by no other founder, envisioned America as a nation of free men and women with a collective destiny. In striving to realize this goal, he tempered his vision with an insightfully realistic understanding of human nature. George Washington was not a brilliant man in the way Thomas Jefferson, Alexander Hamilton, and James Madison were brilliant, but he was an extremely wise man with a remarkably astute judgment on the really important issues of his time.

I am fully cognizant that any effort to recover the flesh-and-blood Washington is difficult and can only be partially successful. Washington's words about the challenge facing an artist painting his portrait apply equally as well to a historian seeking to sketch his likeness with words: "I fancy the skill of this Gentleman's Pencil, will be put to it, in describing to the World what manner of Man I am." Because of his reserve and his caution, Washington was not an easy man to know. He seemed as eager to put up barriers to his inner self as we are eager to peer behind them. In peering behind them, I follow William Safire's suggestion: "Historians try mightily to get inside their subjects' minds. They enliven the written record with intuitive judgment after subjecting it to rigorous professional discipline."

Since my assessments contain a significant amount of informed speculation, some readers will inevitably disagree with my conclusions. (What fun would writing history be if everything were cut and dried and subject to exact measurement?) Some may feel I have been unfair to Thomas Jefferson or too sympathetic to Alexander Hamilton. Others will think that I overemphasized the importance of Sally Cary Fairfax or Martha Custis in his life. I imagine some readers will think I have been too kind to Washington as a slaveholder, while perhaps even more will think I have been too harsh. Probably the most controversial chapter of my book will be the one focusing on Washington and religion, and especially on the question of his Christian beliefs. The current tension between those emphasizing a faith-based knowledge and those emphasizing a fact-based knowledge gives special relevance to Washington's warnings against the dangers of sectarianism and his strong support for complete religious liberty. If we truly wish to follow the Founding Father, we must first accurately understand his views.

Over the past several years, I have been privileged to present a series of lectures on various aspects of George Washington's life and character at historic Gadsby's Tavern in Old Town Alexandria, Virginia, and those lectures form the basis for the chapters in this volume. Whenever George Washington was appointed to a new position, he seemed constrained to point out that he was not properly qualified for the job. Whenever I am about to publish or publicly lecture on George Washington, I feel constrained to point out that I am an eclectic borrower. I owe a tremendous debt to a great many fine scholars. When brilliant wordsmiths like Joseph Ellis, Ron Chernow, and Paul Longmore make important points more effectively and succinctly than I can, I don't hesitate to use their words. Of course, I want to give explicit recognition in all such cases and believe that I have done so. If I have omitted any references, it is due to inadvertence and poor memory, and not from any wish to appropriate another scholar's words as my own.

The following chapters, avoiding both cynicism and sentimentality, endeavor to humanize Washington without diminishing him. Despite his flaws, he was clearly the greatest man of his age and is ultimately an inspirational figure worthy of both admiration and affection. Passionate, ambitious, and determined, Washington was the rarest of men, a realistic visionary who combined a relentlessly realistic view of human nature with a vision of what a free and united America could be for "millions unborn." He dedicated his public life to making that vision a reality.

Acknowledgments

I CAN SYMPATHIZE WITH THE DILEMMA FACING WINNERS OF THE Oscar at the Academy Awards when they start to rattle off a long list of people they wish to thank. I am amazed at how many different people played a role, either large or small, in the completion of this book. It would not have been written if a dear friend, Dean Brundage, then director of the Northern Virginia Center for the University of Virginia, had not created a teaching position for me when I was on the verge of leaving academe. Nor would it have been written without the encouragement of another dear friend, Jack Censer, longtime chairman of the History Department at George Mason University, who discouraged me from an early retirement and encouraged my scholarly pursuits. I am something of a "late bloomer" among Washington scholars, and that blooming, such as it is, owes much to the renowned Washington scholar and good friend Don Higginbotham, whose intercession allowed me to present my views on Washington at various symposiums and gave me confidence that I had something worth sharing. Gretchen Bulova, the curator of Gadsby's Tavern, picked up on my idea for a series of lectures on Alexandria's premier citizen and turned them into a reality, giving the necessary underpinning for this portrait of George Washington.

In the Notes on Sources at the back of this book, I acknowledge those scholars and books that helped me in my preparation of each chapter, but it is necessary for me to single out a number of them here in a more specific fashion. Joe Ellis, who is probably cited more often than anyone else in my work, not only read the entire manuscript and made helpful suggestions, but used his skill as a wordsmith in helping me choose the title of my work. I am indebted to other scholars for reading and commenting on parts or all of the work: Patricia Brady, Richard Brookhiser, Phil Chase, Ron Chernow, Ellen Clark, Joanne Freeman, Frank Grizzard, Don Higginbotham, Ed Lengel, Phil Morgan, Christine Patrick, Mary Thompson, and Roger Wilkins.

The staff at the library of the Mount Vernon Ladies' Association was unfailingly helpful. Dawn Bonner helped me track down many of the illustrations in the work. Mount Vernon's research historian, Mary Thompson, has a cluttered desk but an uncluttered mind whose knowledge about various specific aspects of Washington's life is unsurpassed, and she graciously made available much of her unpublished research on various aspects of Washington's career. I have to single out my good friend Barbara McMillan, who always went out of her way to make me feel welcome and to track down whatever material I requested.

Tracking down quotations can be a challenging task. I wish to particularly thank Anna Berkes at the Library for the Thomas Jefferson Foundation, Frank Grizzard of the Papers of George Washington, and Mary Thompson of the Mount Vernon Ladies' Association for their help in completing the effort. I also wish to offer thanks to the skilled and pleasant staff at the University of Virginia Press for their patience and expertise in taking the raw manuscript and turning it into its final product: Dick Holway, editor; Mark Saunders, director of marketing; Ellen Satrom, managing editor; and Martha Farlow, design and production manager. I would be remiss if I didn't mention the extremely thorough and careful job of copy editing done by Kathryn Krug. The final product is much stronger because of her efforts.

Family members also played an important role in the project. My wife, Marlene, and my sister, Judy Pierce, read over several drafts of the manuscript and caught innumerable minor errors—grammatical, factual, and typographical. (I of course take responsibility for any that still remain.) My cousin and ever-stimulating friend, Diana Henriques, critiqued the entire manuscript with the eye of an award-winning journalist with a flair for stating things clearly. The perceptive insights of my brilliant son Gregg, a clinical psychologist and fellow university professor, greatly enriched my understanding of Washington and his character structure.

I would never be so bold as to compare my life or character with George Washington's except in one area: family. Like him, I have been blessed with a lifelong partner of over forty years who has been a constant source of support and inspiration. Unlike him, I have also been blessed by being the father of four remarkable sons, and have had the joy of watching them grow up into "honorable manhood" and begin families of their own. Thus, I wish to dedicate this work to the core of my world—my dearly beloved wife, Marlene, and to my four sons, Mark, Tom, Gregg, and Tim.

His First Proving Ground

George Washington and
the French and Indian War

> If it be a sin to covet honor, I am the most offending
> soul alive.—*William Shakespeare*

ONE OF THE MOST INSPIRING ASPECTS OF GEORGE WASHING-
ton's life is the growth of the man. He was not, to quote Nathaniel
Hawthorne, "born with his clothes on, and his hair powdered," nor
did he make "a stately bow on his first appearance in the world." Although numerous traits prominent in the mature man are clearly evi-
dent, the George Washington of the French and Indian War was in
many ways not the same man as the George Washington of the American Revolution. Nevertheless, it was the events of the earlier conflict
that shaped his character and philosophy and thrust young Washington into the spotlight, thus setting the stage for him to emerge as the
central and indispensable figure in the founding of America. It is a
fascinating story, with its share of irony and tragedy, and it is perhaps
the best place to begin the search for the flesh-and-blood figure of
history. Lacking significant documentation, much of Washington's
early life will remain forever shrouded in mystery and thus be particularly susceptible to mythical interpretations such as the young boy
who destroyed his father's cherry tree and then brought him to ecstasy
by boldly confessing to the act with the immortal words, "I can't tell
a lie."

George Washington did not become America's greatest leader by
chance. He was not randomly chosen like those lucky winners of the

multimillion-dollar lotteries that seem to fascinate Americans with their promise of great success without great effort. Good fortune certainly played a role. As Thomas Jefferson noted, "Never did nature and fortune combine more perfectly to make a man great." Time and time again, Washington was the right man at the right place at the right time. Yet, if good fortune was involved, George Washington had a great deal to do with the final result. He agreed with those who counseled that it is foolish to expect great results without great effort. Time was limited and not to be wasted. As he later advised his nephew, "every hour mispent is lost forever." George Washington was profoundly ambitious and eager for honor and glory, and his life cannot accurately be understood without grasping these fundamental and absolutely essential facts. In Paul Longmore's telling words, "Throughout his life, the ambition for distinction spun inside George Washington like a dynamo, generating the astounding energy with which he produced his greatest historical achievement, himself."

BOTH GREAT BRITAIN AND FRANCE, the two superpowers of the eighteenth century, claimed the Ohio Country west of the Allegheny Mountains and had vague ambitions for it, but until about the middle of the century, neither of the great powers was in a position to assert control over the area. The driving force in Virginia was a group of expansionists centered in the Northern Neck, part of the vast section of Virginia north of the Rappahannock River controlled by Thomas, 6th Lord Fairfax. Members of the Fairfax, Lee, Washington, and Mason families joined with powerful merchants in London and, enlisting the aid of the future governor of Virginia, Robert Dinwiddie, formed a new land company, the Ohio Company. In 1749, the company was awarded a grant of 500,000 acres of land, contingent upon its building a fort and settling a number of families there within a specified period of time.

Knowing France also claimed the territory, Dinwiddie, now acting governor, sought permission and advice from the home government on how best to proceed against France and received the authorization he sought: "You are to require of Them peaceably to depart . . . & if, notwithstanding Your Admonitions, They do still endeavour to carry on any such unlawfull and unjustifiable Designs, We do hereby strictly charge, & command You, to drive them off by Force of Arms." After receiving this green light in mid-October of 1753, Dinwiddie needed an envoy to carry the message to the French, as well as to ascertain their intentions for the region.

With the advantage of historical hindsight, we can see that George Washington's appointment as Dinwiddie's emissary was one of the truly determining moments of his life. At first glance, he would seem to be an unlikely candidate for such an important mission. He was only twenty-one years old, spoke no French, and had no diplomatic experience. Yet, there were several points in his favor. He was a surveyor with some knowledge and experience of Virginia west of the Blue Ridge Mountains, and he possessed the physique and strength to undergo the difficult and dangerous journey. While certainly not among the first rank of the gentry, he was of gentry standing, and Dinwiddie, having formed a favorable impression of him, had earlier appointed him a major in the militia and adjutant general for southern Virginia. Perhaps most importantly, Washington had the firm support of his major patron, William Fairfax of Belvoir, one of Governor Dinwiddie's most influential counselors. It was Colonel Fairfax who almost certainly alerted him to the opportunity. Washington, who soon professed, "My inclinations are strongly bent to arms," jumped at the chance to enhance his reputation and "offered himself to go" as the Governor's envoy.

Aided by Christopher Gist, an experienced frontiersman who knew the ways of the forest, and a few servants and Indians, Washington undertook a winter journey to deliver Dinwiddie's letter to the commandant of the French forces in the Ohio Country at Fort Le Boeuf near Lake Erie that contained material for future legends. Braving terrible weather, almost unbearably cold temperatures, untracked forests, questionable Indian allies, and French resistance if not outright treachery, Washington survived an apparent assassination attempt by an Indian guide and the capsizing of his raft into the freezing Allegheny River. He reported to the Governor in January of 1754 that the French totally rejected Great Britain's claims and were making plans to seize the still vacant but critical forks of the Ohio River (present-day Pittsburgh). As written in Washington's journal, "They told me it was their absolute Design to take Possession of the Ohio, & by G—— they

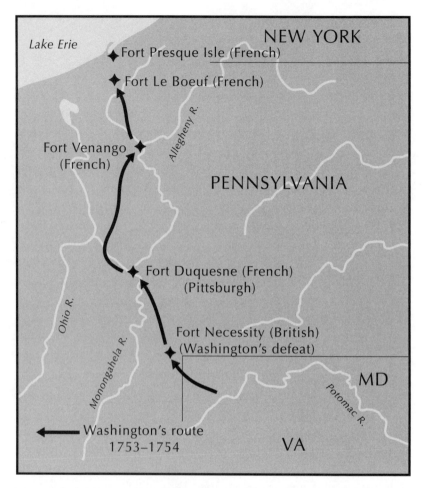

Map of the Ohio Country, 1753-1754. (Adapted from Thomas Bailey and David Kennedy, *The American Pageant* [9th ed., 1991], by permission of Houghton-Mifflin Publishing Company)

would do it." His journal was soon published to considerable acclaim in both America and Great Britain. The House of Burgesses awarded him a sizable bonus of fifty pounds as an expression of their appreciation for his difficult undertaking. Suddenly, George Washington was becoming noteworthy.

The advanced stage of French preparations (Washington had counted well over two hundred canoes ready to ferry men and supplies) induced Dinwiddie to move quickly. He desired to send a group of workmen to build a fort at the forks of the Ohio and also to raise a sufficient military force to protect it from the hostile French. Such designs cost money, and Dinwiddie was hard pressed to win support from the General Assembly. Already angered at Dinwiddie for other reasons, many Burgesses argued over whether the effort was primarily aimed at helping the Ohio Company, whether the disputed land belonged to Pennsylvania instead of Virginia, and even whether the French posed a serious threat to basic Virginia interests. Young George Washington was not among the doubters. The chance to advance the interests of Great Britain, Virginia, and the Ohio Company, to deal a blow to the hated French, and, perhaps most significantly, a chance to advance his own position and perhaps win great honor in the process was irresistible. Words of Shakespeare's Henry V are applicable to Washington: "If it be a sin to covet honor, I am the most offending soul alive."

Honor and glory would not come easily. Ordered to Alexandria in January of 1754 to organize a small force of soldiers to march to the forks of the Ohio, Washington found little enthusiasm for the enterprise and slim pickings for the troops. He quickly informed the Governor, "We daily Experience the great necessity for Cloathing the Men, as we find the generallity of those who are to be Enlisted, are of those loose, Idle Persons that are quite destitute of House, and Home, and I may truely say many of them of Cloaths. . . . There is many of them without Shoes, other's want Stockings, some are without Shirts, and not a few that have Scarce a Coat, or Waistcoat, to their Backs; in short, they are as illy provided as can well be conceiv'd." He commented on what a difficult task it was to "manage a number of selfwill'd, ungovernable People," a theme he would return to on numerous occasions.

Despite the difficulties, Washington, now a lieutenant colonel, marched his motley band of soldiers toward the Ohio River, to Winchester, where work on the fort was already under way. To his great frustration, when he arrived at Winchester, the promised wagons and teamsters were nowhere to be found. Considering the nature of the emergency, he took matters into his own hands. The lengths to which he was willing to go are indicated by a warrant for his arrest, issued

by the Frederick county clerk on April 15, 1754, on charges of tres-
passing. After failing to serve the warrant, the sheriff noted on its
reverse side that "the within named George Washington would not
be taken. He kept me off by force of arms."

Washington soon learned of a significant new development. The
French forces had advanced from their northern strongholds in
sufficient strength to take control of the vital forks of the Ohio River,
although they allowed the beleaguered workmen to return unharmed
to Virginia. (The French quickly built a significant fort there and
named it Fort Duquesne, after their governor of Canada.) Eschewing
a cautious approach, which the changed circumstances warranted, the
callow young officer proceeded toward the fort, seemingly eager to
engage the French. It is unclear what Washington hoped to accomplish by pressing his men forward toward the Ohio River. Perhaps
a contemporary critic had it right: It resulted from his "being too
ambitious of acquiring all the honour, or as much as he could, before
the rest joined him." His rash decision was to have unforeseen consequences.

The Jumonville Affair and Washington's later capitulation at Fort
Necessity caused the first bloodshed of what would become known as
the Seven Years' War, which is referred to more commonly in America
as the French and Indian War. As Sir Horace Walpole, the diarist and
son of the late prime minister, noted, "The volley fired by a young
Virginian in the backwoods of America set the world on fire." In one
of history's greatest ironies, that young Virginian ended up being the
most famous and revered man of the entire age. In the long term, his
volley triggered truly epic events—the removal of France from North
America, the American War for Independence, and the French Revolution. In the short term, the ensuing events revealed just how much
George Washington had to learn in conducting military operations.

His small party of Indian allies, led by Tanacharison, called Half
King by the British, soon discovered a French party of about thirty-
five men camped not far away. Without knowing their intentions and
despite the fact that Great Britain and France were officially at peace,
Washington gave the order to attack. The clash at Jumonville Glen,
named for the commander of this small French party, occurred on
May 28, 1754. Not surprisingly, there are conflicting accounts of what

happened in the brief skirmish that was Washington's baptism by fire. Also not surprising, the French, caught completely unaware, were quickly subdued. Apparently, Jumonville was wounded and captured. He tried to convey as best he could despite the language barrier that he was on a diplomatic mission, not a military one, but his efforts were brutally cut short when the French-speaking Tanacharison, in an effort to bind his tribe irrevocably to the British, tomahawked and scalped him and then ceremoniously washed his hands with Jumonville's brains. It appears that other wounded prisoners were also scalped before Washington, most likely appalled at what he had just witnessed, was able to reassert control. The historian Fred Anderson states that the massacre of the wounded, mentioned in some primary sources, is completely ignored by Washington, but in fact Washington did alert the governor to Indian atrocities: "There were 5, or 6 other Indian, who servd to knock the poor unhappy wounded in the head and beriev'd them of their Scalps." This would help explain the unusually high ratio of dead to wounded reported to Governor Dinwiddie. Washington declared ten Frenchmen were killed and only one was wounded, while normally in such clashes the wounded significantly outnumbered the dead.

Whatever private misgivings or doubts Washington may have had, his public pronouncements were defensive and arrogant, and privately, he seemed excited by the thrill of battle. He confided to his favorite brother, Jack, "I heard Bulletts whistle and believe me there was something charming in the sound." He further boasted to Governor Dinwiddie, "If the whole Detach[men]t of the French behave with no more Risolution than this chosen Party did I flatter myself we shall have no g[rea]t trouble in driving them to . . . Montreal." He certainly did flatter himself. These were the boastful words of a young and inexperienced leader with little sense of the realities he was facing.

Jumonville was a French diplomat, and, in the eyes of the French, had been on a mission comparable to Washington's. Now he had been wantonly murdered, and the French vowed revenge. Washington's augmented but still small force of several hundred men soon found themselves holed up in a quickly constructed fort, aptly named Fort Necessity, facing a combined French and Indian force of about seven hundred men led by Jumonville's irate brother. Catastrophe loomed. Perhaps seeing the course of events more clearly than Washington, his Indian allies deserted. By the end of the first day of the battle at Great Meadows, more than a third of Washington's men lay dead or wounded, and the little fort was flooded by torrential rain. Colonel Washington had every reason to expect his own life might end the next day (July 4th) if the French should storm his inadequate bastion.

Rather than storming the fort, however, the French were willing to parley. Fearful that reinforcements were close by, the French commander decided to seek Washington's sword rather than his life. He offered to allow Washington and his men to capitulate and return to Virginia if Washington signed a document agreeing the French had mounted the attack only to avenge the assassination of their minister, Jumonville. The document was in French, the night was rainy, and the translator, a Dutchman by the name of Jacob van Braam, was less than perfectly fluent in French. Nevertheless, in signing the document, Washington unwittingly gave the French a great diplomatic and propaganda victory, for essentially he admitted that he, not the French, had initiated the conflict. In the words of one Frenchman, "There is nothing more unworthy and lower and even blacker, than the sentiments and the way of thinking of this Washington. . . . he lies a great deal in order to justify the assassination of Sieur Jumonville which . . . he had the stupidity to confess. . . . It would have been a pleasure to read his outrageous journal under his very nose." A British writer mourned that Washington's signing of the articles of capitulation was "the most infamous a British subject ever put his hand to." Stung by the harsh criticism, the young colonel, who was inordinately sensitive to criticism and strongly blame-aversive, declared in his own defense, "That we were wilfully, or ignorently, deceived by our interpreter to the word, *assassination*, I do aver, and will to my dying moment" (emphasis in the original). (Many years later, in 1787, he wrote some remarks on a proposed biography by his aide Colonel David Humphreys. In them, he described Jumonville's party as an advance "detachment to reconnoitre our Camp to obtain intelligence of our strength & position" prior to the attack on Fort Necessity with a force that he now recollected as consisting of fifteen hundred men. In his comments, he conveniently ignored the fact that his attack on Jumonville precipitated the French assault on Fort Necessity.)

Whatever the facts, the war had begun. Officials in Great Britain decided they could not allow the French to control the forks of the Ohio and thus sent over two regiments of British regulars under the command of General Edward Braddock to do what Washington and his ragtag force of colonials had been unable to do. The British were dangerously overconfident. As Fred Anderson notes, "It was a madly ambitious plan approved by men studying maps in London unaware that their ignorance of American geography, politics, and military capacities had foredoomed it to failure."

Surprisingly, Washington emerged from the debacle at Fort Necessity with his reputation intact and in some ways enhanced. In the end, he had returned home with honor after apparently inflicting huge casualties on the hated French. The announced casualty figures were greatly exaggerated, but they made the action at Fort Necessity more palatable. With war now inevitable, Virginia would need soldiers, and George Washington, with his military bearing, his imposing persona, and a knack for seeming to be much older than he was, became a prime candidate to help organize and lead Virginia's defense. Washington was eager to play a role in the upcoming struggle, but only on terms that comported with his sense of honor and fairness. A dispute over pay and rank led to his petulant resignation, but General Braddock's need for competent colonials familiar with the area and his favorable personal impression of Washington landed Washington an unofficial but influential spot in the General's military "family."

Thus Washington rode with Braddock's forces when they were surprised on July 9, 1755, by the French and their Native American allies on the banks of the Monongahela River, only a few miles short of their destination. The Battle of the Wilderness was one of the great British disasters of the eighteenth century, caused in part because Braddock followed Washington's advice and split his advancing army into two divisions. Two-thirds of all the British officers involved were killed or wounded and the army was routed. By all accounts, Washington, who almost missed the battle because he had been sick with dysentery, conducted himself heroically. One of Washington's most salient traits was that death held no terror for him; indeed, a heroic death held a certain attraction. As he later expressed it to Sally Cary Fairfax, "who is there that does not rather Envy, than regret a Death that gives birth to Honour & Glorious memory."

Absolutely fearless in battle (even his most severe critics would not then or later ever question his courage), and able to think clearly in the midst of chaos and death, Washington rallied the Virginia troops and prevented a complete rout. He carried the mortally wounded General Braddock off the field and later buried him under a wagon road so that his body would not be desecrated by the victors. George Washington came very close to losing his own life as well. During the battle, he had two or three horses shot from under him (reports vary) and received four bullet holes in his clothes, one of them through his hat. In his words, "Death was levelling my companions on every side of me," but neither then nor later did a bullet ever pierce his skin, giving rise to stories among some of the Indians and others that he was somehow miraculously immune to gunfire.

Braddock's defeat and the hasty, almost cowardly, withdrawal of the British army into winter headquarters at Philadelphia in the middle of the summer meant that the western frontier of Virginia, now at full-scale war, was more open and accessible to attack than ever before. A new army was needed. Once again emerging from a defeat with his reputation enhanced, George Washington was appointed colonel and commander in chief of the First Virginia Regiment. He was twenty-three years old and now squarely in the spotlight, although the task ahead of him was daunting in the extreme.

How did Washington perform in his first command? Several scholars are very critical. While granting him courage and certain leadership abilities, Thomas Lewis in *For King and Country* depicts Washington as a callow, insecure, grasping, rash, undiplomatic, self-indulgent, untruthful, obstinate, careless, querulous, and rather ordinary young man. Historian John Ferling is not much kinder: "He seemed in the grip of a disturbing and unattractive obsession with his own advancement. No amount of protestation that he soldiered only for patriotic reasons—and he made that claim regularly—is quite convincing. . . . Once in command, . . . he seemed unable to harness his ambition, and his lusts led him to excessive absences, to petulant outbursts, to deceitful and irresponsible conduct, to an unsavory manner that vacillated between obsequiousness and a menacing heavy-handedness, and that, at times, verged even on the treacherous." Even the sympathetic biographer Marcus Cunliffe notes, "There is something unlikable about the George Washington of 1753-1758. He seems a trifle raw and strident, too much on his dignity, too ready to complain, too nakedly concerned with promotion."

There is validity to many of these charges, for George Washington did numerous things that merit criticism and contrast with his nearly spotless record as commander in chief during the War for Independence. He resigned once, threatened to resign a half dozen times, and left his men for long periods of time. Occasionally, his zealous pursuit of honor and glory damaged his virtue. He betrayed two superiors, Governor Robert Dinwiddie and General John Forbes, both of whom had his best interests at heart. As historian Guthrie Sayen expressed it, "His ingratitude and his treachery proceeded from an inability to integrate the prescriptions found in the 'Rules of Civility' and the demands of honor so dear to the warrior. When his ambitions were thwarted, he lost the self-restraint essential to courtesy." His self-assertion in the quest of honor trumped his ability to show proper deference to superiors.

Washington's desire for official British rank and his efforts to obtain a commission in the regular British army bordered on the obsessive and are best illustrated by his obsequious letters to John Campbell, 4th Earl of Loudoun, appointed both commander of the British forces in America and titular governor of Virginia in the summer of 1756. Washington organized a strong letter-writing campaign on his own behalf, but his initial efforts did not lead to a breakthrough. Loudoun was critical of Washington's professed desire to abandon Fort Cumberland: "This Proceeding, I am affraid will have a bad Effect as to the Dominion: & will not have a good Appearance at Home." Washington was deeply upset by the criticism. Self-justification had become a passion; inhumanly fearless against cannon fire, he could become terrified at the threat of a critical word. He complained to Dinwiddie that Loudoun had "imbibed prejudices so unfavourable to my character" because he had not been "thoroughly informed." Of course, the Governor, as Loudoun's principal informant on affairs in Virginia, could not have avoided drawing the intended inference. His protégé was in essence accusing him of treachery.

Washington compounded his error by sending a long, shrill, and ill-advised letter of self-justification to Loudoun, the man he still hoped would give him a royal commission. (The letter fills twelve printed pages in the new edition of the *Papers of George Washington*.) As Sayen points out, Washington blamed everyone but himself: "He condemned local authorities for conniving at desertion. He lambasted the assembly, where he had influential friends, for enacting 'pernicious' laws and mismanaging the colony's finances. He excoriated the militia for disobedience, malingering, and waste. And he denounced the governor and the assembly for ignoring his 'reiterated Letters' on the futility of Virginia's current military strategy." His criticism of Dinwiddie was particularly ill-advised. Not only did he have the gall to criticize his own patron, the man who had advanced him as far as he could and then sponsored his further promotion, but he did the same to his patron's patron.

Washington implied the reason he had not resigned earlier was because of "the dawn of hope that arose" as a result of Loudoun's appointment. He laid it on thick: "Altho' I have not the Honour to be known to your Lordship: Yet, Your Lordship's Name was familiar to my Ear, on account of the Important Services performed to His Majesty in other parts of the World—don't think My Lord I am going to flatter. I have exalted Sentiments of Your Lordships Character, and revere Your Rank. . . . my nature is honest, and Free from Guile." This went beyond deference, which was proper, to servile flattery, which was not. Despite discouragement from the surprisingly tolerant Governor Dinwiddie, Washington pressed and eventually received permission to travel to Philadelphia to make his case to Loudoun directly. After keeping Washington waiting for eleven days, the Earl "dismissed George Washington with the cold, bland, impersonal courtesy of an aristocrat dealing with an inferior." (How different American history would have been had he achieved his goal.)

Washington's stubbornness and backbiting also damaged his standing with another superior, Brigadier General John Forbes, who was given command of the 1758 expedition against Fort Duquesne and who was predisposed to admire him. Washington unsuccessfully tried to convince General Forbes that the only way to capture Fort Duquesne in 1758 was to approach it via Braddock's Road (to the financial benefit of Virginia and Washington, who owned land near the road), instead of moving westward across Pennsylvania. Forbes listened to Washington's arguments and decided against them. That should have been the end of the matter, but Washington bewailed the decision to Speaker of the House John Robinson and accused the expedition's leaders of incompetence, venality, and malfeasance: "I wish," wrote Washington, "I was sent immediately home" (i.e., to London) to denounce Forbes. Forbes learned of Washington's behind-the-scenes actions: "By a very unguarded letter of Col: Washington that Accidentally fell into my hands," Forbes told his second in command, "I am now at the bottom, of their Scheme against this new road, a Scheme that I think was a shame for any officer to be Concerned in." Forbes declared that Washington's "Behaviour about the roads, was no ways like a Soldier." Of course, Washington's dire predictions proved to be false, and Forbes managed to march west with success, capturing the French stronghold of Fort Duquesne near the end of 1758.

Nevertheless, while there are legitimate grounds for criticism, one must not overemphasize them or downplay either Washington's achievements or the acclaim he was accorded. For example, to refer to the young George Washington, as Lewis and others do, as "an ordinary man" caught up in "extraordinary events," is to distort the historical record and do Washington an injustice. The extant record makes clear that George Washington was not only a remarkable mature man but that he was also a remarkable young man. In 1753, the French commander at Fort LeBoeuf, Jacques Legardeur de Saint-Pierre, while rejecting British claims to the Ohio Country, wrote a conciliatory letter to Governor Dinwiddie in which he stated that he received Major Washington "with the distinction owing to your dignity [and] his position." He then went beyond necessary protocol and added *"and his own great merit"* (emphasis added). Washington clearly impressed Legardeur, and the important point to note is how regularly George Washington impressed the important men with whom he came into contact. Colonel William Fairfax, Governor Robert Dinwiddie, General Edward Braddock, Governor William Shirley, General John Forbes, Major Robert Orme, the Reverend Samuel Davies, George William Fairfax, Speaker of the House John Robinson, and leading members of the House of Burgesses and planter elite such as Landon Carter, Charles Carter, William Fitzhugh, and Richard Corbin were all duly impressed and sought to befriend and help the young colonel.

The following sample of quotes, which could be greatly expanded, illustrates Washington's impact and forces us to ask why as such a young man he was able to win such high praise from such a distinguished group of individuals.

Robert Orme: "My Dear Friend: Your aimable Character made me desirous of your Acquaintance and your Acquaintance confirmed the Regard and Opinion your Character had imprinted in my Mind."

Robert Munford: "Our colonel is an example of fortitude in either danger or hardship, and by his easy, polite behavior, has gained not only the regard but affection of both officers and soldiers."

William Ramsay: "Your disinterestedness, your unwearied application and zeal for your country's good determine you to continue in its service at a time there may be the greatest call for you and when probably some signal day may mark you the bravest (as hitherto you have been) of persons."

Governor Robert Dinwiddie: "He is a person much belov'd here and has gone through many hardships in the Service, & I really think he has great Merit."

Governor William Shirley: "No provisional officer upon the continent [is] as deserving of a high position" (as Washington).

Rev. Samuel Davies: Washington's "uncommon bravery, conduct, and knowledge in the art of war, at his age, is superior to what I ever read of." (Davies prophetically wondered whether Providence was sparing his life for an even greater impact later on.)

John Robinson: "I have never heard any man of honor or of reputation speak the least disrespectfully of you or censure your conduct in the least."

George William Fairfax: "[I] beg that you'l freely Command me, being willing and always desirous of serving my Country under so experienced a Commander" as the "brave Colonel Washington." (Washington was eight years his junior and had earlier referred to him in his diary as Mr. Fairfax.)

William Fairfax praised his "heroick Virtue," and declared, "Your good Health and Fortune is the Toast at every table." General Edward Braddock befriended and offered to help him secure a royal commission. General John Forbes put him in charge of one of the three brigades to lead the assault on Duquesne, the only brigade entrusted to a provincial officer. The Virginia House of Burgesses voted him their thanks for "his faithful services to His Majesty and this Colony, and for his brave and steady behaviour from the first encroachments and hostilities of the French and their Indians, to his resignation after the happy reduction of Fort Duquesne." When Washington stammered in response to their words of praise, Speaker Robinson ordered, "Sit down, Mr. Washington, your modesty equals your valor, and that surpasses the power of any language that I possess."

Excerpts from the tribute—and plea—his officers made to him when he told them he was resigning from the service at the end of 1758 simply reinforce the same point. The officers praised "[your] steady adherance to impartial justice, your quick Discernment and invarable Regard to Merit." They declared, "In our earliest Infancy you took us under your Tuition, train'd us up in the Practice of that Discipline which alone can constitute good Troops." They bemoaned the "loss of such an excellent Commander, such a sincere Friend, and so affable a Companion. How rare it is to find those amiable Qualifications blended together in one Man? How great the loss of such a man?" Reading such a tribute, it is easy to forget that the man they were referring to was only twenty-six years old.

How could George Washington garner such lavish praise at such a young age? There is no simple answer to this query, as a number of factors were involved. Part of it stemmed from his remarkable natural bodily endowment, for his physical persona was certainly part of his charm. George Mercer penned a detailed physical description of Washington in 1760:

He may be described as being straight as an Indian, measuring 6 feet 2 inches in his stockings, and weighing 175 lbs. . . . His frame is padded with well developed muscles, indicating great strength. . . . His head is well shaped, though not large, but is gracefully poised on a superb neck. A large and straight rather than a prominent nose; blue-grey penetrating eyes which are widely separated and overhung by a heavy brow. His face is long rather than broad, with high round cheek bones, and terminates in a good firm chin. . . . A pleasing and benevolent tho a commanding countenance, dark brown hair which he wears in a cue. . . . His features are regular and placid with all the muscles of his face under perfect control, tho flexible and expressive of deep feeling when moved by emotions. In conversation he looks you full in the face, is deliberate, deferential and engaging. His demeanor at all times composed and dignified. His movements and gestures are graceful, his walk majestic, and he is a splendid horseman.

Thomas Jefferson's and James Monroe's later comments echo Mercer's description: "His stature was exactly what one would wish, his deportment easy, erect, and noble. . . . the most graceful horseman of his age." And "A deportment so firm, so dignified, but yet so modest and composed, I have never seen in any other person."

Tall and broad-shouldered, Washington had an athlete's body and combined strength and grace in a manner his contemporaries overwhelmingly found attractive. If the exterior were taken as an indication of the interior, Washington already had an advantage. It would, of course, take more than an attractive physique if he was to satisfy his ambitions. Visitors to Mount Vernon today are likely to assume that young George was born into the top ranks of Virginia society, but such was not the case. The Washington family was second-tier gentry. When his father, Augustine, died in 1743, George, only eleven and the eldest of five children by his father's second marriage, saw his future prospects greatly diminished. His inheritance was meager, and the chance for an English education, given to both of his older half brothers, would be denied him. If he was to make something of himself, it would take more than simple ability and hard work. Eighteenth-century Virginia was a deferential and hierarchical society, and advancement would be possible only with the aid of patrons; even more than today, it was not only what you knew but who you knew that mattered. Patronage was the basic means of social mobility in eighteenth-century Virginia, and young Washington would not have been able to rise as he did without key support at crucial points. One of his many talents was stalking men of influence, and he excelled in winning the goodwill of his elders. Thus, he urged his favorite brother, Jack, to "live in perfect Harmony" with Fairfax and his family "as it is in their power to be very serviceable upon many occasion's to us as young beginner's." He made the same point to Jack after his appointment as Braddock's aide: "I have now a good oppertunity, and shall not neglect it, of forming an acquaintance, which may be serviceable hereafter."

George Washington worked hard to fashion for himself a public persona that won praise from those whose praise counted the most, but it was not simply a pose. He was a man of character. In the words of the great Washington biographer Douglas Southall Freeman, "Powerful Virginia elders, who saw much loose living and indolence around them, found stimulation and reassurance in a young man of unassailed morals and of mature, sound judgment, who was full of energetic vigor and was devoted to the defense of a people slow and slothful in defending themselves. These qualities endeared young Washington to most of the potentates and explain in large part his success in dealing with them." He was a man other men admired and wished to emulate and befriend. He merged power (a commanding countenance) with diffidence (affability and deference) in a very engaging and appealing fashion. In Paul Longmore's words, by combining "an acute sense of other people's responses to him, and an actor's craftsmanlike understanding of how to shape his performance, he had begun to create the majestic 'presence' that would constitute one of his chief assets."

In assessing Washington's accomplishments and failures in the French and Indian War, one must keep in mind that he was given a virtually impossible task. His responsibilities were immense, his resources meager. He lamented, "I have been posted . . . upon our cold and Barren Frontiers, to perform I think I may say impossibiltys that is, to protect from the cruel Incursions of a Crafty Savage Enemy a line of Inhabitants of more then 350 Miles extent with a force inadequate to the taske." Ten months after taking command he tersely summarized the situation: "Desolation and murder still increase; and no prospects of Relief. The Blue-Ridge is now our Frontier." The situation was truly desperate, and there was simply no way in the short term to correct it. The frontier boundaries were huge. Washington's troops were few in number, and the Native American foe, savage and

"The People of Winchester Appealing to Washington." (Courtesy of the
Virginia Historical Society)

cunning, was supplied and encouraged by the French, now firmly in
control of the Ohio Country.

Colonel Washington had a grudging respect for the fighting ability of his Native American adversaries: "I cannot conceive the best
white men to be equal to them in the Woods," he wrote; and "No
troops in the universe can guard against the cunning and wiles of
Indians. No one can tell where they will fall, 'till the mischief is done,
and then 'tis in vain to pursue." His overall characterization, however, was negative and tinged with racism. He described some of his
Indian allies, never very numerous, as "the most insolent, most avari-
cious and most dissatisfied wretches I have ever had to deal with." He
seemed to view his Indian foe much the way most modern Americans
view terrorists. They were beyond the pale of civilization and capable
of the most horrific brutalities. Indian warriors "plunder, kill, scalp,
and escape" with virtual impunity. The respect Washington showed
to Indian warriors was similar to that which one would show to a dan-

gerous beast that threatened one's survival. He later compared them to wolves. Differing in shape, they were both beasts of prey as the Indians "prowl about like Wolves; and like them, do their mischief by Stealth." Washington's second in command, Captain Adam Stephen, luridly declared that they spared the lives of the young women in order to gratify their brutal and savage passions. Such reports, combined with terrifying tales of captives being tortured and slowly roasted to death, spread fear across the entire frontier.

While the attacks engendered fear along the frontier, they did not lead to increased enlistment into Washington's Virginia regiment. The lack of cooperation both frustrated and angered Washington: "The timidity of the Inhabitants of this County is to be equalled by nothing but their perverseness," and "You may, with almost equal success, attempt to raize the Dead as the force of this County." He faced the almost impossible task of protecting a people who would not cooperate with him, and indeed often seemed to directly hinder him. In a rather typical letter, he complained to Governor Dinwiddie, "In all things I meet with the greatest opposition no orders are obey'd but what a Party of Soldier's or my own drawn Sword Enforces; without this, a single horse for the most urgent occasion cannot be had, to such a pitch has the insolence of these People arrivd."

If men on the fringes of danger were hesitant to enlist, men farther east were even more reluctant. The war was generally unpopular with many Virginians, and volunteers were hard to find. A vignette illustrating the problems Washington had in obtaining sufficient manpower involved the difficulties he faced with Denis McCarty, a distant cousin and a member of a prominent Fairfax County family. McCarty was quite successful in his recruiting, but he became so by forcibly seizing men from their beds in the night, as well as confining and torturing them until they volunteered. Washington chided him, "I am very sorry you have given me occasion to complain of your conduct in Recruiting; and to tell you, that the methods and unjustifiable means you have practiced, are very unacceptable, and have been of infinite prejudice to the Service: of this I am informed by many Gentlemen, as well as by all the Officers who were ordered to recruit in these parts: and am further assured, that it is next to an impossibility to get a man where you have been; such terror have you occasioned." The sorry

state of Washington's forces is best illustrated by the fact that despite
McCarty's outrages, Washington still recommended that Governor
Dinwiddie commission him as an ensign in the Virginia Regiment.

With volunteers insufficient to fill the ranks, the only recourse was
the draft, and the House of Burgesses, not wishing to anger voters
(basically property-owning males over twenty-one), exempted them
from the draft. The result was a force of generally poor quality made
up of men from the fringes of society, compelled to enlist and eager
to desert. Problems of drunkenness, desertion, and insubordination,
aggravated by supply and pay problems, led Colonel Washington to
ask for ever harsher penalties with up to a thousand lashes for certain
offenses. Washington was perfectly comfortable in executing some of
the more grievous offenders as an example to try to bring the rest
into better compliance with his orders. He experienced little relief
from the militia called out to augment his undermanned Virginia regiment. The harried Commander in Chief's assessment of the militia
was harsh: "They are obstinate, self-willed, perverse; of little or no
service to the people, and very burthensome to the Country."

Given the tools he had to work with, it is little short of amazing that Washington was able to achieve as much success as he did.
His goal was to make himself into a first-rate professional military
man and to make his troops "the first in arms, of any Troops" in the
war. By 1757, he and his men could justly claim, "If it shou'd be said,
the Troops of Virginia are Irregulars, and cannot expect more notice
than other Provincials, I must beg leave to differ, and observe in turn,
that we want nothing but Commissions from His Majesty to make
us as regular a Corps as any upon the Continent—Because, we were
regularly Enlisted, attested and bound, during the King's or Colony's
Pleasure—We have been regularly Regimented and trained, and have
done as regular Duty for upwards of 3 years, as any regiment in His
Majesty's Service." His troops in fact later won praise from British
officers for both their appearance and their performance.

Washington accomplished these feats because he was a very capable military officer. As Fred Anderson notes, Washington "acquired these skills in part by study—he was an indefatigable reader
of military manuals and treatises, devouring everything from Caesar's Commentaries to Col. Humphrey Bland's Treatise of Military

Discipline, and in part by observing experienced officers in action."
He observed how the regulars conducted themselves so that he could
emulate them. Consequently, he acquired their attitudes, copied their
habits of command, and absorbed their prejudices to the point that he
virtually became one of them except for the royal commission. Don
Higginbotham, the leading scholar of Washington as a military man,
concludes, "One has to be impressed in reading Washington's general
orders over his three-year period as colonel of the Virginia Regiment.
They were clear, crisp, and comprehensive, as if they had been issued
by a first-rate officer in the king's army."

Several important discoveries emerge from examining George
Washington in his first command. Certainly the record was mixed,
but he was able to accomplish a considerable amount under the most
trying circumstances. More importantly, the experience did much to
shape his philosophy, both on military matters and on human nature.
Joseph Ellis is particularly effective in demonstrating "a connection
between Washington's character in the most formative stage of its
development and the raw, often savage, conditions in that expansive
area called the Ohio Country. The interior regions of Washington's
personality began to take shape within the interior regions of the colonial frontier." As Ellis so nicely puts it, "Instead of going to college,
Washington went to war. And the kind of education he received, like
the smallpox he had contracted in Barbados, left scars that never went
away, as well as immunities against any and all forms of youthful ide-
alism." The experiences of the war left George Washington with an
unvarnished view of mankind and a distrust of voluntarism as a way
to meet a wartime crisis, a perspective he never lost.

There is evidence that the mature Washington appeared to recognize that the war was the formative phase of his development as a
full man. His "Remarks," prepared for his biographer and former aide
David Humphreys in 1787, are as close as we can get to an autobiography. The disproportionate time he spent on the French and Indian
War demonstrates that he thought it was very important, and what
he chose to focus on is revealing about the impact of the war on his
thinking. One is particularly struck by Washington's focus on death
and his narrow escapes from an early demise. In his "Remarks," he
wrote of the four times he narrowly escaped death. The most interest-

ing focuses on his intervention to break up a "friendly fire" incident among his own troops. (This is an event Washington mentions nowhere else, and we know of it only because Humphreys disobeyed his explicit request to destroy the document.) Colonel Washington described riding in front of his own line, hitting his troops' muskets up with his sword to prevent them from killing their own fellow soldiers. His life, he wrote, was "in as much jeopardy as it had ever been before or since," a point he repeated twice in a single paragraph.

The horrors of the war were still vivid more than thirty years later. Writing of Braddock's defeat, Washington somberly recalled, "The shocking Scenes which presented themselves in this Nights March are not to be described—The dead—the dying—the groans— lamentation and crys along the Road . . . were enough to pierce a heart of adamant [stone]." Part of the frustration that Washington had to face and come to grips with was that there was little he could do in the face of such tragedies. This same sense of anguish is apparent in a passionate letter to Governor Dinwiddie: "The supplicating tears of the women; and moving petitions of the men, melt me into such deadly sorrow, that I solemnly declare, if I know my own mind—I could offer myself a willing Sacrifice to the butchering Enemy, provided that would contribute to the peoples ease. . . . If bleeding, dying! would glut their insatiate revenge—I would be a willing offering to Savage Fury: and die by inches to save a people!" This was not mere rhetoric. To die a heroic death, and to thus win future fame and glory, was something Washington was willing to do; indeed, sometimes one wonders if he was almost eager to do so. As he pondered his own survival, he could only understand it as part of the mysterious working of Providence which was inscrutable and beyond human comprehension. It was a theme to which he would often return.

George Washington at twenty-six was not yet the man he would become, but he was a much wiser, more mature, and more self-controlled man than he was when he declared to his brother that there was something "charming" about the sound of whizzing bullets. He had learned a variety of technical and practical lessons and had learned the less palpable but equally important skills of command as well. Of course, he could not possibly envision at the time that the many difficulties he had experienced and the many lessons he had learned would be the perfect preparation for his Revolutionary War command. In the short term, he essentially viewed his role in the war as a failure.

He had been frustrated in his efforts to attain British rank, had weakened his powerful constitution so much that he thought he would die, and felt unappreciated. In his words, "That appearance of Glory once in view—that hope—that laudable Ambition of Serving Our Country, and meriting its applause, is now no more!" Wounded in body and spirit, Washington decided to retire from military life and seek fulfillment in marriage and the life of a Virginia planter. Not too long after his marriage to Martha Custis in January of 1759, he wrote a relative, "I am now I beleive fixd at this Seat with an agreable Consort for Life and hope to find more happiness in retirement than I ever experiencd amidst a wide and bustling World."

At age twenty-six, George Washington thought his public career was over. Fortunately for the future history of America, he was incorrect.

"Washington Taking Command of the American Army." (Courtesy of the Mount Vernon Ladies' Association)

Taking Command

George Washington and the Beginning of the
War for American Independence

> There is a tide in the affairs of men, which, taken at
> the flood, Leads on to fortune.—*William Shakespeare*

ON THURSDAY, JUNE 15, 1775, THE SECOND CONTINENTAL CONgress, meeting in Philadelphia in the aftermath of the battles at Lexington and Concord, unanimously elected George Washington to be commander in chief of the yet to be raised Continental Army. That they could take such an important action unanimously, in spite of the disagreements that divided Congress into factions, is one of the outstanding facts of the Revolution. In retrospect, it was to be one of the truly fateful and significant moments in all of American history, as over the next twenty-four years George Washington became the indispensable man in the creation of the American republic. How did his unanimous selection come about? What fortuitous combination of "nature" and "fortune" made George Washington exactly the right man at the right place at the right time? Ultimately, Washington would credit his appointment to the mysterious workings of Providence. Whether God-directed or man-directed, it is another interesting chapter in the life of America's greatest hero.

Certainly, in 1758 the idea that he would lead a revolt of the American colonies against the British Empire would have seemed preposterous to George Washington. With his retirement from the military, he thought he was permanently removing himself from the busy world stage. There is no question that the elegant lifestyle of the Virginia gentry that Washington embarked upon following his resignation differed dramatically from his stressful and dangerous life as a soldier. Yet, while his lifestyle was different, his personality was not. His ambition, energy, competitiveness, and drive remained as strong as ever but were simply channeled differently. His relentless drive for distinction would now be directed into excelling in three interconnected areas: society, politics, and economics. By 1775, Washington was extremely successful in all three areas and had evolved into the "complete gentleman" that he had long desired to be but was not in 1758.

Undoubtedly, a major factor in his success and transformation was his marriage to Martha Dandridge Custis in January of 1759. (This absolutely central relationship is examined in chapter 5.) Martha Custis was the wealthiest widow in Virginia, and the marriage provided not only great financial wealth but also the security and prestige that went with it. George Washington would never again write the type of obsequious letter he sent to Lord Loudoun during the recent war. He now had the means to enlarge and refine his home at Mount Vernon as a statement of his emergence as a planter of the very first rank.

A particularly insightful dissertation by Guthrie Sayen examines the genteel ethos of eighteenth-century Great Britain and America and shows how it may be divided into four overlapping types—the court (or amiable) gentlemen, the virtuous gentlemen, the enlightened gentlemen, and the warrior gentlemen. Courtesy (derived from the word "court" to describe how one was to act at court) was an integral part of the genteel ethos. The court gentleman was distinguished by his birth, wealth, looks, manners, taste, skill in dancing, and complaisance—that is, his ability to make himself agreeable to others. Complaisance was central to being a gentleman: "Good Breeding," wrote John Locke, "has no other use or end, but to make People easie and satisfied in their conversation with us." Of the many courtesy books written during this time, *The Rules of Civility*, which George Washington copied as a young man, most influenced his conduct. As Professor Sayen correctly notes, historians have not given enough attention to Washington's "soft side," especially his sociability and amiability that were central to his personality before 1775 and crucial to his success after 1775.

During the years before the American Revolution, Washington led a life of supercharged sociability, dining with friends, playing at cards, billiards, and backgammon, dancing at balls, attending horse races and the theater, and fishing and hunting, especially fox hunting, which appeared to be his favorite form of amusement. The George Washington of this period was not all gravitas but was a much friendlier and approachable person than the stiff, aloof Washington of legend. He enjoyed people and had many friends, among them Robert Orme, Dr. James Craik, Burwell Bassett, John Posey, and Captain Robert Stewart. His complaisance, the ability to make himself agreeable to others, helps explain his charismatic appeal to contemporaries and his superlative leadership ability.

A second illustration of Washington's desire for distinction can be seen by briefly examining his political career. Again, the traditional view is that from 1759 to 1775 Washington mainly concerned himself with his private affairs at Mount Vernon and spent little time on or gave little attention to matters of politics. Frankly, as Paul Longmore effectively demonstrates, such an image was fostered by Washington himself, who wished to have his biography coincide with the preferred image of himself as "disinterested." A reexamination of his career, focusing on his political activities, indicates perpetual interest and involvement in politics throughout his adult life. It reveals him to be both an ambitious and astute politician. For instance, he saved the poll lists from each of the contested elections in which he ran for the House of Burgesses, even keeping one from his brother Lawrence's race. Furthermore, he took the trouble to alphabetize some of them, evidently for more efficient use during future elections. At the age of only twenty-three, in another example of Washington's youthful audacity, he had his brother Jack secretly test the waters in Fairfax County to see if he might be able to run for a seat in the House of Burgesses despite the fact that he held no local offices at the time.

In Virginia, a person could both vote in and represent any county in which he owned property. After a false start in Frederick County in 1755, Washington, at age twenty-six, won election to the House of Burgesses from that county in 1758. (In the process he spent an inordinate amount of money to "treat" the voters to alcoholic refreshment.) Three years later, in one of the less admirable acts of his life, he urged the sheriff of Frederick County to bend the elections law to assist his own reelection and the election of his fellow candidate, George Mercer, against a challenge from his former subordinate, Colonel Adam Stephen: "I hope, and indeed make no doubt that you will contribute your aid towards shutting him [Stephen] out of the Public trust he is seeking, could Mercer's Friends and mine be hurried in at the first of the Poll it might be an advantage, but as Sheriff I know you cannot appear in this, nor would I by any mean have you do any thing that can give so designing a Man as Colo. Stevens the least trouble."

In time, Washington also became increasingly active at the local level as well. He was a vestryman for Truro Parish, a justice of the peace for Fairfax County, and a trustee for the city of Alexandria. His papers reveal a man with a growing sense of civic responsibility and a man of considerable generosity to family, friends, and the community at large. He paid for the education of friends' and relatives' children, lent money without interest, regularly and generously tipped household servants, and gave money to the deserving poor. Washington's great biographer Douglas Southall Freeman expressed it this way:

> [Washington's] code of noblesse oblige would not permit him to turn away perplexed farmers of humble station who valued his judgment above the advice of lawyers and the more so because it cost them nothing, old soldiers who seemed to think their Colonel must remain their counsellor, aging planters of wealth who wanted a prudent executor of their will, or a careful guardian of their sons. All these were beginning now to call on Washington. To hear them took hours; to solve their problems or to relieve their distress sometimes called for days of writing and of riding. It was costly but it was not shunned. Instead, Washington's service for his neighbors daily increased his sense of obligation to them and, at the same time, gave him longer patience and new understanding of men.

George Washington's growing sense of noblesse oblige and service to his community should not lead one to conclude that he was not concerned with his own economic interests, for he certainly desired to stand out in this area as well as socially and politically. Economic wealth meant autonomy and independence, both vital to Washington, who strongly desired to be in control. Personally, I believe it is impossible to read his personal papers without coming away with a strong sense of how powerfully Washington worked to enhance his economic wealth. As Joseph Ellis articulated it, "He was excessively and conspicuously assiduous in the defense of his own interests, especially when he suspected he was being cheated out of money or land." The Master of Mount Vernon had two main financial concerns—to make his tobacco plantations profitable and to make his large investments in western lands a success.

Space prohibits examining this issue in depth, but Washington managed to double the acreage of Mount Vernon to about 6,500 acres, greatly increased his slave force, switched his Mount Vernon farms from tobacco to more profitable grains, started a money-making milling enterprise, engaged in a profitable fisheries business, and traded extensively in the Caribbean, even becoming a ship owner. He used (critics with some justification would say misused) his service in the French and Indian War as a springboard to ultimately acquire over 33,000 acres of land in the west. Much of the land was, in his words, "the cream of the crop." (For example, one of his land acquisitions included forty-two miles of riverfront property.) But Washington argued that he was entitled to it because without his efforts the land would never have become available to the veterans in the first place: "If it had not been for my unremitted attention to every favourable circumstance, not a single acre of Land would ever have been obtained."

Thus, by 1775, there is no question that George Washington had succeeded in his second career as Master of Mount Vernon. Somehow, Washington gradually reconciled honor's conflicting values of self-assertion and self-sacrifice by effectively pursuing both his own interests and the interests of his countrymen. Triumphant at many levels and a planter of the first rank, he had evolved into the "complete gentleman" that he had long wished to be. Why would such a man—successful, wealthy, and essentially conservative—be receptive both to the radical Whig message and to the task of leading armed resistance against what he earlier referred to as "my king and country"?

Like most Virginians of the 1750s, young Washington luxuriated in his patriotism and love of king and country. As British nationalism intensified at mid-century, most Virginians' initial impulse was to join the chorus, affirming their true "Britishness," their unquestioned loyalty to king and constitution, and their deep hostility to France and Catholicism. Certainly, young George Washington was enamored with Great Britain. He was disheartened that his father's untimely demise kept him from obtaining a British education like his older half brothers, long expressed a desire to go to England, and narrowly missed joining the British navy as a teenager. (This is at least one thing for which we can thank his mother, the difficult and irascible Mary Ball Washington.) As we have seen, his quest for a royal commission in the British army during the French and Indian War was relentless. One can't help but speculate how different subsequent history would have been if Washington had achieved any one of these three early goals—a British education, a commission in the British navy, or official rank in the British army.

Over time, George Washington's view of Great Britain soured, and the radical Whig image of a corrupt, power-hungry ministry became more and more resonant and believable to him. While his path to this transformation is a complicated story, a number of things seemed to have converged to bring it about. As Linda Colley has argued, one important result of the surge of aggressive nationalism in Great Britain by the middle of the century was that the English more clearly defined colonial Americans as "other," as a remote people beyond the effective boundaries of the new national imagination. In the French and Indian War, the military contributions of the colonists were downplayed, and the general tone implied that the victory represented more an expansion of empire than the defense of a homeland: "The English now began to regard North American colonists less as fellow Englishmen across the Atlantic and more as another set of people to be ruled."

For men like George Washington, striving to be accepted as a member of the club, the realization that the British really regarded white colonial Americans as second-class beings was a shock. (A young John Adams snarled, "We won't be their Negroes.") Washington believed that Americans of high achievement were just as deserving as Englishmen of high station. Frustrated by his treatment in the French and Indian War, he declared, "We cant conceive, that being Americans shoud deprive us of the benefits of British Subjects," and later further asserted, "I conceive the services of a Provincial Officer as worthy of reward as those of a regular one." Colonel Washington saw British operations up close and was disillusioned by what he experienced. Like viewing the powerful Wizard of Oz, things appeared in a very different light once you looked behind the curtain.

George Washington was disappointed with Great Britain not only in his quest for military rank. In his business pursuits, he soon ran into difficulties with British merchants and policies that parallel his earlier frustrations with the British army. Washington very much wanted to grow fine tobacco, as there were important psychological aspects connected with being a successful tobacco "crop master" as well as economic ones. Yet, despite his best efforts—and Washington was a highly capable and disciplined businessman and an advanced "scientific" farmer—he found his efforts constantly thwarted by legislative acts and other actions of Great Britain and its merchants that seemed increasingly not only short-sighted but also mean-spirited as well.

The Custis plantations produced about 100,000 pounds of tobacco a year during the 1760s, and Washington's correspondence with his agent, Robert Cary and Sons, is a litany of complaints about the low price he received for his tobacco and the high prices he paid for shoddy and outdated products. He felt he was being discriminated against simply because he was an American and people like Cary believed he did not deserve first-class treatment. The whole mercantile system, represented to Washington by the personal face of Robert Cary, seemed designed to foster dependency, and if there was anything the Master of Mount Vernon wished to avoid, it was a sense of dependency.

Earlier and with more clarity than most others, Washington saw that the future of America (and the way to great personal fortune) lay in the huge untapped resources of the country west of the Allegheny Mountains. Here, as in his quest for a British commission and success as a tobacco planter, he found himself thwarted by what he viewed as unjust actions by Great Britain's Parliament and leaders. Washington's vision of a great interior commonwealth was not attractive to the king's principal advisors in London. The obstacles he faced were enough to exasperate a very patient man. The Proclamation Act of 1763 sought to close the vast regions west of the Alleghenies to

Anglo-American settlers. The colonies needed to expand and grow, and the British government was determined to block that expansion and stifle that growth. Washington did not believe that words could stop the inevitable and continued his activities in land speculation: "I can never look upon that Proclamation in any other light . . . than as a temporary expedien[t] to quiet the Minds of the Indians." When he thought his efforts to obtain bounty lands along the Great Kanawha River in western Virginia were to finally be crowned with success after almost two decades, Parliament unceremoniously detached from Virginia the land north of the Ohio River and gave it to Canada, and in so doing created a condition unfavorable to the development of his large tract on the Great Kanawha. At the same time, Lord Hillsborough, the British secretary for the American colonies, ruled that the land granted to veterans of the French and Indian War should be reserved only for British regulars. As a crowning blow, on March 21, 1775, Virginia's governor, Lord Dunmore, suddenly canceled Washington's claim to thousands of acres of prime land—apparently on the pretext that Washington's surveyor, William Crawford, was not qualified and properly licensed to make the surveys.

Thus, as we prepare to examine the course Washington followed on the road to revolution, hopefully the picture sketched above makes the decisions Washington made more understandable. An intensely ambitious man, Washington found his initial outlets blocked and himself treated as a second-class citizen. Denied official British rank, hampered in his efforts to be a great tobacco planter, thwarted in his dream of a western empire, George Washington was understandably receptive to an ideology that warned of corruption and tyranny. He became an avid reader of political treatises (Washington was much more widely read than he is usually credited with being) and long before most of his contemporaries, he linked his personal grievances to the developing constitutional crisis between the colonies and the mother country. Perhaps those historians who argue the Americans overreacted to practical efforts by Great Britain to obtain revenue and control the development of her colonies have a point, but it is easy to see why Washington would have interpreted British actions so negatively. And the colonial radicals' Whig message was not only negative. It also held out the promise of virtuous, liberty-loving freemen living lives of independence and advancing as far as their talents could take them. Perchance in joining and supporting this new cause, George Washington saw both a promising cause and the chance to achieve his long held—and I think still held—desire for fame and glory.

The traditional view of Washington is to portray him as a rather late convert to active resistance. In the words of John Ferling, a recent Washington biographer, "Events were beginning to swirl about the colonies that autumn [1773] that would change Washington's life forever, but he seemed heedless of the course. . . . Washington, typically, had expressed no interest in the politics of the British Empire. For nearly fifteen years the management of his estate and varied business interests had been very nearly his sole concerns."

Certainly, there is some truth in this assessment. Before the summer of 1774, Washington had not been one of the more conspicuous opponents of the British measures that inspired colonial resistance. Washington was neither a writer, orator, constitutional lawyer, nor an organizer of the urban masses. He was in fact primarily a planter and businessman and consequently had not gained the type of notoriety that a Sam Adams did in Massachusetts or a Patrick Henry did in Washington's Old Dominion. Nevertheless, I believe a closer look at the years leading up to the American Revolution, especially the years from 1769 on, will show that George Washington was in fact one of the most forward and determined of all of the colonial leaders. While he was not flamboyant, one is struck by the depth of his opposition and his willingness to follow a course of armed resistance much earlier than most of his fellow Virginians.

The most often quoted letter in support of this position is one Washington wrote to his mentor, George Mason, in April of 1769, supporting the idea of a boycott as a means of pressuring Great Britain to respect the colonists' rights:

At a time when our lordly Masters in Great Britain will be satisfied with nothing less than the deprivation of American freedom, it seems highly necessary that something shou'd be done to avert the stroke and maintain the liberty which we have derived from our Ancestors; . . . That no man shou'd scruple, or hesitate a moment to use a–ms [Washington could not write the emotive word out in its entirety but instead wrote "a", dash, "ms"] in defense of so valuable a blessing, on which all the good and evil of life depends; is clearly my opinion; Yet A–ms I wou'd beg leave to add, should be the last resource, dernier [last] resort.

Willard Sterne Randall might exaggerate but makes a valid point by noting that in writing the letter, "Washington was putting his trust, indeed his life, in the hands of Mason. The letter in the wrong hands was plainly seditious on the face of it." George Washington was going further than almost any other Virginian was to go for the next five years. Not only was a boycott in order, but, if it failed, Americans must be prepared to take up arms in a civil war against a tyrannical Parliament to protect their basic rights.

A much less quoted but interesting letter from Arthur Lee lends additional support for the assertion that Washington from an early period strongly countenanced the use of military resistance under certain circumstances. Writing to the then-famous General Washington in 1777, Lee recollected, "I never forgot your declaration when I had the pleasure of being at your House in [July] 1768 [nine months before Washington's letter to Mason] that you was ready to take your Musket upon your Shoulder, whenever your Country call'd upon you, I heard that declaration with great satisfaction, I recollect it with the Same, & have seen it verify'd to your Immortal honor & the eminent advantage of the Illustrious cause in which we are contending."

Happily for our understanding of Washington's political philosophy during the critical years before the war, his good friend, Bryan Fairfax, son of his patron, William Fairfax, held contrary views. In explaining his position to Fairfax during the summer of 1774, Washington revealed how thoroughly he had thought out the implications of British oppression, as the following excerpts demonstrate. They are a classic statement of the Patriot or Whig position and illustrate how completely Washington embraced this philosophy.

Does it not appear, as clear as the sun in its meridian brightness, that there is a regular, systematic plan formed to fix the right and practice of taxation upon us? Does not the uniform conduct of Parliament for some years past confirm this? Does not . . . [the bill] for transporting offenders . . . to Great Britain for trial, where

it is impossible from the nature of the thing that justice can be obtained, convince us that the administration is determined to stick
at nothing to carry its point? Ought we not, then, to put our virtue
and fortitude to the severest test?

Shall we supinely sit, and see one Provence after another fall a Sacra-
fice to Despotism? . . . [for Parliament has] exhibited unexampled
Testimony of the most despotick System of Tyranny that ever was
practiced in a free Government. . . . I think the Parliament of Great
Britain hath no more Right to put their hands into my Pocket, without my consent, than I have to put my hands into your's, for money.
. . . I . . . should much distrust my own judgment upon the occasion, if my Nature did not recoil at the thought of Submitting to
Measures which I think Subversive of every thing that I ought to
hold dear and valuable—and did I not find, at the same time, that
the voice of Mankind is with me.

An Innate Spirit of freedom first told me, that the Measures which
Administration hath for sometime been, and now are, most vio-
lently pursuing, are repugnant to every principle of natural justice; whilst much abler heads than my own, hath fully convinced
me that it is not only repugnant to natural Right, but Subversive
of the Laws & Constitution of Great Britain itself; . . . the Crisis
is arrivd when we must assert our Rights, or Submit to every Im-
position that can be heap'd upon us; till custom and use, will make
us as tame, & abject Slaves as the Blacks we Rule over with such
arbitrary Sway.

To another correspondent, he lamented that Americans "are every
day receiving fresh proofs of a Systematic ascertion of an arbitrary
power, deeply planned to overturn the Laws & Constitution of their
country, & to violate the most essential & valuable rights of mankind."
George Washington was a reluctant revolutionary who genuinely believed he was being forced into active resistance by Great Britain's
tyrannical actions. Prior to the war, he rejected the British claim that
Americans wanted independence: "I am as well satisfied, as I can be
of my existence, that no such thing is desired by any thinking man in

all North America; on the contrary, that it is the ardent wish of the warmest advocates for liberty, that peace & tranquility, upon Constitutional grounds, may be restored, & the horrors of civil discord prevented." He warned his British correspondent, however, that "more blood will be spilt on this occasion (if the Ministry are determined to push matters to extremity) than history has ever yet furnished instances of in the annals of North America; and such a vital wound given to the peace of this great Country, as time itself cannot cure or eradicate the remembrance of."

Of course, the ministry persisted and blood flowed at Lexington and Concord in April of 1775 as Washington feared it would: "Unhappy it is though to reflect, that a Brother's Sword has been sheathed in a Brother's breast, and that, the once happy and peaceful plains of America are either to be drenched with Blood, or Inhabited by Slaves. Sad alternative! But can a virtuous Man hesitate in his choice?" Even before the outbreak of the fighting Washington informed his brother Jack that, if necessary, he was fully prepared to "devote my Life and Fortune" to the cause of resisting British oppression. Now, in the aftermath of Lexington and Concord, George Washington as a virtuous man had made his choice. Arms might be the last resort, but the time for arms had come.

It was with such thoughts on his mind that George Washington prepared to go back to Philadelphia for the Second Continental Congress. As the likelihood of armed conflict increased, Washington's prominence as a leader rose in Virginia and elsewhere. When the House of Burgesses, meeting as the First Virginia Convention in the fall of 1774, had to choose seven delegates to attend the First Continental Congress in Philadelphia, 95 percent of the members voted for Washington to be one of the delegates. (In passing, Washington received 10 percent more of the vote than did the fiery Patrick Henry.) To attend the Second Continental Congress, Colonel Washington was chosen with more votes than any Virginian save the venerable Peyton Randolph who was the president of the Continental Congress.

The traditional version of what happened next is well known. John Adams nominated a reluctant George Washington to be the commander in chief of the yet to be raised Continental Army. Upon hearing the beginning of the speech, a surprised and embarrassed Washington bolted from the room, encouraged his friend and attorney Edmund Pendleton to oppose the nomination, emphasized to the delegates that he had not sought the nomination and did not think himself capable of doing the job. While most of the facts are accurate, it is not the whole story and conveys an inaccurate rendering of the dynamics at play. Since the decision to take command of the Continental Army most shaped his place in history, it merits a closer examination.

From the beginning George Washington was the leading candidate, and with the advantage of historical hindsight, one might assert the inevitable candidate. It was not by chance that he was unanimously chosen. Let's examine the record. Washington already had a prominent reputation as a military figure both in Virginia and elsewhere. It is significant that six counties from all geographical areas of the colony—Fairfax, Prince William, Albemarle, Spotsylvania, Richmond, and Westmoreland—had all chosen Washington to command their independent companies. In his home county of Fairfax, he and George Mason designed the buff and blue uniforms (later to be adopted for the officers of the new American army) and made Fairfax County a leader in the resistance movement by their innovative actions. Washington had an excellent reputation in New England based on his experience in the French and Indian War. The congressional delegates widely, if inaccurately, believed that following the passage of the Intolerable Acts, Washington had offered to raise and train one thousand men at his own expense and send them to Boston's aid. On the way to Philadelphia in May of 1775, Washington was feted as a military expert in Baltimore and asked to review their volunteer units. His arrival in Philadelphia was greeted by a large turnout unmatched by any other delegate. Congress immediately put him on several important military committees overseeing such tasks as how to defend New York City and find ammunition and supplies for the coming conflict.

Politically, visually, and in terms of character, Washington was virtually the ideal choice. Certainly, there were "political" considerations to take into account. Virginia was by far the largest, most populous, and wealthiest of the thirteen colonies, and New England leaders desired and needed Virginia's support and active participation in the upcoming struggle. If Washington had been from Delaware, he might not have been chosen. Being a Virginian, however important, was not sufficient. Other factors were also important. In comparison with other native-born Americans, he had significant military experience. At the age of forty-three he was mature but still very vigorous and in the prime of his manhood. Equally important, George Washington looked the part. His military air and bearing, augmented by the wearing of his brand-new uniform, impressed virtually everyone: "He has so much martial dignity in his deportment," said Dr. Benjamin Rush of Philadelphia, "that you would distinguish him to be a general and a soldier from among ten thousand people. There is not a king in Europe that would not look like a valet de chambre by his side."

Perhaps most importantly, George Washington was the type of leader in which the American patriots could take great pride. A devoted family man of great wealth and moderate views, he was nevertheless fully committed to the patriot cause. Washington's character and demeanor clearly impressed his fellow delegates, and his appeal grew with exposure. As Silas Deane, a delegate from Connecticut, expressed it, "The more I am acquainted with, the more I esteem him. . . . His Virtues do not shine in the View of the World by reason of his great Modesty but when discovered by the discerning Eye, shine proportionably brighter." "He seems discre[e]t & Virtuous," said Eliphalet Dyer of Connecticut, "no harum Starum ranting fellow but Sober, steady, & calm." One of the delegates, Thomas Cushing of Massachusetts, succinctly summarized George Washington's character: "He is a complete gentleman. He is sensible, amiable, virtuous, modest, and brave. I assure myself that your acquaintance with him will afford you great pleasure, and I doubt not his agreeable behaviour and good conduct will give great satisfaction to our people of all denominations."

As Guthrie Sayen explains, Cushing ascribed to Washington the cardinal qualities of the four major aspects of the gentry ethos. Washington's good sense marked him as an enlightened gentleman: intelligent, reasonable, judicious. His amiability showed him to be a court gentleman, whose social address and deferential manners made him agreeable to all. His virtue identified him as a gentleman who was willing to sacrifice private interest for public good. His bravery revealed him a warrior, which is what the leaders of the American resistance movement needed in June 1775. And his modesty, as Deane noted, made the other qualities shine brighter.

No one person could personify all facets of gentility, but Washington's American peers were deeply impressed by the degree to which he exemplified the genteel ethos. In Abigail Adams's phrase, he agreeably blended the gentleman and the soldier. Put another way, George Washington combined in an exceptional fashion the courtesy and complaisance of the courtier with the appearance and record of a warrior. This compelling blend of apparent diffidence and power made him attractive to many and acceptable to all: "The Master of Mount Vernon gave lie to the notion that all provincials lacked grace, refinement and the finest amenities." It was his character, rather than his military knowledge or experience, that made him the perfect choice to lead America's new army. As Silas Deane put it, he was selected because "he removes all jealousies, and that is the main point."

How did Washington feel about these developments? Did he want the appointment? Both publicly and privately, he denied any such desire. Perhaps we can come closest to understanding Washington's perspective from words he wrote his wife, Martha (one of the very rare letters that have survived): "I have used every endeavour in my power to avoid it, not only from my unwillingness to part with you and the Family, but from a consciousness of its being a trust too great for my Capacity and that I should enjoy more real happiness and felicity in one month with you, at home, than I have the most distant prospect of reaping abroad, if my stay were to be Seven times Seven years. But, as it has been a kind of destiny that has thrown me upon this Service, I shall hope that my undertaking of it, is designd to answer some good purpose."

At one level, this is all true—a major part of Washington did not want the appointment (what sane man would, considering the difficulties to be surmounted) and, certainly, he feared he would fail and ruin his hard-earned reputation. But I do not think it is the whole story. I would suggest, though it is impossible to prove, that another part of George Washington wanted the position and made it very likely that it would be offered to him. Let me briefly indicate why I think this may be the case. There is no disputing his desire for military glory in the French and Indian War. In his words, "My inclinations are strongly bent to arms," and he hoped to "be distinguished in some measure from the general run of provincial officers." Even at the end of that frightful war, he still expressed his belief in the benefits of a heroic death, "Who is there that does not rather Envy, than regret a Death that gives birth to Honour & Glorious memory?"

Personally, I am not convinced Washington ever completely put out of his mind dreams of military glory. I think it is worth noting that after he resigned and married, he tried (unsuccessfully, as it turned out) to buy a number of busts of military heroes for Mount Vernon, including those of Julius Caesar, Alexander the Great, and Frederick the Great. When he prepared to have his first (and what he probably thought at the time would be his only) portrait painted in 1772 by Charles Willson Peale, he significantly donned his old uniform from the French and Indian War, now fourteen years in the past. Before he left Mount Vernon for the Second Continental Congress, he was visited by Horatio Gates, a companion in arms from the French and Indian War and a former British officer, who wondered no doubt, what place, if war came, he could find in the armed forces of the colonies whose cause he had resolved to support. (The controversial Charles Lee had come earlier on a similar mission.) It is hard to believe that George Washington did not think about the same things. He was simply too smart and too ambitious not to do so.

And, of course, George Washington wore his military uniform to the sessions of Congress. While there has been some dispute on which military uniform he wore, it now seems clear that it was the buff and blue uniform he had designed for the Fairfax County militia. (Washington loved uniforms, and buff and blue were the colors of the Whig party in Great Britain.) And, of all the members attending the convention, as far as we know only he wore a uniform. When you are over six feet tall, of imposing martial bearing and wearing a brand-new uniform, and you know there is virtual unanimity among the delegates that an army is to be formed, it can't come as a total shock to discover that you are being seriously considered for a leadership position.

George Washington throughout his life proved himself a master of the effective gesture. (Washington had a life-long fascination with the theater and he saw himself as "a figure on the stage" and wanted desperately to play his part well.) From the days of his awkward, ambitious youth, Washington was intensely conscious of the symbolic importance of behavior and image. If we look at his subsequent life, it is clear that modeling—to use a modern term—was important to him—actually critical to understanding his relationships with almost everyone. He was not a quick or outstanding orator and he was conscious of his "defective education." What he could not articulate, he offered as example. Deeds speak louder than words, Washington believed with all his heart and, over time, he became a master of the correct gesture.

Wasn't donning his military regalia an effective gesture? On one level, wearing the uniform was a statement of his commitment to American rights, but it also sent a signal of his availability. Of course, Washington did not actively campaign for the position—this would have gone against the Whiggish fear of power. But I do not think it is accurate to say Washington did everything in his power to keep from being appointed. His letter to Martha makes explicit that he knew he was seriously being considered for the position for some time prior to his actual nomination. (One wonders if that realization prompted him in early June to buy five books on the military art and a tomahawk, several cartouch boxes, and new coverings for his holsters.) Significantly, although he knew he was the leading candidate, he did little if anything to discourage such talk. For example, he might have proposed another candidate for the position, but it is clear that he did not do so.

Of course, a genuine part of George Washington did not want to be chosen, as he was ambivalent about power—eager for it and at the same time fearful of failure. In psychological terms, it may be seen as an "approach–avoidance" dilemma (or a wish/fear tension). For whatever reason or combination of reasons, Washington had a deep and burning desire for fame and glory. He was drawn to power and the chance to win that fame and glory. This would be difficult for Washington to verbalize or even consciously acknowledge. Joseph Ellis is correct when he argues that Washington had considerable trouble acknowledging his own ambitions: "His claim that he had no interest in the commander-in-chief post was not so much a lie as essential fabrication that shielded him from the recognition that, within a Continental Congress filled with ambitious delegates, he was the most ambitious—not just the tallest—man in the room. He needed to convince himself that the summons came from outside rather than inside his own soul."

An additional factor increasing his hesitation, Washington had internalized the Whig distrust of power and how dangerous it can be. He knew accepting his new appointment would threaten his autonomy, and a very strong part of him desired to live in peace and security under his own vine and fig tree at Mount Vernon. Failure to achieve his mission would cost him his autonomy and his dearly desired reputation—and perhaps his life. Yet the chance to lead America in what soon became the "glorious cause," to defend and strengthen liberty and republicanism *and* to earn glory and fame for George Washington was a "win-win" situation. I think he wanted the job and acted to get it but sought it in a very subtle and wise way. As Longmore observes, he carefully regarded appearances; how will his audience perceive and interpret his conduct? He protested his inadequacy. He avoided actively soliciting the job. And finally, by making the offer come to him, rather than actively promoting himself, he increased his influence and authority.

George Washington's understanding of the mind-set of the Continental Congress is brilliantly demonstrated by his very first act on accepting command. He offered to serve without pay. He knew that the Continental Congress feared military power and the man on horseback. Even as they voted to raise an army to defend their rights they were nervous that it could turn on them. (The Whig ideology posited that a standing army in a time of peace was a major threat to liberty and should not be tolerated.) By offering to serve without pay, Washington went far to demonstrate he was a man who could be trusted with power because he took it reluctantly, would not abuse it, and would relinquish it when the task was done. And frankly, Washington would prove in the Revolution and later that he could be trusted with power. He, unlike many revolutionaries, had a basically healthy psyche. He had a plantation that he loved and a family that he loved and to whom he wished to return. Even as part of him desired fame and glory, it was fame and glory won not by achieving great power but rather by performing service for the greater good, a service which would earn him the affection and admiration of his fellow men that he so desperately desired.

That is, of course, if he could carry out the mission successfully. The task was daunting in the extreme. I by no means wish to deny the reality and genuineness of Washington's professed concerns and worries. Success had to seem a very long shot indeed. Shortly after his nomination he talked with Patrick Henry and told the great rebel to remember his words, that with this nomination, "I date my fall and the ruin of my reputation." Happily for George Washington, and the country he came to love, he once again could not have been more mistaken!

The inauguration of Washington as president. (Courtesy of the Mount Vernon Ladies' Association)

3

"A Kind of Inevitable Necessity"

The Presidency of George Washington

Necessity so bow'd the state that I and greatness were
compelled to kiss.—*William Shakespeare*

He had done it! However improbable it might have seemed,
George Washington had led his ragtag forces to victory over the
greatest military power of the eighteenth century. After a protracted
and bitter struggle lasting over eight years, Washington had achieved
something like total victory both for his country and for himself.
(Washington could only credit such an unlikely result to the mysterious workings of a benign Providence.) America's independence
from Great Britain, assured by his victory over General Cornwallis at
Yorktown in 1781, was formally recognized in the Treaty of Paris of
1783. On a personal level, George Washington emerged from the tax-
ing struggle as the unrivaled hero and savior of his country—far and
away the most beloved and admired man in America as well as one of
the most famous men in the Western world. Rather typically, a French
chaplain wrote, "Throughout all [this country] he appears like a benevolent God; old men, women, children all flock eagerly to catch a
glimpse of him; people follow him through the towns with torches."
The president of Yale, Ezra Stiles, declared in 1783, "Oh, Washington,
how I do love thy name! How I have often adored and blessed thy God
for creating and forming thee, the great ornament of humankind!"
The poet Francis Hopkins declared George Washington was "the best
and greatest man the world ever knew," adding that "had he lived in

the lap of idolatry, he had been worshipped as a god." And so it went. No American before or since has ever been so revered.

The fame and honor he had sought were now his in a way that must have exceeded even his fondest expectations. Douglas South-all Freeman understood Washington's motivation: "Other men might want ships or mistresses, or race horses and luck at cards; his ambition was that of deserving, winning, and retaining the goodwill of right-minded Americans." With victory achieved and fame assured, Washington was determined to perform what he certainly thought was the last, and, many since have declared, the greatest act of his life. He would return his commission to Congress, walk away from the power, and live out the remaining years of his life as a farmer on his beloved Mount Vernon. The voluntary surrender of unprecedented power struck observers as the last act of a great historical drama. King George III declared that if Washington did that, he would be the greatest man of his age. He did. It was perhaps, as Joseph Ellis put it, the greatest exit in American history.

George Washington understood that the purity of a perfect heroism was the willingness to be rewarded *only in fame*, not in material awards. That is what made his voluntary retirement and return to Mount Vernon and private life so special and drew comment from around the world. As the Pulitzer Prize–winning historian Gordon Wood perceptively notes, "Washington was not naïve. He was well aware of the effect his resignation would have. He was trying to live up to the age's image of a classical disinterested patriot who devotes his life to his country" and then retires to his farm.

As it turned out, the length of Washington's retirement would be directly connected to the success of the new country and its experiment in republican government. Whether the thirteen former colonies— now independent states but jealous of their rights and privileges and fearful of anything that seemed to give too much power to a central government—could remain one single country was very much an open question. In his Circular Letter to the States, his first farewell address, Washington gave advice to his beloved country on how it could prosper and thrive. He explained that America was particularly blessed on many different levels and the future was bright. Yet, His Excellency added a warning and note of caution: "At this auspicious period, the United States came into existence as a Nation, and if their Citizens should not be completely free and happy, the fault will be intirely their own." The General feared that excessive localism would undercut the effort at nation building.

The war had shaped Washington's philosophy and attitude toward a strong central government. He emerged from that conflict as an ultranationalist with a profound skepticism about the virtues of state sovereignty. Too often he had witnessed how the states' actions or lack of action had impaired the good of the nation as a whole. As historian Glenn Phelps summarized it, "Their local views, jealousy of the national government, unjustified fear of the army, and self-interest combined to make them the greatest obstacle to attaining the unity necessary for winning the war." Now these same forces seemed to combine to keep the Revolution from working out as Washington had hoped.

The General's letters during the mid 1780s are full of pessimism and foreboding. The country was fast approaching "the brink of the precipice," "a sea of trouble," "some awful crisis," "anarchy and confusion," or some other similarly gloomy metaphor. Instead of a quiet retirement, His Excellency found himself engaged in an active correspondence with friends and leaders around the country, arguing only a stronger and more energetic central government could preserve the union. The ultimate result of the growing concern among an increasingly large number of those Americans who, like Washington, "thought continentally," was what some have called the "Miracle at Philadelphia." There, with His Excellency presiding (he was again the unanimous choice), a new constitution was drawn up in 1787 and eventually ratified by a sufficient number of states by 1788 for the new government to go into effect. Washington's support was absolutely essential in the ratification struggle. In the words of an opponent in Virginia, William Grayson, "I think that were it not for one great character in America so many would not be for this government." Another declared he was sure Washington's support "had a secret and powerful influence in disposing the minds of the people to embrace the new constitution." James Monroe wrote to Thomas Jefferson in France, "Be assured, his influence carried the government."

The new Constitution of the United States, while leaving many questions unanswered, significantly strengthened the powers of the central government. Additionally, it created a brand-new office, the President of the United States, which was based on the assumption that "Energy in the executive is a leading character in the definition of good government." While definitely hedged, as everything the founders constructed was hedged, the presidency was an unexpectedly powerful office, especially in view of the authors' Whiggish fear of excessive political power. The president would serve for an unlimited number of four-year terms, appoint and supervise the heads of departments, be commander in chief of the army, and have veto power, the right to call Congress into special session, and a surprisingly large amount of latitude in directing the government in the conduct of its foreign relations.

There was simply no doubt in the minds of the delegates that the man who was presiding over their deliberations at Philadelphia would be the first president. As one of the delegates accurately put it, "Entre nous, I do not believe they [the powers of the president] would have been so great had not many of the members cast their eyes toward General Washington as President and shaped their ideas of the powers to be given a President by their opinions of his virtue." Interestingly then, and often overlooked, George Washington did a great deal to shape the office of president even before he occupied it.

Apparently, they all concluded that only Washington had the requisite skills and support to do the job. Gouverneur Morris, penman of the final version of the Constitution and one of America's most perceptive, if sarcastic and witty, founding fathers, explained to America's hero why he must accept the office.

> Your cool steady Temper is *indispensibly necessary* to give a firm and manly Tone to the new Government. . . . No Constitution is the same on Paper and in Life. The Exercise of Authority depends on personal Character; and the Whips and Reins by which an able Character governs unruly steeds will only hurl the unskilful Presumer with more speedy & headlong Violence to the Earth. The Horses once trained may be managed by a Woman or a Child; not so when they first feel the Bit. And indeed among these thirteen Horses now about to be coupled together there are some of every Race and Character. They will listen to your Voice, and submit to

your Control; you therefore must I say *must* mount this seat. (emphasis in the original)

Morris had to write such a letter, as did many others, because George Washington was genuinely reluctant to accept the office. In fact, no president in the over two hundred years since has wished to avoid the office more than George Washington did. In this instance, to borrow words that are more commonly used to describe his neighbor, George Mason, Washington was truly a "reluctant statesman." While one of course cannot read Washington's mind, my sense is that he was genuinely reluctant to become president in 1789 in a way that he had not been to become commander in chief in 1775. In both cases, the task facing him was daunting in the extreme, but there were some differences. Washington, now aging and past the prime of his life, declared he had no desire to face "the ten thousand embarrassments, perplexities & troubles to which I must again be exposed in the evening of a life, already near consumed in public cares." Additionally, at the conclusion of the War for Independence, Washington had solemnly pledged to permanently retire from public life, and he did not want to do anything that might cheapen or undercut the sincerity of that pledge. Believing his time on earth was short (he was very conscious that he was from a short-lived family), he did not want to leave his much-loved Mount Vernon yet again. Furthermore, his reputation and fame were already secure and could, in his view, only be weakened in the new position. His letters of the time have a plaintive quality to them—I don't want the position. Please don't choose me: "The great Searcher of human hearts knows there is no wish in mine, beyond that of living and dying an honest man, on my own farm."

In the final analysis, there was no other choice. A quote from Shakespeare's Henry IV seems applicable to Washington: "Necessity so bow'd the state that I and greatness were compelled to kiss." Whether aware of it or not, Washington's own words paralleled those of Henry. He wrote a close friend that "a kind of inevitable necessity" might eventually compel his acceptance. Washington was faced with a conundrum. How could he refuse, he worried, if "my refusal might induce a belief that I prefered the conservation of my own reputation & private ease to the good of my Country." Ultimately then, for Washington, it was a "sacrifice of inclination to the opinion of duty." Like the great Roman patriot Cato, Washington's life was grafted on to the fate of his country. It was not his own when his country demanded it. As he shared with Lafayette, "Like you, my dear Sir, I sighed for retirement; like me, I am afraid, you must continue the sacrifice." He confided in his diary that he prepared to leave Mount Vernon for his inauguration in New York City "with a mind oppressed with more anxious & painful sensations than I have words to express." He came close, however, in a letter to a friend: "My movements to the chair of Government will be accompanied with feelings not unlike those of a culprit who is going to the place of his execution."

If George Washington's feelings were like those of a man going to his execution, the actual journey from Mount Vernon to New York was one long triumphal march with rituals strikingly similar to those employed to welcome English monarchs on their "royal progresses" to their coronations in London. One of Washington's former aides noted, "You are now a King, under a different name," and wished that he "may reign long and happy over us." Washington was the central figure in an extended rite which lasted eight days and gave a kind of spontaneous legitimacy to his election. The president-elect's wish for a quiet entry into New York City, the nation's temporary capital, was completely ignored, as he must have known it would be. One correspondent noted, "The whole city was one scene of triumphal re-joicing." Shouts of "Long Live George Washington" rang out every-where. The fondest wish of every man, woman, and child seemed to be to simply get a glimpse of their hero. Some participants declared that they could now die happy, having seen the great Washington with their own eyes.

If no president entered office with more personal prestige and af-fection than George Washington, only Abraham Lincoln and Frank-lin Roosevelt faced comparable crises. At first glance, the crisis facing the first president might not seem so extreme. As Ellis reminds us, Washington's "achievement must be recovered before it can be appre-ciated, which means that we must recognize that there was no such thing as a viable American nation when he took office as president." His core achievement as president, much as it had been as commander in chief, was to transform the improbable into the inevitable and to create the nation that Lincoln and FDR could rescue later.

Washington's determination to secure the *union* defined his presidency. The President was first and foremost a supreme nationalist and approached his task as president with the mind-set of a strong nation builder. As Washington scholar Don Higginbotham expressed it, "George Washington, more than any member of the Revolutionary generation, both by word and deed, advanced the concept of an American nation, and pressed for the creation of an institutional umbrella to bind America together." Higginbotham suggests that Washington should be known by the nickname the Unifier, a phrase that nicely encapsulates what he wanted to accomplish. To achieve his overarching goal of a strong union, it was essential that the central government must be given enough power and authority to effectively govern, but other specific goals would have to be realized as well. The grave problem of the national debt and sufficient funding must be solved. Commerce must be encouraged. The western frontier must be secured from both Native Americans and foreign influence. Peace must be maintained with European powers. Partisanship and sectionalism must be minimized even if they could not be eliminated. It was a tall order indeed.

How successfully the experiment began was crucial. The first president was particularly sensitive that he and his administration were walking on "untrodden ground." As he explained, "Many things which appear of little importance of themselves at the beginning may have great & durable consequences from their having been established at the commencement of a new general government." Washington knew he personally would be closely scrutinized: "My political conduct . . . must be exceedingly circumspect and proof against just criticism, for the eyes of Argus [the hundred-eyed guardian of the gods in Greek mythology] are upon me, and no slip will pass unnoticed." That is why a great deal of time was spent on apparently trivial matters such as how the president should be addressed (John Adams suggested "His Exalted High Mightiness") and the manner in which the president should receive the general public. It was initially decided that the President and his wife, Martha, would make a brief appearance to greet invited guests in a rather stiff and formal way before retiring to seclusion. Washington thought that hand-shaking was much too familiar for the president to engage in; consequently, he kept one hand occupied holding a fake hat and the other resting on his dress sword. (Later, Martha held her own, less formal levees.) It was thought necessary that a certain distance be kept, although Washington carried out such rituals for reasons of state, not from any personal preference. Additionally, historian Joanne Freeman notes that the President self-consciously maintained a middle ground between authority and modesty, most strikingly, perhaps, in his daily walk: at two o'clock each afternoon, he dispensed with his beautiful, elaborately ornamented carriage and strolled around the block in the muck of the streets like anyone else—a seemingly trivial gesture with a powerful impact. Its graphic egalitarianism proved that Washington was no king.

George Washington, blessed with his majestic bearing, was able to endow the presidency with dignity and a certain formality and ceremony necessary to the rituals of governing. (Future presidents would be respected because of the office they held, but in Washington's case the office would become respected because of the man.) Initially, except in the minds of his relatively few critics, he managed to do so without slipping into the dangerous trappings of monarchy. It was a fine line to draw because Americans, used to the traditions and the royal pomp and ceremony attending monarchy and royal government, needed something in their place. Washington's personal magnetism and "modest dignity which excited involuntary respect, and inspired the purest attachment" helped the country move relatively easily from monarchy to republicanism. As James Flexner expressed it, Americans got charisma at hardly any cost.

Washington was very aware of his ceremonial role as president. He sat for innumerable portraits, delivered numerous proclamations and exchanged salutations with all sorts of religious and government groups, all actions intended to increase his visibility. He consciously employed his status as military leader and hero of the Revolution to create respect for national authority and to bolster the legitimacy of the new nation. In the absence of long-existing feelings of nationalism in the 1790s, popular celebrations of Washington became a substitute for patriotism. Despite the difficulties involved, he traveled to every state in the Union, the embodiment of the new nation and of revolutionary virtue. As he approached various towns on his southern tour in 1791, the President left his coach and mounted Prescott, his white parade steed, for a ceremonial and choreographed entry that gave lasting memories to many of the inhabitants.

Politics is theater, and Washington was America's first great actor-president, a man who very much saw himself as a figure on the stage and often used theatrical images to convey his thoughts. The image of George Washington as an "actor" is both very useful and also potentially misleading. The Greek word for "actor" has come almost unchanged into English: hypocrite, one pretending to be who he is not. Washington was not an actor in that sense. He believed in and absorbed the role he played (based primarily on the Roman patriot Cato as portrayed by the British essayist Joseph Addison) and was able to be exactly the type of leader the people desired.

While such ceremonial events were of critical importance, Washington would also have to be the chief executive and manage the affairs of state. The President was generally successful because he possessed a bundle of talents. He has been too commonly portrayed as a figurehead and passive political leader, when in fact he was the central politician of his age. In reality, he was not an icon but an energetic and shrewd activist. Few men, as Edmund Morgan has demonstrated, have understood power and effective leadership better than George Washington. Indeed, the word Morgan employs, "genius," is appropriate. The President had a vision and knew what he wanted to accomplish. A very astute judge of character and ability, and comfortable enough in his own persona, he actively sought the support of the "best and the brightest" to aid him in his mission. He was an excellent administrator. Perhaps nine-tenths of his time as commander in chief had been spent in administration. Managing Mount Vernon, his extensive land holdings in the west, and hundreds of slaves also honed these skills. Additionally, Washington had made no bargains to attain the presidency, and he had no debts to pay off or special interests to mollify. John Adams, an occasional critic of the first president, declared, "No man, I believe, has influence with the president. He seeks information from all quarters & judges more independently than any man I ever knew."

Washington's sensitivity to the difficulties he faced are indicated in an interesting and thoughtful personal letter he wrote a female admirer in Great Britain: "The establishment of our new Government seemed to be the last great experiment, for promoting human happiness, by reasonable compact, in civil Society. It was to be, in the first instance, in a considerable degree, a government of accommodation as well as a government of Laws. Much was to be done by *prudence*, much by *conciliation*, much by *firmness*. Few, who are not philosophical Spectators, can realise the difficult and delicate part which a man in my situation had to act" (emphasis in the original). Few historians connect George Washington with "philosophical spectators," but this letter proves just how aware Washington was of the complicated challenges he faced and the need to utilize various strategies to achieve his goals.

The President always weighed carefully what was politically feasible. Washington had to contend with the fact that at the very core of America's philosophy there was a deep distrust and fear of a consolidated, central government. We must remember that the national government, in the Revolutionary decade, had been built from the bottom up, with local bodies stingily endowing higher branches of government with certain necessary powers, so that not only was the structure as a whole fragile but its ultimate authority was no more than a bundle of concessions subject to withdrawal. Patriots like Patrick Henry and many others regarded any projection of executive power as a betrayal of the spirit of '76. While acutely aware of the fears many felt, George Washington simply viewed things differently. Not only was a strong national government absolutely essential to preserving an effective and genuine union, it was, however paradoxically, equally important in preserving the rights and liberties of both the states and citizens. Excessive parochialism and individualism would ultimately lead to the loss of the rights they were meant to protect.

The President faced a real dilemma. What was politically essential for the survival of the infant nation was ideologically at odds with what it claimed to stand for. In the face of this reality, where most Americans viewed government as "them" and not "us," Washington "fashioned a kind of Fabian presidency (the Roman general Fabius achieved his goals by delay and avoiding conflicts he might lose) that

sustained the credibility of the federal government by avoiding political battles that threatened to push federal sovereignty further and
faster than public opinion allowed." Two examples were on the question of slavery and on the power of the federal judiciary. On slavery,
for example, Washington, although increasingly personally critical
of the institution (this topic is examined in chapter 8), opposed the
Quaker petitions attacking slavery and was glad to see the issue buried. As Ellis notes, "What strikes us as a poignant failure of moral
leadership appeared to Washington as a prudent exercise in political
judgment. There is no evidence that he struggled over the decision.
Whatever his personal views on slavery may have been, his highest
public priority was the creation of a unified American nation."

If the nation were to prosper and survive, the economic crisis had
to be eased if not resolved. The President gave Alexander Hamilton
virtually total responsibility to rescue the debt-burdened American
economy. The secretary of the treasury's bold and brilliant plan involving funding, assumption of state debts, tariffs, and a national
bank solved the immediate financial crisis facing the young nation.
Indeed, Washington was soon boasting, "Our public credit stands
on that ground which three years ago it would have been considered
as a species of madness to have foretold." Yet, the success was purchased at a grave price. In the eyes of a growing number of his critics
(led by Washington's brilliant secretary of state, Thomas Jefferson,
and Hamilton's former collaborator, James Madison), the program
benefited mainly the speculators and the wealthy, concentrated in the
northern states, to the detriment of ordinary soldiers and farmers
throughout the country. In effect, in the view of these opponents, the
moneychangers had taken over the temple, and the original promise
of the American Revolution had fallen into enemy hands. Additionally,
in the eyes of his critics, Hamilton's plan enhanced the power of the
national government to a dangerous level, threatening the rights of
the states and endangering the liberties of the people.

The effort to block Hamilton's program was a major impetus in
the development of political parties, although there were never parties in the modern sense of the term during Washington's tenure as
president. Washington himself never accepted the idea of the "loyal

opposition" and viewed the nascent development of political parties as a dangerous threat to his vision of a united America. As historian Glenn Phelps points out, Washington, a classical republican, had a vision that "implied that there was something called the public interest to which virtuous men could unanimously subscribe. The idea that there could be equally valid, but different, notions of the public interest was utter nonsense to Washington—a heresy upon good republican precepts." He never understood the value of the two-party system, and while he succeeded in developing national unity, he failed in his goal of promoting political unity. Indeed, many of his actions and decisions, perhaps inevitably, led to increased partisanship.

Even graver threats to Washington's vision of a united America originated overseas. As president, George Washington's goals were national unity, social stability, sound money, and flourishing commerce. Ultimately, the French Revolution, breaking out in 1789, threatened all of them. Washington found himself confronted with perhaps the greatest test of his statesmanship. Not only did he have to deal with grave foreign policy crises associated with the general war in Europe but also with the domestic crises brought about by divergent American attitudes toward the French Revolution and the European war. Space does not allow examination of this story in the depth it deserves, but it merits some attention because it so clearly demonstrates Washington's mature leadership.

By 1793, France and England were at full scale war, and the President recognized that a war of such magnitude would inevitably dramatically impact the young and relatively weak United States, since she was deeply involved in international commerce. The challenge was to keep America from being destroyed by the conflagration: "It will be our prudence to cultivate a spirit of self-dependence—and to endeavour by unremitting vigilance and exertion under the blessing of providence to hold the scales of our destiny in our own hands. Standing, as it were, in the midst of falling empires, it should be our aim to assume a station and attitude which will preserve us from being overwhelmed in their ruins." Washington consequently issued a Proclamation of Neutrality, itself a controversial and precedent-setting action. While few Americans wanted war, most favored the French and wanted our neutrality slanted in a way favorable to that

President George Washington. Portrait by Gilbert Stuart.
(Courtesy of the Mount Vernon Ladies' Association)

nation. After all, France stood for "Liberty, Fraternity, and Equality"
and Great Britain was our recent foe who had tried to brutally crush
our just struggle for independence.

In seeking additional American support, the new and controversial
French ambassador, Edmund Genet, annoyed at the cautious policy
of the President, whom he referred to as "old Washington," argued
that the cause of liberty was essentially the cause of mankind, and
neutrality in such a cause was basically desertion. Washington, who
was, in Joseph Ellis's concise phrase, a "rock-ribbed realist" and certainly not a universalist, disagreed. He greatly feared that excessive
enthusiasm for France might lead America to take steps that would

put her on a collision course with Great Britain. Indeed, there was a growing move in Congress, spearheaded by the Republicans, to pass legislation imposing commercial penalties on Great Britain in order to compel her to better respect our neutral rights. And, in fairness, Great Britain was violating our rights—seizing not only our ships but also our seamen, retaining armed forts within the territorial boundaries of the United States, and actively aiding the Indians (the terrorists of the day in the eyes of most Americans) in their struggle against America's advancing western settlers. Washington, however, feared that any such contemplated legislative action against Great Britain might ultimately drag the country into the war.

His efforts to diffuse the situation set the stage for the gravest crisis of his presidency and for what became both his most beleaguered but in many ways his finest hour. Seeking, at least temporarily, to take the crisis out of the hands of Congress, the President appointed John Jay, still chief justice of the Supreme Court but the young nation's most experienced diplomat, as his special envoy and sent him to England in the hopes of negotiating outstanding differences and avoiding a potential war. In so doing, George Washington seized the initiative, took responsibility for resolving the crisis, and consequently established a far-reaching precedent that made the President the unrivaled leader in conducting American foreign policy. (Jay's appointment was criticized as "contrary to the spirit and meaning of the Constitution" and the "most unconstitutional and dangerous measure in the annals of the United States.")

George Washington was willing to directly involve himself in foreign affairs in a way he would not do in economic questions. Few realize how well educated Washington was for dealing with foreign events. He had served with the officers of both "superpowers" of his day and had learned much about international relations and the intricacies of foreign affairs. As early as the American Revolution, when he warned of the dangers of allowing France to help America invade Canada (France's former possession), Washington expressed the view that would control his actions in foreign affairs for the rest of his career. It was the obverse of the idealistic school and showed he had few illusions about international relations: "No nation is to be trusted farther than it is bound by its interest, and no prudent statesman or politician will venture to depart from it." (Later, in his Farewell Address, he made exactly the same point: "There can be no greater error to expect, or calculate upon real favours from Nation to Nation. 'Tis an illusion which experience must cure.")

John Jay did obtain a treaty, but it disappointed the President, as it won few concrete concessions beyond the promise that Great Britain would withdraw its troops from American territory, something that they had earlier agreed to do in the Treaty of Paris of 1783. More significantly, the Jay Treaty basically accepted the British interpretation of neutral rights and granted them favored nation status, eliminating future commercial discrimination against them while the treaty was in effect, a period of ten years. To the Republicans, led by Jefferson and Madison, this was a blatant sellout of American interests by an Anglophile—a toadying to Great Britain and a betrayal of France. From their perspective, it put America back into virtually a colonial position and all but negated its independence.

Given such views, it is not surprising that when the terms of the treaty became public, a huge outpouring of dissent and protest quickly followed. There was a deluge of petitions to Washington urging him not to sign it. The unpopular Jay was often burned in effigy. A rather obscene poem emphasized how Jay had groveled before George III:

> May it please your highness, I John Jay
> Have traveled all this mighty way,
> To inquire if you, good Lord will please
> To suffer me while on my knees,
> To show all others I surpass,
> In love, by kissing of your ___.

The bitter words of one newspaper expressed the mood of many in the country: "Damn John Jay. Damn everyone who won't damn John Jay. Damn everyone who won't put lights in their window and stay up all night damning John Jay." Washington mirrored the prevailing tension in a letter to Alexander Hamilton, who incidentally was stoned while trying to defend the treaty: "At present the cry against the Treaty is like that against a mad dog; and everyone, in a manner, seems engaged in running it down." He declared the treaty agitated "the public mind in a higher degree than it has been at any period since the Revolution."

Nevertheless, after much thought, the President decided to sign the treaty, which earlier had been ratified by exactly the necessary two-thirds vote (20-10) in the United States Senate. While many factors were at work, including a confrontation with his new secretary of state, Edmund Randolph, the fundamental reasons why Washington signed the treaty were simple. Despite its shortcomings, the treaty avoided war with Great Britain, facilitated our trade, and gave the young nation crucial time to grow and mature. War, on the other hand, would undermine Washington's vision for a glorious American future and most likely snuff out what he so eloquently had called "the sacred fire of liberty." Washington was convinced that a time of peace was absolutely crucial to the fragile country's survival as an independent nation: "For sure I am, if this country is preserved in tranquility twenty years longer, it may bid defiance, in a just cause, to any power whatever, such, in that time, will be its population, wealth, and resources." Basically, to gain precious time Washington was willing to go down the road of appeasement, a dirty word ever since Neville Chamberlain's concessions to Hitler at Munich in 1939, but not necessarily always a poor policy. As the President explained, "Men in responsible situations cannot, like those in private life, be governed solely by the dictates of their own inclinations, or by such motives as can only affect themselves."

His action caused widespread criticism, and no leader was more desirous of public approval and more sensitive to criticism than George Washington. Nevertheless, the mature Washington was willing, in the manner of the high-minded Roman patriot of classical times, to trade on his personal reputation and the deep admiration most Americans had for him in order to promote what he firmly believed was the greater good of the country. His view is well articulated in the following quotes:

> While I feel the most lively gratitude for the many instances of approbation from my country; I can no otherwise deserve it, than by obeying the dictates of my conscience.

Next to a conscientious discharge of my public duties, to carry along with me the approbation of my Constituents, would be the highest gratification my mind is susceptible of; but the latter being subordinate, I cannot make the former yield to it; unless some criterian more infallible than partial (if they are not party) meetings, can be discovered as the touch stone of public sentiment. If any power on earth could, or the great power above would, erect the standard of infallibility in political opinions, there is no being that inhabits this terrestrial globe that would resort to it with more eagerness than myself. . . . But as I have found no better guide hitherto than upright intentions, and close investigation, I shall adhere to these maxims while I keep the watch; leaving it to those who will come after me to explore new ways, if they like; or think them better.

Historian Todd Estes effectively demonstrates how Washington, sometimes acting behind the scenes and sometimes publicly, eventually managed to swing public opinion behind the treaty. He concludes that Washington "acted boldly and forthrightly at several key junctures in the public debate, each time strongly helping the pro-treaty side." Of course, his most potent weapon was the confidence most Americans had in his judgment. In the words of one, "The President will not see the country wronged, much less wrong it himself." Benjamin Rush recalled, "No sooner did General Washington ratify it than a majority of our citizens defended it." As James Madison later grumbled, "The name of the President is everywhere used with the most wonderful success . . . in subduing . . . Popular objections." It was not, however, only George Washington's great stature and influence but also his artful deployment of political skills that turned the tide.

Although the treaty had been signed by the President and ratified by the Senate, it could not go into effect without the House of Representatives (controlled by the Republicans) voting the funds necessary to carry it out. Many in the House sought to derail the treaty which they believed was so harmful to American independence. Arguing its authority to vote funds for a treaty implied a right to assess a treaty's value, the House requested the President to send them the papers involved in negotiating the treaty. Interestingly, James Madison, the

"Father of the Constitution," implied that the founders expected the House of Representatives to play a role in the treaty-making process.

George Washington (as virtually all constitutional scholars since) saw it differently. Invoking the Constitution, he insisted that when the framers gave the president and the Senate the power to make treaties it was not their intention to give the House of Representatives a veto on their decision. Indeed, the request would set a "dangerous precedent." Washington not only refused the request from the House but also did so by portraying it as a blatantly partisan political act: "Brilliantly fusing constitutionality with his own stature and reputation, Washington deployed this address to reframe the public contest almost as one of personalities between the House and the president so as to maximize his transcendent position." He made the constitutionality of the request rather than the merits of the treaty the central issue, and that was an easier case to win. In absolutely refusing the House's request, he established the right of executive privilege in certain cases. (When Congress demanded papers investigating a military disaster, the President complied fully with their request.)

Even with the President's support the vote was extremely close. Aided by Washington's timely release of the terms of the universally popular Pinckney's Treaty with Spain that opened the mighty Mississippi River to American trade and a moving speech by Federalist Fisher Ames, the House by a vote of 51-48 narrowly agreed to the necessary funding. In retrospect, most scholars concur that Washington's course during the events surrounding the Jay Treaty was the correct one. Interestingly, that is almost always the case in studying George Washington. In retrospect, when passions have cooled, we see he made the correct decision, and it is an indication of his greatness. To identify, while deep in the trenches of conflict, what the future would consider obvious, is a towering intellectual achievement.

Washington's final significant action as president was his justifiably famous Farewell Address, printed in newspapers in the fall of 1796 and never actually given verbally. Prepared with great care, it was essentially Washington's final sermon to the American people and what he hoped would be his lasting legacy. Written in part by James Madison (Washington had asked for Madison's help when he thought he would retire after one term), and in a larger part by Alexander

Hamilton, the ideas were George Washington's. Covering many topics, although significantly ignoring the questions of slavery and of Native Americans, the Farewell Address stressed two central points: unity at home and independence abroad.

His advice in conducting foreign affairs still rings true. He warned: "The Nation, which indulges towards another nation an habitual hatred, or an habitual fondness, is in some degree a slave. It is a slave to its animosity or to its affection, either of which is sufficient to lead it astray from its duty and its interest." (In other words, don't love any country too much or hate any country too much—for it may lead you to act against your own interests.) Finally, in yet one last plea, George Washington emphasized once again his belief in the importance of a strong American union, "The Unity of Government which constitutes you one people is also now dear to you. It is justly so. . . it is of infinite moment, that you should properly estimate the immense value of your national Union to your collective & individual happiness; that you should cherish a cordial, habitual & immoveable attachment to it."

Such advice seems rather obvious and commonplace to most Americans today who have long thought of themselves as one united nation. We forget that for Washington unity was a vision, not a reality. As Ellis reminds us, "these national exhortations were not affirmations of what we were, but rather pleadings for what we must become." In this sense, the Farewell Address was primarily a great prophecy that the term "United States" was destined to become a singular rather than a plural noun (which happens after the Civil War) in which the first word (United) eventually would trump the second (States).

With the publication of the Farewell Address, George Washington made his decision official: After eight long and difficult years in office, he yet again voluntarily withdrew from power, proving once more that his deepest allegiance was thoroughly republican. Washington was not philosophically a champion of a mandatory two-term limit for the presidency. Rather, he believed that it was important for him to set a precedent exemplifying a proper republican approach to the problem of succession, and that meant he must not die in office before formal retirement. The result was another precedent-setting tradition: the peaceful transfer of power from one administration to another. The president at the end of his term would once again become simply an ordinary private citizen. At the conclusion of the inaugural ceremony of John Adams, Washington consciously emphasized this fact by pointedly insisting that Thomas Jefferson, the new vice president, precede him in exiting the building.

After the inauguration, Washington went back to his Philadelphia residence to put some of his papers in order. Then he decided to walk to the Francis Hotel, where President Adams was staying, to pay his respects. Suddenly behind him the streets were full of people: "An immense company," one eyewitness called them, "going as one man in total silence as escort all the way." At the door of the hotel, Washington turned and looked at them, his cheeks wet with tears. "No man ever saw him so moved," declared another eyewitness. For a long moment he stood face to face with his people in solemn silence. Then he turned and when the door closed behind him, a great smothered sigh went through the crowd, something between a sob and a groan. It was the tribute of grief from the voiceless common man, who knew that he was saying goodbye to his greatest friend.

With his long-awaited departure to the joys of life at Mount Vernon, the presidential term of George Washington became part of the historical record. How should it be assessed? It was not an unqualified success, and problems naturally persisted. Like a seesaw, as our relations with Great Britain improved, those with France deteriorated. Partisanship was intense, and His Excellency was no longer universally beloved. Many men peremptorily refused to drink to his health. He was perceived by some as chief of a party rather than chief of a nation. The old Revolutionary, Thomas Paine, was particularly harsh toward the man he called a "treacherous . . . hypocrite": "The world will be puzzled to decide whether you are an impostate [apostate] or an imposter, whether you have abandoned good principles or whether you ever had any." One newspaper, the *Aurora*, editorialized, "If ever there was a period of rejoicing this is the moment—every heart, in unison . . . ought to beat high with exultation that the name of WASHINGTON from this day ceases to give currency to political inequity and to legalize corruption. . . . It is a subject of greatest astonishment that a single individual should have cankered [corrupted] the principles of republicanism . . . so far as to have put in jeopardy its very existence." The impending crisis over slavery had figuratively been swept under the carpet. The President could not insure fair treatment for Native Americans, hampered by what he acknowledged was the common western view that to kill an Indian was a minor crime if it were a crime at all.

Nevertheless, given the harsh realities he had to face, and the limited resources at his disposal, George Washington was remarkably successful on a number of different fronts. The financial crisis had been solved and commerce was thriving. A Bill of Rights had been added to the Constitution, an event which could not have occurred without his support. A serious challenge to the national government, the Whiskey Rebellion, had been successfully crushed. Thanks to his diplomacy and the victory by General "Mad Anthony" Wayne in the Battle of Fallen Timbers, the Ohio Country had been secured for settlement. Freedom to use the Mississippi River had been achieved by gaining a favorable treaty from Spain. The nation had avoided a costly and crippling war.

Perhaps most significantly, the new government was now a going concern, and many important precedents had been established. As Morris earlier noted to Washington, no constitution is the same in life as it is on paper. The President's actions gave life to the paper. His establishment of the cabinet, his relations with Congress, his use of annual messages and appointment powers, his vetoes for both constitutional and practical grounds, his issuing proclamations such as ordering a day of thanksgiving, his actions in foreign affairs in matters such as negotiating treaties and declaring neutrality, and his claims for executive privilege were some of the many precedents that influence the presidency down to the present day. Furthermore, Washington bequeathed to all future presidents a potentially powerful office—and at the same time he set the highest standards for conducting the affairs of that office.

George Washington was the rarest of men, a multitalented, realistic visionary who envisioned a grand future for the United States and worked to realize that vision with resourcefulness, ability, and remarkably steadfast determination. He did it not only for his generation of countrymen but also for "millions unborn." He firmly believed that the "destiny of the republican model of government [is] 'deeply' [and] 'finally' staked on the experiment entrusted to the hands of the American people." The gift he gave his beloved country was priceless. How the citizens would use it was up to them.

4

"A Votary to Love"

George Washington's Relationship with Sally Cary Fairfax

Tis true, I profess myself a Votary to Love.
—*George Washington*

GEORGE WASHINGTON'S LETTER OF SEPTEMBER 12, 1758, IN which he apparently professed his love for Sally Cary Fairfax, is perhaps the most interesting and controversial letter that has survived from his hand. For well over a hundred years after its composition, virtually no one knew of its existence. It was first published in the newspaper the New York *Herald,* in 1877, and sold at auction for a pittance to an unknown buyer. It immediately disappeared from public view. During the first half of the twentieth century, prominent Washington scholars dismissed it as a forgery: "If it still exists, its owner is keeping it carefully hidden. No writer on Washington has ever seen it—or, at least, will not say that he has. None of them has subjected it to the tests that any careful student insists on having made by experts in the matter of a doubtful manuscript—tests of paper, ink, handwriting. . . . The Romantics [those believing Washington was in love with Sally Fairfax] are zealously holding in air an arch without a keystone."

Then in the late 1950s, indefatigable Washington scholar and former attorney Bernard Knollenberg tracked the letter to Harvard University's Houghton Library, where its authenticity was confirmed beyond doubt. Even so, some Washington scholars continue to ignore or play down the significance of the letter. (Sally Cary Fairfax is virtually ignored at Mount Vernon.) Washington hagiographer Harrison Clark, in his study under the revealing title *All Cloudless Glory*, does not even include Sally Fairfax in his index. In a much more balanced and enlightening treatment of Washington, Richard Brookhiser downplays the relationship with the assessment: "the surviving letters are ambiguous." Most recently, the distinguished Washington scholar Don Higginbotham puts forth the case for minimizing the importance of the letter: "We know that in September 1758 George Washington and Sally Cary Fairfax exchanged playful, quite possibly flirtatious letters." He concludes by asserting that Washington's "flirtatious behavior . . . hardly seems out of character for the age when men and women engaged in playful language replete with innuendo."

Why is the letter so interesting and controversial? It is interesting in part because it reveals an intensely passionate George Washington, very different from the man traditionally portrayed as cold and remote. It is controversial because Washington apparently professed his love to the wife of his close friend, George William Fairfax, the son of his patron and major benefactor. As if that were not shocking enough, he made the confession at the time when he was apparently engaged to marry the young widow, Martha Dandridge Custis. Thus, some have concluded that, if true, the incident significantly tarnishes Washington's character and undermines his life as a role model for others to follow. John C. Fitzpatrick, the editor of the first main edition of the Washington Papers and author of the book *George Washington Himself*, worried, "If Washington were so completely lacking in gentlemanly instincts as these writers would have us believe, he would be fundamentally . . . a worthless scoundrel."

Was George Washington in love with Sally? Did she reciprocate? Was their relationship physical? What does the relationship reveal about Washington's character? This chapter will focus on these questions, but an initial caveat must be offered. While there is more evidence on these questions than many people realize, there is much we simply do not know and most likely will never know. Our only recourse is informed speculation, but one need not apologize for that effort as long as it is made clear what one is doing. As William Safire reminds us, "Historians try mightily to get inside their subjects' minds. They enliven the written record with intuitive judgment after subjecting

Sally Cary Fairfax. Copy of portrait by an unknown artist.
(Courtesy of the Virginia Historical Society)

it to rigorous professional discipline." That is what I try to do. The
argument presented below is a plausible one, but one thing all good
historians know is that something may be plausible but not necessarily accurate.

The best place to begin is with the controversial letter. Written on
September 12, 1758, and addressed to an unidentified "Dear Madam,"
the epistle is not easy to completely understand as the syntax is convoluted and some references are deliberately vague. (As a general
rule, the more excited or upset George Washington became, the more
convoluted his syntax became.) Nevertheless, it can only be properly
called a love letter. Indeed, however surprising and out of character
it may seem, George Washington described himself as "a Votary to

Love." The eighteenth-century Oxford Dictionary defines "votary" as "One who is devoted to or passionately addicted to some particular pursuit, occupation, study or aim" or "A devoted adherent or admirer of some person, institution, etc."

Here are the most salient passages of the letter:

> Tis true, I profess myself a Votary to Love—I acknowledge that a Lady is in the Case—and further I confess, that this Lady is known to you,—Yes, Madam, as well as she is to one, who is too sensible of her Charms to deny the Power, whose Influence he feels and must ever Submit to. I feel the force of her amiable beauties in the recollection of a thousand tender passages that I could wish to obliterate, till I am bid to revive them—but experience alas! sadly reminds me how Impossible this is. . . . You have drawn me dear Madam, or rather I have drawn myself, into an honest confession of a Simple Fact—misconstrue not my meaning—doubt it not, nor expose it—The World has no business to know the object of my Love, declared in this manner to—you, when I want to conceal it.

It should be carefully noted what Washington wrote. He admitted that he was enthralled by "her charms," the power of which he "must ever submit to." He recalled "a thousand tender passages" that he might try but was unable "to obliterate." He wanted his confession kept secret: "The World has no business to know the object of my Love . . . when I want to conceal it."

Are these words consistent with a playful, flirtatious letter? Professor Higginbotham is certainly correct in asserting flirtatious letters with sexual innuendos were common and must not be taken at face value. The intellectual historian Peter Gay notes that eighteenth-century writers "peppered their letters with exaggerations that seem cloying today, but were ritual formulas then." George Washington himself often engaged in just such banter as the following examples clearly illustrate.

The wife of a Virginia colonel wrote her sister-in-law that the General "can be downright impudent sometimes—such impudence, Fanny, as you and I like." When the poet, Annis Boudinot Stockton, an ardent admirer of Washington, asked for absolution for her poetry to him, Washington responded that "if you will come and dine with me on Thursday and go through the proper course of penitence, which shall be prescribed, I will strive hard to assist you in expiating these poetical trespasses on this side of purgatory." He continued in the same letter, "Once the Woman has tempted us and we have tasted the forbidden fruit, there is no such thing as checking our appetites, whatever the consequences may be." When one of his closest female friends, Eliza Powel, invited him to the theater to see a production of the play *School for Scandal*, Washington had to refuse but commented that he could "but regret that matters have turned out so unluckily, after waiting so long to receive a lesson in the School for Scandal." In a final example, His Excellency wrote Lafayette to have him warn his wife that "I have a heart susceptable of the tenderest passion, and that it is already so strongly impressed with the most favourable ideas of her, that she must be cautious of putting loves torch to it."

I would contend that George Washington's missive to Sally Cary Fairfax is of a different genre. A fair reading of Washington's September 12th letter indicates that he was not joking. This is simply not a "playful, flirtatious letter." This is a deadly serious—if somewhat awkward and veiled—assertion of love, which he wanted to be kept secret. He emphasized that the world had no business knowing anything about it. Including this type of request seems incongruous with a joking, tongue-in-cheek type of letter. George Washington was essentially a very honest man, and it seems perfectly reasonable to take him at his word. Indeed, the serious nature of the confession has led some scholars to argue that the letter was addressed to someone else, apparently on the grounds that it is not quite as troubling if it were to someone other than the wife of his good friend. Another tack to exonerate Washington is to acknowledge that he was writing to Sally but argue that he is informing her that he is a votary of love to his fiancée, Martha.

Neither argument can hold up to close scrutiny. Internal evidence from another letter proves beyond a doubt that the famous "votary to love" epistle of September 12th was written to Sally Cary Fairfax. On September 1, 1758, George William Fairfax responded to two earlier letters from Washington. Fairfax wrote, "The first [letter] Mrs. Fairfax undertakes to answer as I don't care to detain the bearer," whom he later describes as the "impatient man at my elbow." In other words,

Sally Fairfax definitely wrote to Washington on September 1st. Then, in his famous September 12th letter to "Dear Madam," Washington referred to receiving "the short, but very agreeable favor of the 1ˢᵗ" and further wrote, "I cannot easily forgive the unseasonable haste of my last Express [messenger] if he deprived me thereby of a single word you intended to add."

The position put forth by John Fitzpatrick that Washington was really expressing his love for Martha leads to all sorts of strange twists and turns and what Freeman calls "absurdities of misinterpretation." To cite one example, Washington would not be able to recall "a thousand tender passages" with Martha Custis, with whom he had spent very little time. Additionally, the entire tone of the letter, which includes comments such as "I wish I was happy also," makes no sense if he is writing about Martha. The letter is remarkable among Washington's writings, but it clearly conveyed his emotions about Sally Fairfax, not anyone else. The "keystone of the arch" that critics said was missing has been found and is revealing. Right or wrong, admirable or not, George Washington was at this moment of his life in love with Sally Cary Fairfax. People sometimes fall in love with people they are not supposed to. This seems to be one of those cases.

Why he fell in love with her—and why he chose to write and confess his love for her in September of 1758—are impossible to answer with any kind of certainty, but there are a number of points, which taken together help us understand why such events occurred. Sally was born Sarah Cary in 1730, the eldest daughter of a very wealthy and influential family, the Carys of Ceely, Virginia, just north of Hampton. Her father, Wilson Cary, was one of the most important members of the Virginia House of Burgesses. Sally grew up in a world of wealth and sociability and was given many opportunities available only to the elite. Intellectually gifted, she wrote in French as well as English and quoted Juvenal. On the blank pages of a volume at Belvoir, her father-in-law's mansion, guests occasionally inscribed their thoughts. There, on September 6, 1757, writing in French and in beautiful handwriting, Sally inscribed her thoughts following the death of her father-in-law four days earlier: "Misfortunes never come singly," and "We never prize a blessing until we have lost it."

In December of 1748, at the age of eighteen, she had married

George William Fairfax, six years her senior and the son of William Fairfax of Belvoir. William was the land agent for his cousin Thomas, 6th Lord Fairfax, the sole proprietor of the huge five-million-acre grant of land known as the Northern Neck Proprietary. He also was a member of the governor's council and the most important man in northern Virginia. The inventory of items for sale from his beautiful mansion, Belvoir, in 1773 confirm the great affluence of the owners whose home must have matched many gentry interiors in London. The home, whose foundation is still visible on the grounds of the military base of the same name, was located south of Mount Vernon. There, George's half brother Lawrence lived with his bride, Anne Fairfax Washington, George William's sister.

Through regular visits to Lawrence, George was often at Belvoir, where he learned much of what it meant to be a true Virginia gentleman: "In all he did, young Washington shaped himself to the pattern prescribed by his culture." The Fairfax family, including the mesmerizing Sally Cary Fairfax, was his finishing school. Given the circumstances, it is hard to imagine young George, an awkward sixteen- or seventeen-year-old youth when he first met Sally, not being smitten with her. Here was a beautiful and cultured young woman, only two years older in age but many years older in terms of her knowledge of genteel society. A few hints indicate his feelings for her. As touched on in chapter 1, Washington hurried back from his winter mission to the French to warn the Governor of France's nefarious plans: "Although he had given in to no need for rest between bouts with nature at her most violent," he decided to stop for a day at Belvoir to take necessary rest. Once the war began, he begged Sally for a letter, asserting her reply would "make me happier than the Day is long." Professor Higginbotham concedes their relationship was important in Washington's development: "He undoubtedly learned a great deal about interacting with the fairer sex, including the social graces, from Sally Fairfax."

And it should be noted that Washington learned to interact extremely well with the fairer sex. We know precious little about his youth. It is clear he had some early unsuccessful encounters with women, but emphasis on this point can easily distort the fact that over time Washington became increasingly attractive to women. Additionally, most Washington biographers tend to ignore the fact that he was powerfully attracted to the female sex. One exception is John Alden, who writes,

> Washington was almost twenty-seven years of age when he married. He was a lusty young male, and one is tempted to infer that he had long been deeply interested in women, in legal or illegal unions with them. Moreover, despite his devotion to war, he had had time in which to pursue attractive ladies in the older settlements of Virginia and less sophisticated girls in the Valley. There were camp women who followed the soldiers in his campaigns. One may speculate that his unsuccessful courtship of Betsy Fauntleroy was accompanied by other less formal enterprises in which he did not fail to achieve success.

Several surviving letters from his fellow officers imply that the Colonel had an eye for "the fair Ones," and that his subordinates were comfortable writing to him about such matters. One wrote he thought that Bryan Fairfax, another son of William who joined the Virginia regiment at his father's urging, was about to soften "his austerity in the arms of some fair nymph—could he reconcile the Toying, Trifling, Billing Sports of Love to the solemnity and gravity of his deportment—amusements and joys unbecoming of his philosophic Temper." George Mercer, then a captain in the Virginia Regiment, wrote Washington a long letter from Charleston, South Carolina, describing its women: "A great Imperfection here too is the bad Shape of the Ladies, many of Them are crooked & have a very bad Air & not the enticing heaving throbbing alluring . . . exciting plump Breasts common with our Northern Belles." Another letter from an officer who served under Washington during the French and Indian War clearly suggests that before his marriage Washington did more than admire women from afar: "I imagine you By this time, plung'd in the midst of delight heaven can aford: & enchanted By Charms even stranger to the Ciprian Dame." (A Cyprian dame was a sexually available or licentious woman, especially a prostitute. This particular one was called Nell.)

George Washington was many things, but one thing he was not, and would not want to be, was a Puritan. He was tolerant of lapses in sexual conduct, as illustrated by his treatment of Alexander Hamilton (chapter 7) and his close relationship with the witty Gouverneur

Morris, a known profligate, who could write about making love to his French mistress and celebrating "the Cyprian mystery" to her great satisfaction. Morris felt comfortable joking with President Washington about a lovesick Chinese pig, a sow that had been overlooked by the boar of the same species: "To asswage her Melancholy (for what alas can helpless Widows do) took up with a Paramour of Vulgar Race [i.e., an ordinary boar] and thus her grunting Progeny have jowls and Bellies less big by Half than their Dam."

Washington likewise often exhibited what we might call a rather "earthy" sense of humor with sexual connotations. For example, a letter written in 1786 concerns the failure of Royal Gift, the jackass presented to Washington by the king of Spain, to perform stud service according to expectations: "At present, tho' young, he follows what one may suppose to be the example of his late royal Master, who cannot, tho' past his grand climacterick, perform seldomer, or with more Majestic solemnity, than he does. However, I am not without hope, that when he becomes a little better acquainted with republican enjoyments, he will amend his manners, and fall into a better & more expeditious mode of doing business." To another neighbor who sent his jenny to Mount Vernon for a similar reason, Washington replied, "I feel myself much obliged by your polite offer of the first fruits of your Jenny. Tho' in appearance quite unequal to the match—yet, like a true female, she was not to be terrified at the disproportionate size of her paramour—& having renewed the conflict twice or thrice, it is hoped the issue will be favourable." In time, it should be noted to Royal Gift's credit, he eventually did produce offspring with a jenny belonging to Washington.

The best example of this type of humor (which again goes against what many might expect from the staid General) comes from a letter His Excellency sent to the Reverend William Gordon.

I am glad to hear that my old acquaintance Colo. Ward is yet under the influence of vigorous passions—I will not ascribe the intrepidity of his late enterprize [Ward had just married] to a mere *flash* of desires, because, in his military career he would have learnt how to distinguish between false alarms & a serious movement. Charity therefore induces me to suppose that like a prudent general, he had reviewed his *strength*, his arms, & ammunition before he got involved in an action—But if these have been neglected, & he has been precipitated into the measure, let me advise him to make the *first* onset upon his fair [lady] del Tobosa, with vigor, that the impression may be deep, if it cannot be lasting, or frequently renewed. (emphasis in the original)

While there is no creditable evidence that Washington ever strayed from his marriage vows to Martha, that does not mean he did not enjoy the company of the female sex, as countless references in his diaries and letters make clear. George Washington liked women! He was extremely attractive to them and found himself equally attracted to them as a mature, married man, just as he had undoubtedly found himself attracted to them as a young unmarried adult male in the midst of fighting for his king and country.

If, in his early twenties, Washington was "a lusty young male," he was also, as shown in chapter 1, an increasingly important and charismatic one. The transformation can be illustrated in his changing relationship with George William Fairfax and indubitably with Sally as well. In his journal entries of his first trip west in 1748 as part of a surveying party, Washington referred to George William as Mr. Fairfax and clearly looked up to the older man, then twenty-four, as another mentor. By the time of the French and Indian War, however, the relationship had undergone a noticeable shift. Washington was now commander of the Virginia regiment. George William appeared eager to join the fray (although he never did) and wrote to Washington, "I beg that you'll freely command me, being willing to serve under so experienced an officer and Commander." Certainly, Washington biographer James Flexner exaggerates when he describes George William Fairfax "as a quivering white rabbit" in comparison to the dashing Virginia colonel, but Washington had a definite presence about him, and it is not going beyond the evidence to assert that Sally felt it as well as others.

When did Washington's almost inevitable infatuation with Sally, childless in her marriage to George William, grow into something more powerful? Again, we can only engage in informed speculation, but there are several known facts which may shed light on the story.

Near the end of 1757, Colonel Washington, severely ill, took a leave of absence from the army and returned to Mount Vernon in the hopes of winning his struggle with the "Grim King," as he once referred to death. Washington felt comfortable enough in his relationship with Sally to ask for her help in procuring various medicines, wines, and special jellies. During the several months of Washington's illness and slow recovery, George William Fairfax was in Great Britain, attempting to protect his claims to the Fairfax title. We don't know how often George and Sally corresponded or how often Sally visited him at Mount Vernon during this time period. Unfortunately for the curious, Washington routinely and regularly destroyed all of Sally's letters to him, apparently following the advice he gave Sally that the "world has no business" knowing his thoughts in this matter. The only fragment of a letter from her to Washington that survives does so because it was added as a postscript to a letter from her husband in 1755. Ironically, in that letter, Sally thanked heaven for his safe return following Braddock's debacle and referred to Washington's "great unkindness" in refusing to stop at Belvoir. She added, "if you will not come to us tomorrow at morning very early we shall be at Mount Vernon."

There can be little doubt that Sally went to Mount Vernon and tried to nurse Washington back to health during her husband's absence in Great Britain. What happened on those visits will never be known. Did she offer more than soup and sympathy? The tantalizing question, did they or didn't they, will have to remain unanswered. There is certainly no concrete or convincing evidence that they had a sexual relationship, and accounts of them meeting in the woods for brief assignations are complete fabrications, the stuff of novels but not serious history. On the other hand, it is also true that Washington soon wrote her that he felt "the force of her amiable beauties in the recollection of a thousand tender passages." One cannot help but wonder what the phrase, "a thousand tender passages," refers to, but I am afraid we will simply have to wonder.

At the very least, there was a window of opportunity for Washington, recovering from a near fatal illness, to become more deeply enmeshed with a woman for whom he had long felt a strong attachment. Their bond may well have been strengthened since Sally was now acting as a caregiver, for it is not uncommon for people to feel a special closeness to those who care for them when they are ill. Washington later gave much wise advice to his granddaughters about love and passion. Perhaps it came from his personal experiences as well as from his general observation on the human condition:

> In the composition of the human frame there is a great deal of inflammable matter. . . . when the torch is put to it, that which is within you may burst into a blaze.

> A hint here; men and women feel the same inclinations to each other now that they always have done, and which they will continue to do until there is a new order of things, and you, as others have done, may find, perhaps, that the passions of your sex are easier raised than allayed.

> Experience will convince you that there is no truth more certain than that all our enjoyments fall short of our expectation; and to none does it apply with more force than the gratifications of the passions.

Two factors may well have played a role in the timing of Washington's decision to send his remarkable—and frankly very dangerous—letter to Sally. One was that he was about to embark upon the campaign to take Fort Duquesne, a very dangerous mission (Washington could not have foreseen that the French would abandon their stronghold without a fight). Many of his men had recently been killed in action, and he knew his own life would soon once again be put at risk, and in fact he nearly lost his life a couple of months later. Isn't it at least plausible to assume that, facing death, he wanted Sally to know just how deeply he cared for her?

Second, and more significant, there was the matter of his likely upcoming marriage to Martha. Most historians assume that they were formally engaged, and they may well have been. In his famous letter of September 12th, Washington makes reference to the "animating prospect of possessing Mrs Custis," clearly in response to something Sally said in her missing epistle. Interestingly, this is the only reference he makes to Martha in all his extant correspondence prior to their marriage. In extended correspondence over the last half of 1758, his close friend Captain Robert Stewart makes numerous personal allusions but gives no hint that he is aware that his commander is engaged. Thus, it is at least possible that he had not yet finalized his commitment to marry Martha when he confessed his love to Sally. Whether formally engaged or not, isn't it plausible to argue that Washington, realizing he was about to enter the permanent state of matrimony and end one chapter of his life, desperately wanted to know how Sally felt about him and whether she reciprocated his love? While it might not in fact change anything, it was still important to find out. In the words of Douglas Southall Freeman, "George Washington was going to marry Martha but was hopelessly in love with Sally and wished above everything else to know whether she loved him."

How did Sally feel? Again, the evidence is incomplete but tantalizing. First, and of crucial importance, *she kept the letter.* The only reason anything is known about this story is that Sally kept this letter in her personal possession for *over fifty years,* until her death in 1811. A relative, Constance Cary Harrison, wrote in *Scribner's Monthly,* July 1876, "Upon her death, at the age of eighty-one, letters (still in possession of the Fairfax family) were found among her effects, showing that Washington had never forgotten the influence of his youthful disappointment." Does one keep for over fifty years a playful, flirtatious letter from a man not yet that famous? Certainly one does not keep such a letter if its purpose was to say how much the author cared for another woman! Or, rather, isn't it much more likely for one to keep such a letter because it means a great deal to the person and one does not want to part with it? As far as the record is concerned, Sally never told *anyone* of Washington's love letter to her. She was not part of the present kiss-and-tell generation; today, the recipient would most likely make the rounds of the various TV talk shows and publish a tell-all book. For whatever reason or combination of reasons, it is indisputable that she kept the letter in her possession for her entire life.

Hidden in the midst of Washington's correspondence, there is one other hint of Sally's strong feelings on the subject. Shortly after the war for American independence ended (1785), Washington wrote George William Fairfax about visiting the ruins of Belvoir, which had been destroyed by fire during the war: "When I viewed them [the rooms]—when I considered the happiest moments of my life had been spent there—when I could not trace a room in the house (now all rubbish) that did not bring to my mind the recollection of pleasing scenes; I was obliged to fly from them." George William commented in his reply that his wife, Sally, expressed no shock at hearing of the destruction of Belvoir by fire. Yet, he added that hearing Washington describe the present pathetic condition of Belvoir and that his time there had been the happiest of his life "produced many tears & sighs from the former Mistress of it." It was not the destruction of Belvoir but rather hearing Washington describe his time at Belvoir as the "happiest of his life" that brought forth such a strong emotional response from Sally.

However strong her personal feelings might have been for Washington, his profession of love presented Sally with a very difficult dilemma. She may even have encouraged him to write as he had, and was most likely deeply touched by the great tribute he had paid her in his confession of his love for her. But now that he had done so, what should she do? How should she respond? How could she respond without jeopardizing her marriage and her whole lifestyle? This was a love affair that had no future—to pursue it would be disastrous to all involved. Coincidentally, there had been an earlier sex scandal involving the Fairfax and Washington families. Lawrence Washington accused the Reverend Charles Green, the rector of Truro parish, of having sexually assaulted his wife, Anne Fairfax, in the years before her marriage to Lawrence. While hushed up after the fact and almost lost to history, at the time the scandal was sensational news, drawing press attention even in Pennsylvania. (Sexual scandal involving prominent people has always seemed irresistible to the American public.) "Another sex-scandal involving a Fairfax woman and a Washington man would have been unthinkable."

Comprehending this, Sally responded as if she did not understand what Washington was *clearly* trying to convey. Exactly how she responded is unknown because, as was his habit, Washington destroyed her letter. We can, however, partially reconstruct it from the way he responded to it on September 25, 1758, the second very interesting epistle he wrote Sally, which she also kept in her possession. Washington wrote in some frustration: "Dear Madam: Do we still misunderstand the true meaning of each others Letters? I think it must appear so, tho' I woud feign hope the contrary as I cannot speak plainer without—but I'll say no more, and leave you to guess the rest." Of course the only way Washington could speak plainer was to explicitly say he loved her, and he does not want to do that because she is his friend's wife and he plans to marry Martha, but he wants her to know it nonetheless. He concluded his missive declaring that he was "most unalterably" her obliging servant, the only time he ever added these words to his traditional ending.

While not easy for modern readers to understand, the most inter-esting—and thought-provoking—sentence in George Washington's September 25th letter is "I should think my time more agreeably spent believe me, in playing a part in Cato with the company you mention, and myself doubly happy in being the Juba to such a Marcia as you must make." Apparently, in Sally's missing letter, she referred to a play, *Cato: A Tragedy* by Joseph Addison, in which she played or read the part of Marcia. *Cato*, the story of a selfless Roman patriot who preferred death to tyranny under Caesar, was George Washington's favorite play. He knew it very well, quoted from it often, used Cato as a role model, and later even had the play performed to inspire his troops at Valley Forge.

The connection to the apparently doomed love affair between Mar-cia and Juba has enough parallels to the one between Washington and Sally that one must wonder if Sally used the reference to Marcia with a specific purpose in mind. Indeed, one Washington biographer goes so far as to suggest that Sally's reference to her role as Marcia sent Washington a coded message. Marcia was the daughter of Cato, and Juba was the African Prince of Numidia who had to hide his unaccept-able love for Marcia. The play is full of Juba's rhapsodies on the beauty and virtue of the object of his love. In the first meeting together in act 1, Marcia bids farewell to Juba, who must keep hidden his forbidden love as he goes off to war against Caesar. In the fourth act, Marcia, believing Juba has been killed, proclaims her love for him while he is hiding nearby. (There are shades of Romeo and Juliet in the play.) Juba then declares to Marcia: "Juba will never at his fate repine; Let Caesar have the world if Marcia's mine." But their love cannot be. It is Marcia who ultimately declares, "While Cato lives, his daughter has no right to love or hate but as his choice directs." (In this rendering, Sally's husband is "Cato" and she his "daughter.") She was therefore not available to Juba, whom Marcia declares is fated to make "any of womankind but Marcia happy." Is this putting greater freight on the words of their letters than can be properly placed? Perhaps. Nevertheless, the connection is striking and at least worth considering.

Despite his happy and satisfying marriage to Martha (examined in the next chapter), the evidence indicates that Sally always held a special spot in George Washington's heart. The last time he saw Sally was in 1773, fifteen long and eventful years after his awkward profession of love. At that time, George William and Sally returned to Great Britain, never, as it turned out, to return to America. In time, their possessions at Belvoir, some of the most valuable in America, were auctioned off. By far, the largest purchaser of items was George Washington. Undoubtedly, most, if not all, of the items purchased were for their utilitarian value or to make a statement of Washington's standing at the top of the Virginia gentry. Those who enjoy psychohistory, however, might put special emphasis on the fact that Washington also purchased the pillows that had graced Sally's bed. It might also be noted that he bought Sally's handsome mahogany double chest of drawers that had stood in her bedchamber. The chest was a beautiful and valuable piece of furniture, and Washington placed it in his master bedroom—leading one wag to point out that Martha's drawers were in Sally's drawers. Don Higginbotham correctly points out that some people make much too much out of such purchases: "It has been suggested that Washington received some sentimental, if not sensual, pleasure from having Sally's bureau in his bedroom. The 'romantics' have seemingly been unaware that another furniture item in the Washington bedchamber, a small bureau, came from Martha's boudoir during her first marriage to Daniel Parke Custis. One hazards to guess whether there is meaning in their standing on opposite sides of the bedroom!" There is no question that some authors do exaggerate the psychological impact of Washington's feelings for Sally on the other actions of his life. One goes so far as to write that George Washington was never "for the rest of his life" able to think of Sally "without choking up." Such distortions do not, in my judgment, negate the claim that the relationship was a very important part of his life.

This is confirmed by a final letter that the retired President wrote Sally, now long widowed, in 1798. After not having seen her for twenty-

five years, after experiencing the glory of winning the war for American independence and being the nation's first chief executive and un-
challenged national hero, Washington could still write Sally that none
of the great events of his career "nor all of them together, have been
able to eradicate from my mind, the recollection of those happy moments—the happiest of my life—which I have enjoyed in your company." The fact that he enclosed a letter from Martha with his letter does
not in my view detract from the fact that Washington looked back at his
relationship with Sally as unique in his long and remarkable life.

Despite his love for Sally as a young man, it did not negatively impact on his relationship with either Martha or with George William.
Washington and George William remained good friends with a deep
sense of respect and admiration for each other. Certainly that would
not have been the case if the latter believed Washington overstepped
himself. It was one thing to know Washington particularly admired his
wife. It would have been a very different story if he thought Washington had acted improperly. Additionally, Martha became good friends
with Sally although it is difficult to imagine that she did not sense her
husband's affection for Sally. It is notable that not one echo of gossip
survives to indicate that there had been anything amiss in their relations. James Flexner takes up this idea: "Surely it was no small and
easy matter, in a situation so complicated and intimate, involving so
many people they admired, and beset with such desperate quick sands,
to find and traverse, year after year, a path that made trouble for none
but themselves. Here surely was education for a man who was eventually to steer a new nation through history's quick sands!"

What if they had traversed a different path? What if Sally had
answered differently than she did? Would Washington, like Juba, have
not repined at his fate as long as he had Sally? Was he willing to throw
away his future, give up his dreams of fame and glory, and publicly
shame a friend for the joys of having Sally profess her love for him?
"George William was not just another husband, he was the emotional
legatee of Lawrence and of William Fairfax; to betray him would be
the height of that unnatural and sordid vice, ingratitude; moreover,
it would be unjust." The mature George Washington would never do
such a thing. Might the twenty-six-year-old Virginia colonel facing
death on the Virginia frontier have done so?

George Washington had not yet matured into the man of remarkable self-control that he would become. He needed time to do so, and he was lucky that he was given the time to do so. Think of how often he came close to losing his life as he sought honor and glory. What if, for example, one of the four bullets that pierced his clothes in the Battle of the Wilderness in 1755 had been a few inches off in one direction or another? The future of America would have been very different. Washington's love for Sally Cary Fairfax was as dangerous to his future as any bullet that ripped through his clothes on the banks of the Monongahela. It could have destroyed it. We cannot know how Washington ultimately would have acted if Sally had encouraged him to do something reckless. Fortunately, as historian John Alden notes, "In the end, however much Sally may have encouraged his addresses, she saved him from disgrace and preserved a great future for him."

Perhaps some people will harshly judge George Washington as a "worthless scoundrel" for his confession of love to his friend's wife. More, I suspect, will agree with the conclusion of Rupert Hughes: "His letter, however confusing to his idolaters, redeems him to humanity [his vulnerability makes him more appealing than the man who is always in control] and, however pitiful as a confession, [the letter] is magnificent as passion." And that is what George Washington's letter to Sally demonstrates. He was a man of the most intense passion, but ultimately, aided by Sally's restraint, he was able to both control and channel his passions into founding a great republic. If his country owes a great debt of gratitude to George Washington, it also owes one to Sally Cary Fairfax as well.

From an "Agreable Consort" to "My Dear Patsy"

The Relationship between George and Martha Washington

> I have always considered marriage as the most inter-
> esting event of ones life. The foundation of happiness
> or misery.—*George Washington*

WITH THE ADVANTAGE OF HINDSIGHT (THE ONE BIG ADVANTAGE historians have), the most important event in George Washington's public career occurred on June 15, 1775. Acting more wisely than they could have known, on that date the Second Continental Congress unanimously elected him commander in chief of the Continental Army, propelling him to center stage in the story of the birth of the American republic. With the advantage of hindsight, the most important event in George Washington's private life occurred on January 6, 1759. Acting more wisely than he could have known, on that date, George Washington married the young widow, Martha Dandridge Custis. It turned out to be perhaps the best decision of his life.

There is a vignette, which if not literally true, certainly conveys a truth. Following the President's rise to fame, one of his critics yelled out to the great man, "What would you have been if you had not married the widow Custis?" The question makes the important point that George Washington's remarkable success owed much to his marriage to Martha.

What was their relationship? Did Martha always hold second place in Washington's heart behind his first true love, Sally Cary Fairfax? What kind of woman was Martha and how influential was she? As with Sally Cary Fairfax, the task of answering such questions is not an easy one. Sources are limited. Martha, most likely shortly after Washington's death, or possibly with his help during his lifetime, burned all of their personal correspondence. Why? Probably not because there was some deep secret, but rather because this was one part of their life they believed "the World has no business to know." There was likely a frankness and openness about people and events in their letters that the circumspect public figures would rather not share with the world. George Washington wished to be remembered and judged for his public contributions and preferred that his private life remain just that. Martha had been forced to share her husband with the world for most of their marriage. Their private letters were one aspect of her life she would not share. Ironically, however, in burning the letters, she most likely did herself a disservice by setting the stage for rumors and by making it more difficult for people to realize the important role she played in her husband's life.

The task of accurately reconstructing the relationship between a husband and a wife is incredibly difficult, even if extensive records survive. We like to say, "Everyone knows," but in many ways, "nobody knows." There is just so much that we do not know and cannot know about a marital relationship spanning forty years—and the missing letters simply make a complex task that much more difficult. Having entered that caveat, there is nevertheless, upon close examination, a considerable amount of evidence and many vignettes which, while not telling the whole story, are both revealing and interesting. They shed light not only on George and Martha Washington and their relationship but also on the times in which they lived.

George Washington's marriage to Martha Dandridge Custis was to a significant degree a marriage of convenience. However, it should be emphasized that it was a marriage of convenience for both of them. For if Martha was a good catch, so was the Virginia colonel. Similar in age (she was nearly a year older, having been born on June 2, 1731), the Virginia colonel was a handsome and widely respected war hero with a bright future and excellent administrative skills. The scanty evidence indicates the young widow was quickly and deeply smitten by Washington. Of course, Martha was a good catch because she was, quite frankly, the richest widow in Virginia. Her husband, Daniel Parke Custis, had died suddenly in 1757, leaving no will but leaving a young widow, twenty-six, with two very young surviving children, aged one and three (two others had died in early childhood), and a large fortune in slaves, land, and surprisingly liquid capital. Under Virginia law, since Custis died intestate, one-third of his assets went directly to Martha with the other two-thirds being managed in trust for the two children until they became of age. Also, under eighteenth-century Virginia law, Martha as a *feme sole* controlled her money, but once married she would be a *feme covert* and her wealth would be completely under the control of whomever she should marry.

It is always difficult to translate wealth in eighteenth-century Virginia into modern dollars, but the inheritance certainly made Martha the equivalent of a modern millionaire several times over. The Custis estate, besides slaves and personal property, included nearly 18,000 acres within a forty-mile radius of Williamsburg. The General Court assigned Mrs. Custis three plantations, totaling nearly 4,000 acres, a gristmill, a house with gardens on a four-acre plot in Williamsburg, property in Jamestown, 85 slaves, 324 cattle, 225 hogs, and 97 sheep. Whoever controlled such an estate would immediately be thrust into the top echelon of the Virginia gentry.

Martha's wealth was undoubtedly a major attraction to George Washington. There is no question he hoped to marry a wealthy woman, as he had tried to do so unsuccessfully in the past. It is probably safe to assert he would not have married Martha if she had not been wealthy. We know very little about their courtship except that it was very brief and took place in 1758 while Washington was on sick leave from his position as commander in chief of the First Virginia Regiment. Washington's records show that he made three separate visits to Martha's home, White House on the Pamunkey River, during the first half of 1758. It is more than likely, in a social environment as small as that of the great planters, that he had met Martha and her husband on his various earlier trips to Williamsburg, but nothing concrete from the historical record has survived. The couple spent only a relatively few days together prior to their engagement, which was most likely entered into by June of 1758 (Washington's ledger records payment of sixteen shillings for a "Ring from Phila[delphia]"), but, as discussed in the previous chapter, it might not have been formalized until later in the fall.

The courtship of George and Martha Washington. (Courtesy of the
Virginia Historical Society)

There was, however, more than money that attracted George Washington to Martha Custis. In the first place, Martha was physically attractive. While she was perhaps not a great beauty, there are many
descriptions that indicate that her portraits don't do her justice, and
the later image of her as a "plain Jane" is unwarranted. Later descriptions vary but most are very positive. A Polish nobleman described
the General's wife as "small with lively eyes, a gay air and extremely
kind. . . . She was at one time one of the most beautiful women in
America and today there remains something extremely agreeable and
attractive about her." The British architect Benjamin Latrobe agreed,
adding that nearly forty years after her marriage, she still "retains
strong remains of physical beauty." Another architect and physician,
William Thornton, wrote she "has the remains of great beauty." Martha conformed to the eighteenth-century ideal of femininity: "buxom,
yet small and delicate." As her current biographer Patricia Brady once
commented, Martha was "a real cutie."

More importantly, perhaps, Martha had an extremely winning personality. Warm and talkative, she exercised her influence through a deferential style that focused on making others feel comfortable, happy, and well taken care of. Her new and best biographer declares that she "raised emotional support to an art form." The result was that she was beloved by almost everyone with whom she came into contact. In the words of Tobias Lear, family tutor and personal secretary, "Mrs. Washington is everything that is benevolent and good." The always perceptive and candid Abigail Adams reported, "Mrs. Washington is one of those unassuming characters which create love and esteem." Another acquaintance commented that she "appeared to me to be one of the best women in the world, and beloved by all about her." (A very rare critical comment came from a disgruntled visitor to Mount Vernon in 1784 who criticized her for a "damnable squeaky voice" and said that Martha and her niece, Fanny, mewed at each other "like two cats.")

An indication of her winning personality comes through in the story of how Martha Dandridge, a woman from a perfectly respectable but certainly not a top tier Virginia family, married into one of the most wealthy and renowned families in Virginia. Her husband, Daniel Parke Custis, appeared to be a confirmed bachelor. He was thirty-nine at the time of their marriage, apparently in part because no woman that he was interested in was ever good enough to win the approval of his eccentric and dominating father, John Custis IV. Although Martha's family standing was suspect and he had originally severely criticized the match, meeting Martha in person changed the father's mind. Word of this surprising shift is indicated in a letter to Daniel Custis from a friend: "This comes at last to bring you the news that I believe will be most agreeable to you of any you have heard—that you may not be long in suspense I shall tell you at once—I am empowered by your father to let you know that he heartily and willingly consents to your marriage to Miss Dandridge—that he has so good a character of her, that he had rather you should have her than any lady in Virginia—nay, if possible, he is as much as enamored with her character as you are with her person."

Thus, Martha scored high in three important areas: wealth, physical attractiveness, and character. No wonder that George Washington, shortly after his marriage, told a friend, "I am now I beleive fixd at this Seat [Mount Vernon] with an agreable Consort for Life and hope to find more happiness in retirement than I ever experiencd amidst a wide and bustling World." Martha may have started out being an "agreable consort," but in time she became much more than that. If the Washingtons' marriage began as one of convenience for both of them, there is no doubt that over the years it developed into a marriage of deep affection and love. Sally Cary Fairfax may have been the first real love *in* George Washington's life, but Martha Custis Washington was the real love *of* his life. It appears that, over time, Washington's anguished fascination for Sally cooled into a special friendship as he became more deeply attached to his wife. There are several indicators demonstrating the depth of their affection and closeness during their marriage.

Fortunately, two of Washington's many letters to Patsy, as he called Martha, escaped the flames and were later found by a granddaughter in the back drawer of a desk that she purchased following her grandmother's death. The most important, significantly addressed to "my dearest," was written immediately after Washington's appointment as commander in chief and gives an indication of his deep affection for his wife, and the other was composed a few days later as he prepared to depart for Boston. Here are the most salient passages from the two epistles:

> My Dearest, I am now set down to write to you on a subject which fills me with inexpressable concern—and this concern is greatly aggravated and Increased when I reflect on the uneasiness I know it will give you—It has been determined in Congress, that the whole Army raised for the defence of the American Cause shall be put under my care. . . . I should enjoy more real happiness and felicity in one month with you, at home, than I have the most distant prospect of reaping abroad, if my stay was to be Seven times Seven years. . . . it was utterly out of my power to refuse this appointment without exposing my Character to such censures as would have reflected dishonour upon myself, and given pain to my friends— this I am sure could not, and ought not to be pleasing to you, . . . My dear Patcy . . . I retain an unalterable affection for you, which neither time or distance can change.

He knew what a blow his departure would be because of their very close relationship, and he wrote to his brother, his brother-in-law, and his stepson and urged them all in the strongest language to do what they could to visit and ease Martha's pain. Typically: "I shall hope that my Friends will visit, & endeavour to keep up the Spirits of my Wife as much as they can, as my departure will, I know, be *a cutting stroke* upon her" (emphasis added). (Throughout their marriage, Washington was constantly concerned with his wife's safety and comfort.)

In his effort to reassure Martha, Washington expressed confidence that he would return to her and Mount Vernon in the fall. In fact, it would be *over six years* before he came back to his beloved Mount Vernon. An extremely telling indicator of the closeness of their relationship grew out of this reality. Since the conditions of war did not allow the General to go to his wife, he asked her to spend the winters of the war years with him. If there is ever a good justification for being away from your wife, it is that you are at war: "Washington, age 43 when he first beseeched her to come and stay as many months as possible, had reached a stage in life that finds countless men growing restless and feeling a void in their intimate spousal relations—what the French call *le demon de midi*, the devil at high noon." Yet, the General wanted her to come, and she did come *every single year* of the war. Of course, traveling in the winter was a difficult if not a dangerous undertaking. And these were not brief visits. Mary Thompson, the research historian at Mount Vernon, has computed that, in total, Lady Washington (as she was called by the troops) spent 52-54 of the roughly 114 months of the war either with her husband in camp, or nearby, in the hopes that they could spend more time together. (No wonder Martha referred to herself as the "the great perambulator.")

Perhaps a major reason the General so desired Martha's visits to his winter encampments was that, over time, Martha gave George Washington a gift every bit as valuable as the economic security her wealth conferred on him—the gift of *psychic security*. She gave him the type of unconditional support and love that his personality, perhaps in part because of his difficult childhood, seemed so desperately to need. Martha's care and devotion proved a balm for a man who had lost his father at a young age and had a troubled relationship with his mother. Indeed, in many ways, Martha was the opposite of his strong-willed, demanding, and apparently never-satisfied mother, Mary Ball Washington. Martha was calm and faithful, and rarely, if ever, burdened her husband with troubles or complaints. (It is interesting to note in passing that Martha, who seemed to get along well with everyone, apparently never established any kind of close rapport with her mother-in-law. One surprising fact is that in the over thirty years between her son's marriage to Martha and her own death from breast cancer in 1789, Mary Ball Washington, as far as the record reveals, never once visited Mount Vernon.)

When Washington went off to war against France in the 1750s, his mother had complained that he was ignoring her needs and, by implication, was not being a good son. Washington desperately hoped his wife would not attempt to put a similar guilt trip on him for accepting command of the Continental Army. His letter emphasized his uneasiness: "I know you will feel at being left alone—I therefore beg of you to summon your whole fortitude & Resolution, and pass your time as agreeably as possible—nothing will give me so much sincere satisfaction as to hear this, and to hear it from your own Pen. . . . my earnest, & ardent desire is, that you would pursue any Plan that is most likely to produce content, and a tolerable degree of Tranquility as it must add greatly to my uneasy feelings to hear that you are dissatisfied, and complaining at what I really could not avoid." Unlike his mother, Martha never disappointed him. What the General asked her to do she did, and, as far as the record shows, did it with little or no complaining.

One of the most revealing, if inadvertent, statements that Washington made about marriage occurred when he worried that his stepson, Jacky Custis, was about to embark on a marriage before he was mature enough to realize that "his own Peace, & the happiness of another" was dependent on how the marriage worked out. The choice of words is instructive. In short, Washington viewed marriage in part as the event that determines a man's "Peace" for the future. That is what he received from his marriage to Martha. Martha gave him peace—at least as much as possible, considering the challenges he often faced. Undoubtedly, it was a comfort for the General, always on show, to be able to unburden himself to one whose love and support was unconditional. With Martha, Washington could let his guard down and be himself. In Mercy Otis Warren's words, "the benevolence of her

Martha Washington. Miniature by Charles Willson Peale, 1772.
(Courtesy of the Mount Vernon Ladies' Association)

heart, and her affability, candor and gentleness qualify her to soften
the hours of private life or to sweeten the care of the Hero and smooth
the rugged scenes of war."

The Master of Mount Vernon made numerous other comments
that give further clues into how he viewed marriage and how important he thought it was: "I have always considered Marriage as the most
interesting event of ones life. The foundation of happiness or misery."
When his niece and nephew married, Washington commented that
they were "now one bone, and one flesh." In another letter, he referred
to the "sweets of Matrimony" and in a third called marriage one of
life's "greatest blessings."

Always the realist, the President cautioned his granddaughter, "Do not then in your contemplation of the marriage state, look for perfect felicity before you consent to wed. Nor conceive, from the fine tales the Poets & lovers of old have told us, of the transports of mutual love, that heaven has taken its abode on earth." Nonetheless, he believed, "In my estimation more permanent & genuine happiness is to be found in the sequestered walks of connubial life, than in the giddy rounds of promiscuous pleasure."

Occasionally, he expressed his views on marriage in a humorous fashion, such as when he wrote to a French companion in arms about the latter's decision to wed:

> So your day has, at length, come. I am glad of it with all my heart and soul. It is quite good enough for you. Now you are well served for coming to fight in favour of the American Rebels, all the way across the Atlantic Ocean, by catching that terrible Contagion—domestic felicity—which time like the small pox or the plague, a man can have only once in his life: because it commonly lasts him—(at least with us in America—I dont know how you manage these matters in France) for his whole life time. And yet after all the maledictions you so richly merit on the subject, the worst wish which I can find in my heart to make against Madame de Chastelux and yourself is, that you may neither of you ever get the better of this same—domestic felicity—during the entire course of your mortal exestence.

There is no denying the importance Washington placed on marriage, and comments by others strengthen the assertion that the Washingtons enjoyed an affectionate and close marriage. In the words of a female friend, "His Worthy Lady seems to be in perfect felicity while she is by the side of her Old Man as she calls him." General Nathanael Greene wrote his wife, "Mrs. Washington is excessive fond of the General and he of her. . . . They are happy in each other." Lafayette wrote that Martha loved the General "madly." Perhaps symbolic of Washington's affection, he most likely wore a painted miniature of Martha around his neck during the war, as did Martha of him. Her locket included a lock of her husband's hair and was very dear to her.

George Washington's final significant document confirms his deep love for his wife of forty years. Washington, who wrote his entire twenty-nine-page last will and testament completely by himself over the summer of 1799, chose his words carefully throughout. Twice in the will he referred to Martha not as "my wife" or even as "my beloved wife" but rather as "my dearly beloved wife." He described her as "the partner of all my Domestic enjoyments" and made very ample provision for her in the will, much larger than he had to do by law. He gave her "the use, profit and benefit of my whole estate, real and personal, for the term of her natural life."

If marriage was a great blessing to George Washington, what was the nature of the relationship with his wife? Did he simply dominate the marriage, with Martha meekly agreeing to go along with whatever he wanted to do? Or was she influential in her own right and able to influence her husband to do what she wanted him to do? There are two essentially opposite views of Martha, both of which appear to miss the reality behind the relationship. One sees Martha as little more than a minor prop in the great saga of George Washington, someone who knew her place and kept it. She did what her husband wanted her to do and was essentially a cipher in the grand scheme of his life and accomplishments. The opposite view, most recently put forth in a 2002 biography of Martha, *The First Lady of Liberty* by Helen Bryan, essentially sees Martha as a proto-feminist and an early champion of women's issues and rights. An article on the Web gives a clear example of this type of Martha, and it sounds very appealing to many modern-day readers:

By her actions as First Lady, Martha Washington also nurtured the idea of independence for women. She surrounded herself with the wives of leading politicians and army officers, whom she regaled with stories she alone had access to as her husband's most trusted confidant. Her commitment to equal education for women inspired her to make sure that all her nieces and grandchildren had the best private schooling available. Few things were more important to her than her own independence of mind, and she seldom lost the opportunity to drive the point home to her female friends and relatives. Not only must women think for themselves, she of-

ten exclaimed to anyone who would listen, they also should keep
their business affairs—from managing the household to overseeing accounts—in their own hands.

There is little evidence that Martha did these things in the manner described, and this appears to be an example of the common case of believing what is pleasant over what is displeasing in spite of the evidence.

We always have to be careful of forcing a twenty-first-century
mind-set back on the eighteenth century. It was a different world with
a different worldview, a worldview in which domination by males was
taken for granted by both sexes. The then widely accepted view is
well illustrated by comments in a journal kept by Elizabeth Washington of Hayfield, the wife of George Washington's distant cousin
and farm-manager, Lund, and a woman who incidentally received a
mourning ring from Washington, a clear sign of his admiration and
affection for her. Elizabeth indicated that failures of a wife include
"teasing" and "disputing with her husband," and declared it has "ever
given me pleasure to please" Lund. In one passage she wrote, "There
was never married people who lived happier than we do . . . so entirely
free from disputing." The reason: "the Lordly Sex, they can never be in
the wrong in their own opinion—therefore cannot give up to a woman.
. . . I never thought it degraded my understanding to give up my opinion to my husband's. . . . A desire to do my duty, to conform with Scripture direction [namely, 'wives, obey your husbands'] has been the rul-
ing principal that has conducted my actions in the married state."

Martha most likely would have essentially echoed those sentiments. George Washington was the dominant partner, and I think
Martha was very comfortable with that arrangement. A conversation
between the couple on their wedding day at Martha's home, taken
from a historical novel, accurately illustrates this aspect of their relationship, even though the quote is a fictitious one. Martha, in response to Washington's comment that Governor Francis Fauquier attended the ceremony to honor the bride, expressed a different view: "'I
think the bride fitted in rather nicely into the long shadow cast by the
groom.' . . . Taking his right hand with both of hers, she raised it to
her face. 'The bride is quite content always to live like that.'" In other
words, she would happily live in his shadow and give him whatever

support she could. This is basically how she in fact lived their married life of over forty years together. Martha would defer to her husband on most matters whether it was on major alterations to Mount Vernon, when she should visit him in camp, or what she should include in her letters, which he often wrote and she simply copied. Her devotion and behind-the-scenes support of her husband in all of his pursuits characterized her entire married life. His pain was her pain. After the fall of Philadelphia, she wrote, "The pore General was so unhappy that it distressed me exceedingly." A later observer, Henrietta Liston, noted that Abigail Adams as First Lady had "spirit enough to laugh at the abuse of her husband" by the opposition press but noted "poor Mrs. Washington could not."

While Washington was the dominant partner, as much emphasis must be placed on the word "partner" as on the word "dominant." There are numerous vignettes to illustrate that it was very much a partnership and that what Martha wanted counted for a great deal. Sometimes Washington acquiesced in actions that he did not agree with because of Martha's desires. This was particularly true concerning the children. The Washingtons essentially raised two families. The first consisted of Martha's two children, Jacky and Patsy, by her first husband; the second consisted of George Washington Parke Custis (Wash) and Eleanor Parke Custis (Nelly), the two youngest children of Jacky, who died unexpectedly in 1781.

In the area of the children, Martha was generally the dominant partner. (Washington was very disappointed he and Martha did not have children, but he did not think of himself as sterile and speculated that it was theoretically possible that he might play the fool if Martha were to die and become a father with a much younger woman as his wife.) Martha can only be described as a doting mother. For whatever reasons, she spoiled the children—at least the males, Jacky and Wash. Speaking about her grandson, she confessed, "I cannot say but it makes me miserable if ever he complains let the cause be ever so trifeling." Why didn't Washington intervene more actively? Perhaps because he was the stepfather rather than the natural father, but I think the following quote by Tobias Lear expresses the most salient reason: "Mrs. W's happiness is bound up in the boy—and rigidity used toward him would perhaps be productive of grievous effects on her." In short, Washington preferred spoiled youngsters to an unhappy wife.

Two vignettes involving Jacky are revealing. One involves his being vaccinated against smallpox and the other involves his marriage to Nelly Calvert. When Jacky was vaccinated for smallpox in 1771, Washington wrote his tutor, the Reverend Jonathan Boucher, that Martha was not aware of the inoculation of the boy (Washington wanted to shield his overprotective wife from worry), and that any information about Jacky's reaction to it should be sent to him by way of his manager, Lund Washington. Why not have Boucher write directly to Colonel Washington? The Master of Mount Vernon gave the reason. Martha, he was sure, "could not rest satisfied without knowing the Contents of any Letter to this Family of your writing." This casual comment flashes a ray of light on their marital relationship. It was certainly not one of a domineering husband and a cowed wife. While Washington might decide on his own to keep the inoculation from Martha, their relationship was also such that Martha would not hesitate to open a letter addressed to her husband if she felt it might contain information about her precious Jacky. And there is no hint that Washington could or would order his wife not to open such mail.

The second involves Jacky's hasty marriage. Washington put great emphasis on education, perhaps in part because he so keenly felt the effects of his own "defective education." He managed to get his stepson enrolled at Columbia, then called King's College, only to soon discover that Jacky, still in his teens, had become engaged to Nelly Calvert of the wealthy Maryland Calverts. While not opposing an eventual union, Washington refused to give his blessing until Jack finished his schooling: "As his Guardian, I conceive it to be my indispensable duty (to endeavour) to carry him through a regular course of Education, many Branches of which, sorry I am to add, he is totally difficient of, and, to guard his youth to a more advancd age before an Event, on which his own Peace, & the happiness of another is to depend."

Yet, later in the same year in which he sent his explicit refusal, he wrote the following letter to the president of King's College: "At length, I have yielded, contrary to my judgment, & much against my wishes, to his quitting College; in order that he may enter soon into a new scene of Life, which I think he would be much fitter for some years hence, than now; but having his own inclination—the desires of his mother—& the acquiescence of almost all his relatives, to encounter, I did not care, as he is the last of the family, to push my opposition too far; & therefore have submitted to a Kind of necessity."

Washington's comment, "he is the last of the family," may well have played a role in his change of heart. Tragically, Jacky's younger sister, Patsy, at the tender age of seventeen, had died a short time earlier as a result of one of her many epileptic seizures. Patsy's long illness, "the afflicted path" she had been forced to tread for at least five years, had been an emotional and financial drain on the family. (They consulted at least eight different doctors.) In the summer of 1770, Washington kept a log of these episodes in the margins of a printed calendar in his almanac. Of the eighty-six days in this period, Patsy had seizures on twenty-six, often as many as two per day. He wrote his brother-in-law about her sad demise: "She rose from Dinner about four Oclock, in better health and spirits than she appeard to have been in for some time; soon after which she was seizd with one of her usual Fits, & expired in it, in less than two Minutes without uttering a Word, a groan, or scarce a Sigh." Hard as it was on Washington, he knew it was even more difficult on his beloved wife: "This Sudden, and unexpected blow . . . has almost reduced my poor Wife to the lowest ebb of Misery." Washington changed his schedule and did not leave Mount Vernon for some time after Patsy's death in order to be there for his wife. His diary for the next couple of weeks includes brief but telling entries: "Went with Mrs. Washington and Dind at Belvoir. . . Rid with Mrs. Washington to the Ferry Plantn. . . . Rid with Mrs. Washington to Muddy hole, Doeg Run, and Mill Plantations. . . . Mrs. Washington and self went to Belvoir to see them take shipping." It was apparently impossible, under the circumstances of her bereavement over Patsy, to deny his wife's wishes when she indicated she supported Jacky's decision to drop out of school, return to the area, and marry. (Martha was very fond of Jacky's fiancée, a girl of about Patsy's age who spent considerable time at Mount Vernon and undoubtedly was a comfort to the grieving mother.)

Martha influenced Washington's actions in areas other than the children. One case involves the efforts to recapture a fugitive slave, Ona Judge, one of Martha's dower slaves, a seamstress who was a "perfect Mistress of her needle." Martha was particularly outraged at Ona's actions, her "ingratitude," because as Washington expressed it,

Ona was "treated more like a child than a Servant." In his efforts to reclaim the young fugitive, Washington repeatedly stated that Martha wanted her back. He may well have been willing to let her go, given the potential political embarrassment of reclaiming her from freedom in New Hampshire, but Martha insisted on trying. (The efforts failed, and Ona later left the only first-person account by a fugitive slave from eighteenth-century Virginia.)

Thus, like most married couples, the Washingtons did not see eye to eye on everything. Their views on child rearing, slavery, and religion (discussed in chapter 9) may have been somewhat different, but such differences did not keep them from having a close and comfortable marriage. Martha wrote and enticed her sister to visit by describing the "mirth and gaity" at Mount Vernon. Her references to Washington as "my Old Man" or "Pappa" (perhaps her most common sobriquet) are also revealing. A brief note from Martha to her husband about the weight of a silver cup was recently discovered by the editors of the *Papers of George Washington*. It had been scribbled on the back of another letter, thus avoiding destruction. Significantly, it begins with the revealing words: "my love." (The only other extant note from Martha begins, "My dearest.") One of Washington's letters to a friend also indicates the tone of their conversation as man and wife. Discussing a proposed visit by Charles Thompson, he wrote that if Martha knew of the invitation, she would "I am certain, adduce arguments to prove that I ought to include Mrs Thompson; but before she should have half spun the thread of her discourse, it is more than probable I should have nonplused her, by yielding readily to the force of her reasoning."

The gaiety and mirth experienced at Mount Vernon meant that Martha would, like her famous husband, have to sacrifice her personal pleasure for the good of the nation when Washington reluctantly agreed to accept the presidency. How she wished that they had been allowed to remain at Mount Vernon where she hoped "we should have been left to grow old in solitude & tranquility together." She knew, however, as she expressed to another friend, that such thoughts were wishful thinking: "I have been so long accustomed to conform to events which are governed by the public voice that I hardly dare indulge any personal wishes which cannot yield to that."

By virtually all accounts, she publicly acquitted herself very well as the nation's first "First Lady." (The actual term "First Lady" would not gain currency for another century.) She seemed able to charm almost everyone with whom she came into contact. Abigail Adams again helps us understand why: "Her manners are modest and unassuming, dignified and femenine, not a tincture of ha'ture [haughtiness] about her." Martha Washington's levees, called her "republican court," were less formal than the President's, and it appears that they were used by many as a kind of high-class dating society. Supposedly, Mrs. Washington helped broker a number of marriages (including that of James and Dolley Madison) that were at least partly connected to these gatherings.

The fact that she was successful didn't mean that she was not frustrated in her new position as the wife of the nation's first president. Some of the frustration is made clear in private letters: "I live a very dull life hear and know nothing that passes in the town—I never goe to any public place, indeed I think I am more like a state prisoner than anything else, there is certain bounds set for me which I must not depart from—and as I can not doe as I like I am obstinate and stay at home a great deal." This sense of captivity is echoed by the recollection of her friend, "Betsy" Hamilton, wife of the secretary of the treasury: "Mrs. Washington who, like myself, had a passionate love of home and domestic life, often complained of the 'waste of time' she was compelled to endure. 'They call me the first lady in the land and think I must be extremely happy,' she would say almost bitterly at times and add, 'They might more properly call me the chief state prisoner.'"

One reason historians mourn the loss of George Washington's letters to Martha is because there is clear evidence that Martha was his confidant. From one of his two surviving letters to her, and nowhere else, we learn that Washington expected to be nominated as commander in chief for a period of time prior to his actual nomination. As president, he did something he did not want the public to know about. Under false pretenses, he sent his slaves back to Virginia so that they would not be able to take advantage of a new Pennsylvania law, which declared any slave being kept in Pennsylvania beyond six months could claim his or her freedom. In instructing his trusted personal secretary, Tobias Lear, to carry out the subterfuge, the President wrote that except for the two of them, only his wife knew the real reason. Unlike Lear, Martha had "no need" to know; it is simply an example of how much the President confided in her.

Thus, the letters would undoubtedly have revealed many interesting facts and tidbits of information, but they would not have revealed a passionate exchange between the correspondents. Washington's view of an established marriage is revealed in a letter to his granddaughter:

> Love [i.e. passionate love] is a mighty pretty thing, but, like all other delicious things it is cloying; and when the first transports of passion begin to subside, which it assuredly will do, and yield, oftentimes, too late, to more sober reflections, it serves to evince that love is too dainty a food to live on alone, and ought not to be considered further than as a necessary ingredient [in] that matrimonial happiness which results from a combination of causes: none of which are greater importance than that the partner should have good sense, a good disposition, a good reputation, and financial means. [Martha would score very high in each area.] Such qualifications cannot fail to attract (after Marriage) your esteem and regard into which, or into disgust, sooner or later love naturally resolves itself.

There is a fascinating exchange of letters between President Washington and his close female friend and admirer, Eliza Powel, which gives us our best insight into the tone of the correspondence that was burned. When Washington left the presidency in 1797, he sold his desk to the Powels, and Eliza soon discovered a large packet of letters from Martha to her husband, which had inadvertently been left in one of the drawers. Eliza teased the retired chief executive that she now had in her possession, "the love Letters of a Lady addressed to you." In responding, the retired President declared that if anyone had in fact read Martha's letters, they would have discovered that the missives were "more fraught with expressions of friendship, than of *enamoured* love" (emphasis in the original). If one expected "warmth" from the letters in question, Washington joked, the person would have to put them in a fire.

George Washington's final encounter with his wife neatly encapsulates key aspects of their relationship. It shows him as the dominant partner, but it also demonstrates his trust in her, her unwavering support for him whatever the crisis, and the great strength of character they both possessed. (Washington's death is examined in chapter 10.) By the early hours of Saturday morning, the 14th of December, 1799, the President, already stricken with the disease that would claim his life before the day ended, awoke with a high fever, labored breathing, and in considerable discomfort. Greatly alarmed, Martha wanted to seek help, but Washington, concerned that her going out into the cold night air might lead to a relapse (she had only recently recovered from a serious illness), told her not to do so. Martha's acquiescence to her husband's request, despite her deep concern for his well-being, sheds light on their relationship. Even in the face of a grave illness, Martha yielded to her husband's wishes. For approximately four long hours, they waited together, Washington laboring for breath, Martha sick with worry, until Caroline, one of the household slaves, finally arrived sometime around 7 A.M. to light the fire in their room. Martha could at last send her to summon Colonel Lear and help.

Sadly, there was nothing eighteenth-century medicine could do as George Washington essentially slowly and painfully choked to death. Martha remained faithfully by his side throughout the long ordeal, but often apparently stayed at the foot of the bed while Washington spoke to others about things that needed doing. Nevertheless, on his deathbed, he entrusted his precious final will and testament, which he had devoted so many hours to composing, into her hands with instructions to burn the old one. She maintained a Spartan-like composure during the long ordeal, never adding to the General's discomfort by breaking down under her own great grief. Words that an aide of General Steuben wrote earlier seem applicable: "She reminded me of the Roman matrons of whom I read so much." She could be as much of a Stoic as her husband.

Tobias Lear wrote about how she faced the moment of her husband's demise. Keeping a silent and prayerful vigil at the foot of the bed (she and her husband shared a single bed together for over forty years), Martha grasped what had happened. Somehow managing to speak in a firm voice, she asked, "Is he gone?" Lear, struck dumb with

grief, could only lift his hand as a way of answering. Echoing her husband's last words, Martha replied in the same firm tone of voice, "Tis
well. All is now over. I shall soon follow him and I shall rejoice when
the moment arrives! I have no more trials to pass through." Certainly,
Martha faced the terrible ordeal with courage worthy of the First
Lady of the land, and although she lived until 1802, in many ways her
life ended when his did. Her grief was intense, and her major biographer poignantly notes, "Sorrow had turned this woman, all movement
and smiles and lighthearted talk, to stone." She never slept in their
bedroom again, and when death came, a granddaughter's husband,
Thomas Law, noted, "She met death as relief from the infirmities and
melancholy of old age."

In summarizing their relationship, quotes from contemporaries
appear justified and accurate: "I thought she well deserved to be the
companion and friend of the greatest man of the age." "The first of
men chose her as his wife—the companion of a life of glory, and well
did she repay his confidence and attachment." Few men, famous or
not, are fortunate enough to have such a loving and devoted wife. She
was indeed, as her obituary in an Alexandria newspaper noted, "The
worthy partner of the worthiest of men."

6

Reluctant Enemies

The Increasingly Strained Relationship between George Washington and Thomas Jefferson

[Thomas Jefferson] is a man of whom I early imbibed
the highest opinion—I am much pleased therefore to
meet confirmations of my discernment in these matters, as I am mortfied when I find myself mistaken.
—*George Washington*

MARTHA WASHINGTON MAY HAVE GIVEN GEORGE WASHINGTON
psychic security and provided a peaceful haven amidst the many
troubles he faced as commander in chief and later as president of the
United States. She had, however, neither the skills nor inclination to
give him guidance or solutions for dealing with those troubles and
challenges. For that type of assistance, Washington had to look elsewhere. Always sensitive about his "defective education," Washington
was also fully cognizant that some of his peers possessed quicker and
better trained minds than his. Consequently, throughout his life, he
sought mentors, among them William Fairfax, George Mason, James
Madison, and Alexander Hamilton, although it should be noted that
he was always willing to discard them as well. One of his most important mentors was the brilliant, multitalented genius, Thomas Jefferson, whom most historians rank second only to George Washington
in their list of the most important founding fathers.

This lofty pairing of the two great patriots is reflected in the design of the grand ballroom of the Library of Congress in Washington, D.C. Placed in large niches on opposite walls of the ballroom
are facsimiles of Jean-Antoine Houdon's famous busts of George
Washington and Thomas Jefferson. As the author of the immortal
Declaration of Independence and the almost as far-reaching and im-

portant Virginia Statute for Religious Freedom, as the father of the
University of Virginia and the eloquent champion of the Enlightenment and human reason, Jefferson was the most important of all the
revolutionary spokesmen. Better than anyone else, he articulated the
basic American ideology—belief in liberty and equality, confidence in
education, and faith in the common sense of ordinary people.

This chapter will focus primarily on the increasingly stressful
relationship between these two remarkable individuals. Ultimately,
significant differences in their philosophies in combination with
significant differences in their personalities led to a complete break,
but one must not allow their ultimate rupture to color how one views
their relationship in an earlier period. In fact, throughout the large
majority of the approximately thirty years they knew each other, they
were friends, with each man holding an extremely favorable opinion
of the other. Each saw traits in the other that he admired and undoubtedly wished he possessed as well.

At first glance, when examining the two men, one is struck by

Houdon busts of Thomas Jefferson and George Washington. (Courtesy
of the Boston Museum of Fine Arts and the Mount Vernon Ladies'
Association)

the great many things that George Washington and Thomas Jefferson shared in common. They first met each other in Williamsburg in 1769, when Jefferson won election to the Virginia House of Burgesses, where Washington had been a member since 1758. These tall Virginians were both members of the planter elite; both were early supporters of the patriot cause, served on committees together, and were intensely ambitious; both devoted almost their entire adult lives to public service; both were fascinated with the west and expansion; both disliked public speaking; and both reached the pinnacle of national political power. There were other striking similarities as well. Both were born into families that were not quite in the first ranks of Virginia society; both lost their fathers as young boys; both had strained relationships with their mothers; both became romantically involved with the wives of close friends (Jefferson with Betsy Walker); both married wealthy widows named Martha and had unusually happy marriages (although Jefferson's was cut short by the untimely death of his wife in 1782); both spent a lifetime working on their respective homes which reflected their personalities; both were compulsive record-keepers; both pined (without great success) for the life of an independent planter; and both detested slavery but nevertheless continued to live with it and off it.

During the War for Independence, their relationship was essentially a deferential one, with Jefferson having an almost filial reverence for General Washington, eleven years his senior and commander in chief of the Continental Army. In his *Notes on the State of Virginia,* published in 1781, Jefferson included Washington as one of the three men of genius produced in America. (The other two were Benjamin Franklin and David Rittenhouse.) Based on his earlier contact with Jefferson, Washington recognized him as a man of unique ability, and he purchased Jefferson's important pamphlet, *A Summary View of the Rights of British America.* When Jefferson seemed to remove himself from public service, Washington asked rhetorically, "Where is . . . Jefferson?" Most of their contact during the Revolution was through mail, especially while Jefferson was governor of Virginia during the difficult years from 1779 to 1781. One of Governor Jefferson's first problems was how to deal with the recently captured Sir Henry Hamilton, former lieutenant governor of Detroit, and notorious as the

"Hair Buyer General" for his policy of encouraging Indian attacks on the frontier. Jefferson initially approved the harsh sentence of keeping Hamilton confined in irons in a small dungeon and denied writing material or conversation, but he worried about British reprisals and sought General Washington's advice. Washington urged second thoughts and, based on this advice, Jefferson reduced the severity of Hamilton's condition while he was in captivity.

While severely hampered by numerous problems, Jefferson as governor of the Commonwealth did what he could to help Washington, and the General wrote several letters praising Jefferson's conduct as governor. Jefferson was in Annapolis during what he described as the "affecting scene" of Washington's resignation of his commission at the end of the war, and he declared that the General's final address "was worthy of him." Jefferson desired a statue of General Washington to grace the rotunda of the new state capital at Richmond and was instrumental in working out the details for the greatest sculptor of the eighteenth century, Jean-Antoine Houdon, to travel from France to Mount Vernon to create a life mask of America's hero. The resulting statue, even according to the famous painter Gilbert Stuart, was the greatest lifelike rendering of Washington ever produced.

The friendship between Washington and Jefferson blossomed in the years after the war. Both men were extremely interested in opening up the Potomac River and connecting it to the west. It was a magnificent obsession with Washington throughout his adult life, and he was flattered that Jefferson, whom he described as a man "of discernment and liberality," agreed with his views. Washington began to ask Jefferson for advice and asked that it be rendered with the "fullest latitude of a friend." Once, asking for additional advice, Washington wrote, "I have accustomed myself to communicate matters of difficulty to you, & have met forgiveness for it." Jefferson, always in a very deferential manner, began to offer advice to Washington on such matters as how best to respond to a large gift of stock in the James River Canal Company and to the fact that the membership in the Society of Cincinnati was based on heredity.

Thus, as Jefferson scholar Andrew Burstein notes, "It was not just Jefferson's cosmopolitan connections and diplomatic experience [he was our minister to France] but his character and their common stance on public morality and dignified behavior that led the president to appoint his fellow Virginian as Secretary of State." Acknowledging his friend Lafayette's praise for Jefferson, Washington responded to the Frenchman, "The favourable terms in which you speak of Mr. Jefferson gives me great pleasure: he is a man of whom I early imbibed the highest opinion—I am much pleased, therefore, to meet confirmations of my discernment in these matters, as I am mortified when I find myself mistaken."

Wanting Jefferson as his secretary of state, Washington exercised remarkable patience as Jefferson initially expressed great reluctance. The President sought to be persuasive, but he left the final decision up to Jefferson and never went so far as to argue that a sense of duty should compel him to accept the job: "I consider the Office of Secretary for the Department of State *very* important on many accts: and I know of no person, who, in my judgment, could better execute the Duties of it than yourself" (emphasis in the original). Encouraged by Madison and other friends, and undoubtedly moved by Washington's praise and by a sense of loyalty to him, Jefferson accepted the President's nomination, but it was not until March of 1790 that he finally arrived in New York to take up his post. Prior to his arrival he assured Washington, "You are to marshal us as may be best for the public good," and he pledged to loyally execute "whatever you may be pleased to decide." Neither man anticipated the bitter divisions that were soon to threaten the unity of the new country.

There is no doubt that as Thomas Jefferson began his position as George Washington's first secretary of state there was a great deal of mutual admiration and respect between the two men. Jefferson, for example, had been extremely critical of the Constitution's failure to limit the number of terms an individual could be president, for he feared it would lead to monarchy, and, if there was anything that Jefferson opposed, it was monarchy. Nevertheless, he argued that there was no need to correct the error while Washington was president, for the nation needed him to start the experiment successfully, thus making governing by lesser men possible later on. Washington's respect for Jefferson was shown in the great patience he demonstrated in getting him to join his administration. As they worked together, the President manifested genuine affection for his secretary of state.

In his book *Founding Friendship*, Stuart Leibiger observes that one can obtain a good sense about Washington's relationship with an individual by the words he used in the salutations of his letters: "Sir" for those with whom he was not close or barely knew; "Dear Sir" for those with whom he was closer; and "My Dear Sir" for those closest to him. Washington used the phrase "My Dear Sir" with only a few individuals, but by 1792 he would on occasion use that term with Thomas Jefferson.

What happened to lead to dire misunderstandings between the two men and, eventually, to a complete rupture in the years after Jefferson resigned his post as secretary of state? Part of the answer lies in the development of competing visions of America and what the American Revolution was all about. In time, it seemed that an unbridgeable gulf opened between the friends of Order who wished to harness some of the energies released by the revolution, and the friends of Liberty who feared any such effort was a betrayal of the revolution itself. At the core of their beliefs, and to a degree neither man recognized or acknowledged, George Washington and Thomas Jefferson had significantly differing political philosophies and visions for the future of America. At heart, Washington was a friend of Order and Jefferson a friend of Liberty. Washington viewed a strong government as a necessary means of strengthening the union and protecting liberty. Jefferson viewed a strong government as a dangerous threat to liberty: "The natural progress of things is for liberty to yield and government to gain ground." In his own words, Jefferson always had "more confidence" than Washington "in the natural integrity and discretion of the people, and in the safety and extent to which they might trust themselves with a control of their government."

There were early indications of their differences in the 1780s. Washington asked for Jefferson's advice concerning the Society of Cincinnati, which had been created by officers of the American Revolution and was to be a hereditary society. (Washington was elected its first president.) Jefferson was candid in his criticism of the Society when Washington asked his opinion, and later he was even more outspoken. In Jefferson's gloomy prophecy, the Society of Cincinnati would lead to a "hereditary aristocracy" and ultimately "change the form of our government from the best to the worst." This exchange provides good insight into Jefferson's mind-set that would later cause him to see such danger in the ideas of Alexander Hamilton. It is interesting to note, however, that Washington, although in agreement with some specific criticisms made by Jefferson, wrote at roughly the same time about "the most unreasonable prejudice against an innocent institution" and asserted that he was in basic agreement with its philosophy. In short, Jefferson saw great dangers where Washington saw none.

Jefferson's mental focus was on the way things ought to be rather than on how they were. He was convinced that in a Golden Age long ago they were once right, and that they could and would once again be that way. In his Pulitzer Prize–winning work, *Founding Brothers*, Joseph Ellis contrasts Washington and Jefferson: Washington "was a rock-ribbed realist, who instinctively mistrusted all visionary schemes dependent on seductive ideals that floated dreamily in men's minds, unmoored to the more prosaic but palpable realities that invariably spelled the difference between victory and defeat. . . . At its intellectual core, it meant he was the mirror image of Jefferson, for whom ideals were the supreme reality and whose inspirational prowess derived from his confidence that the world would eventually come around to fit the pictures he had in his head. Washington regarded such pictures as dangerous dreams."

It was, of course, the rise to prominence of Jefferson's archrival, Alexander Hamilton, the brilliant secretary of the treasury, that brought about a crisis. (Hamilton is the focus of the next chapter.) Hamilton's vision of America seemed to Jefferson and his supporters to take America in exactly the wrong direction. It threatened to undo the great experiment in republicanism by a return to monarchy and aristocracy. One scholar summarized Jefferson's view: "With devious brilliance, Hamilton set out, by a program of class legislation, to unite the propertied interests of the eastern seaboard into a cohesive administration party, while at the same time he attempted to make the executive dominant over the Congress by a lavish use of the spoils system." Another wrote: "The instruments of government Hamilton favored were all too familiar to Jefferson: a large and more or less permanent national debt; a national bank; the vigorous promotion of manufactures by the national government; and a substantial military establishment, all to be paid for by a system of duties and excise taxes." It seemed to be the re-creation of the hated system Robert Walpole had built in England seventy years earlier and that had more recently been used to attempt to crush American liberties. In short, Jefferson asserted the machinery of the new government was tragically being used to exploit the mass of the people in the interest of a small minority.

Prone to view the world as divided between good and evil, Jefferson soon developed a full-blooded conspiracy theory in which these actions portended, as he warned Washington in 1792, the "change from the present republican form of government to that of a monarchy of which the British Constitution is to be the model." In his *Anas*, a quasi autobiography full of gossip and stories, Jefferson went further. Alexander Hamilton "was not only a monarchist but a monarchist bottomed on corruption." He sought to alert Washington to the grave dangers posed by Hamilton. Yet, "to Jefferson's utter astonishment, the President remained unconvinced. . . . What was patently obvious to Jefferson was invisible to Washington. This failed conversation between the two men, one of many in the 'Anas,' suggests one reason for Jefferson's increasing distance from the President. In his mind, Washington was unwilling to face the truth." How to deal with the fact that the man he deeply admired could seem to agree with the man he deeply despised would be for Jefferson an ever increasingly difficult dilemma.

Jefferson faced a related dilemma. He was part of an administration that was pursuing policies that he thought were detrimental to the health of the republic. Consequently, he acted in ways that many Washington scholars have found offensive, essentially secretly supporting efforts opposed to the Washington administration and its policies. A prime example was Jefferson's involvement in supporting Philip Freneau and his anti-administration newspaper, the *National Gazette*. Jefferson's sympathetic biographer Noble Cunningham concludes that "attracting Freneau to Philadelphia, putting him on the payroll of the State Department, and giving him privileges denied to other editors, left Jefferson vulnerable to charges difficult to refute." Professor Higginbotham recounts a personal story of meeting Dr. Gertrude Richards, the senior member of Douglas Southall Freeman's research team as Freeman worked on his monumental and still in many ways unsurpassed biography of Washington. She informed him that both she and Dr. Freeman had concluded that Jefferson was "little short of being a fiend" for the way he undercut the administration of which he was a major part.

To Washington, the bitter and increasingly personal feud between his two premier cabinet members was deeply troubling and worrisome. The President wrote of his deep concern "that internal dissentions [were] . . . tearing [at] our vitals." He pleaded, "My earnest wish, and my fondest hope therefore is, that instead of wounding suspicions, & irritable charges, there may be liberal allowances—mutual forbearances—and temporising yieldings on *all* sides. . . . Without them every thing must rub—the Wheels of Government will clog—our enemies will triumph—& . . . the fairest prospect of happiness & prosperity that ever was presented to man, will be lost—perhaps for ever!" Washington urged cooperation because he was "persuaded there is no discordance in your views." He was, of course, mistaken in his assessment. The feud between Jefferson and Hamilton was much more than a personal one. There was, in fact, a major and fundamental dissonance in their views about where America should be headed.

About the only thing the two men did agree on is that George Washington, however much he might long for retirement, had to remain in office for a second term. In Jefferson's words to the President, "North and South will hang together, if they can hang on you." That mission accomplished, Jefferson, increasingly frustrated by Hamilton, announced his intention to resign, which, after some slight postponement, he did at the end of 1793. The parting, at least on the surface, was amiable with nice things written by both parties, although it is plausible to argue that Washington felt that in some manner Jefferson, in leaving at a critical time (during the crisis with the new French ambassador, Edmund Genet), left him in the lurch, especially after Jefferson had convinced him that he had to serve a second term. (And Jefferson seemed to rub salt in the wounds by almost taunting Washington with the bright prospects he looked forward to at Monticello while Washington was fated to struggle on as chief executive in Philadelphia.) At any rate, it is perhaps significant to note that never again did Washington refer to Jefferson as "My dear sir."

Jefferson's posture toward Washington shifted perceptibly during his second administration. His concern was raised to a fever pitch—first by the President's manner of putting down the Whiskey Rebellion, then by his attack on the Democratic Societies and, most importantly, by his support for the Jay Treaty. Washington viewed the Whiskey Rebellion, an uprising of farmers in western Pennsylvania against what they viewed as unjust taxes, as a threat to the viability of the national government and marshaled a massive thirteen-thousand-man force to crush it. Jefferson, seeing the threat as grossly exaggerated for domestic considerations, was shocked at Washington's speech defending his actions, and declared it contained "shreds of stuff from Aesop's fables."

Washington's criticism of the Democratic Societies (about thirty-five in number, liberal in ideology, and sympathetic to the French Revolution)—blaming them in effect for causing the Whiskey Rebellion—was particularly upsetting: "Washington spoke in the name of law and order, without distinguishing between resistance to the government and criticism of the government." Jefferson told Madison it was a sad day when the President permitted himself to be the instrument of an attack on the freedom of discussion. Presidential scholar Richard Norton Smith concluded, "The great champion of free speech and free thought apprehended in Washington's strident words confirmation of his worst fears—the monocrats had at last captured the president. What a tragedy, thought Jefferson, that George Washington, the symbol of man's age-old desire to taste the fruits of liberty, should now permit himself to become an instrument in the suppression of basic rights to discuss and dissent and publish."

Worse was yet to come. Washington's support for the initially extremely unpopular Jay Treaty between the United States and Great Britain brought Jefferson to the nadir of his relationship with Washington and caused him to write a letter, a paragraph of which was to plague him for the rest of his life. Despite few concessions from Great Britain, Washington decided to sign the treaty because approval of the treaty would mean peace with Great Britain and continuation of America's commercial prosperity. (This is expanded on in chapter 3.) In Thomas Jefferson's view, the Jay Treaty belonged more properly in the annals of treason than in the annals of diplomacy. It was a deal between Great Britain and the Anglomen in America against the people of America: "As Jefferson saw it, the Jay Treaty was a repudiation of the Declaration of Independence, the Franco-American alliance, the revolutionary movement sweeping through Europe and all the political principles on which he had staked his public career as an American statesman."

The danger of the treaty was crystal clear to Jefferson and yet the President would not—or could not—see it. If the President was not moved by what Jefferson considered to be unassailable logic, then, to Jefferson, there had to be something wrong with the President's perception of reality. How could the man who led the fight for American liberty support such a blatantly poor and dangerous treaty? How could he become the patron, however unwillingly, of oppression? The only acceptable answer for Jefferson was that the George Washington supporting the Jay Treaty was no longer the *real* George Washington: "His memory was already sensibly impaired by age, the firm tone of mind for which he had been remarkable was beginning to relax, it's energy was abated; a listlessness of labor, a desire for tranquility had crept on him and a willingness to let others act and even think for him." In effect, he was becoming senile. "In his private correspondence with trusted Republicans, he developed the image of an old soldier past his prime, reading speeches he did not write and could not comprehend, . . . a hollow hunk of his former greatness."

Based in strong measure on Jefferson's characterization, the image of a tired, mentally failing George Washington is strongly entrenched in many scholarly portrayals. Undoubtedly, there is an element of truth in it, and certainly some of Washington's comments may be marshaled to give credence to the assertion. In my view, this image has been greatly exaggerated, distorts reality, and is a major reason why so many historians fail to give Washington the credit he deserves. In the first place, we must remember that Washington was always self-deprecating and constantly downplayed his abilities to others. As Eliza Powel noted, "He appears to have an invincible Diffidence of his own Abilities." Additionally, he wanted very much to retire from the office of president after one term; stressing his failing health and declining mental acuity (such as a failing memory and loss of hearing) was a way of justifying why his leaving office made sense. The extant records demonstrate that in fact Washington had lost none of his mental sharpness and memory, at least beyond what would be considered normal in a man in his sixties. The best proof of this is found in examining his correspondence. His remarkably detailed letters to plantation managers at Mount Vernon while he was president, his scathing, detailed critique of James Monroe's book attacking his administration, his amazingly detailed last will and testament, and his final exhaustive letter, written just days before his own demise, to his plantation manager James Anderson sketching in vivid detail his vision for future changes at Mount Vernon, all combine to give lie to the charge that Washington was suffering from any serious type of mental impairment. In fact, they demonstrate just the opposite and portray a man with a remarkable grasp of detail and a very clear idea of what he wanted to accomplish.

Of course, from Jefferson's perspective, portraying Washington in failing mental health helped explain why Alexander Hamilton was able to have such powerful, if nefarious, influence on a man Jefferson liked, respected, and wanted to admire. No doubt, it was psychologically easier for him to impute the President's behavior to a sinister advisor rather than to conclude that he and the President disagreed so fundamentally. In the words of historian Joanne Freeman, "Washington's blindness to the Federalist threat was born of fatigue and corrupt ministers; it was surely *not* the result of simple disagreement, which would either depict Federalism as a viable alternative or place Washington among the politically damned." Describing the aging president as a good man hoodwinked by a more clever and sinister man enabled Jefferson to admire the man and oppose his administration. In short, Washington was "deceived" but he was not "depraved."

In time, the President learned that Jefferson had authored more damning words than that Washington was suffering from old age and sinister advisors. In private correspondence, Jefferson, temporarily tormented and disillusioned with Washington's actions on the Jay Treaty and its aftermath, went so far as to call him an "apostate" (one who rejects previous beliefs) to republican values. In what became a famous—or infamous—letter to his Italian friend, Philip Mazzei, Jefferson wrote,

My Dear Friend: The aspect of our politics has wonderfully changed since you left us. In place of that noble love of liberty and republican government which carried us triumphantly through the war, a . . . monarchical . . . party has sprung up whose avowed object is to draw over the substance, as they have already done the forms of the British government. . . . It would give you a fever were I to name to you *the apostates* who have gone over to these heresies, men who *were Samsons in the field and Solomons in the council, but who have had their head shaved by the harlot England.* (emphasis added)

This letter, written in April of 1796, did not become public until May of 1797, by which time Washington had left the presidency. Washington never deigned to comment on it publicly. Nevertheless, there is no doubt in my mind that it was the main catalyst in Washington's decision to sever all ties with Jefferson. It is worth noting that as far as the record shows, and Jefferson later confirmed, they had no contact, written or in person, after the letter became public knowledge. It was not simply because they disagreed on issues that Washington severed his relationship with Thomas Jefferson. Washington was not naive on that score. He knew that men disagreed and, like Jefferson, wrote eloquently on why that was bound to be the case: "[Shall I] set up my judgment as the standard of perfection? And shall I arrogantly pronounce that whosoever differs from me, must discern the subject through a distorting medium, or be influenced by some nefarious scheme? The mind is so formed in different persons as to contemplate the same objects in different points of view. Hence originates the difference on questions of the greatest import, human and divine." In several letters to individuals like Benjamin Harrison, Bryan Fairfax, and Gouverneur Morris, he made clear that disagreeing on issues had no impact on his friendship for them. Indeed, Washington wrote a remarkably critical letter to Gouverneur Morris, and did it as a sign of his friendship: "I do it on the presumption, that a mind conscious of its own rectitude, fears not what is said of it; but will bid defiance to and dispise shafts that are not barbed with accusations against honor or integrity."

Washington's perspective is clear. Criticism and disagreement are perfectly legitimate but, if they are "barbed with accusations against honor or integrity," that is another story. Whether accurately or not, over time His Excellency came to view Jefferson's words and actions against him in that light. Exactly when he did so is a matter of dispute. Certainly, a number of friends, including Jefferson's adversary, Henry Lee, had written and warned Washington that Jefferson was privately critical of him. Jefferson, for example, had declared that the President would not be under undue British influence as long as he was "influenced by the wise advisers." In his response, the President expressed doubt that Jefferson would make such a charge unless "he has set me down as one of the most deceitful, and uncandid men living," because both in private and in cabinet meetings Jefferson had heard Washington often say that he wanted America to develop her own character and not be under any other nation's influence. (An examination of Jefferson's private correspondence demonstrates that he in fact believed the President was overly sympathetic to Great Britain.)

Then in 1796, Jefferson, apparently aware of the suspicions about him, wrote Washington to assure him that specific attacks in Benjamin Franklin Bache's Philadelphia *Aurora* had not come from his pen. (Technically, Jefferson was correct, since they had not come directly from his "pen," but he was being disingenuous, since he was involved in the attack.) Washington's response is subject to differing interpretations. Gracious on the surface, he wrote, "I had never discovered any thing in the conduct of Mr. Jefferson to raise suspicions, in my mind, of his insincerity." But the tone of the letter was such that Joseph Ellis concludes, "Washington's response was a masterful example of how one Virginia gentleman tells another he has violated the unspoken code." However Washington felt about Jefferson and his opposition in 1796, the publication of the Mazzei letter in 1797 settled the issue. Thomas Jefferson not only disagreed with his policies, but he also leveled attacks barbed with accusations against Washington's honor and character.

In short, it was the manner of the opposition and Jefferson's attacks on him that were the key ingredient in embittering Washington. (Interestingly, over time, he ended his contact with four other famous Virginians—George Mason, James Madison, James Monroe, and Edmund Randolph—for essentially similar reasons.) One of Washington's central character traits was a very strong need for approval (possibly connected to not winning approval from his mother as a youngster), and as a consequence, he was very sensitive to criticism, especially criticism about his intentions. He could not tolerate outside criticism in addition to his own fierce inner critic. It was not only important for Washington to act honorably, but it was also equally important that he be recognized for doing so. From his perspective, he was essentially sacrificing himself for the good of his country, accepting the call of duty over his personal pleasure and ease. (He referred to himself as "a perfect Slave.") How much more would he prefer to be on his farm at Mount Vernon than at his desk in Philadelphia dealing with a myriad of almost unsolvable problems! Thus to have his intentions questioned, or to have the purity of his motivation attacked, was something that was sure to bring forth the fury of the squire of Mount Vernon.

There was probably no more serious charge in Washington's mind than to be viewed, either implicitly or explicitly, as an "apostate" to republicanism. Jefferson himself recounted a rare incident of Washington's losing his temper when an opposition newspaper printed a satire, "The Funeral of George Washington and James Wilson, King and Judge," depicting a tyrannical executive laid low on the guillotine: "The President was much inflamed, got into one of those passions when he cannot command himself; ran on much on the personal abuse which had been bestowed on him, defied any man on earth to produce one single act of his since he had been in the government which was not done on the purest motives." Imagine how George Washington must have felt when he learned that Thomas Jefferson, a man who knew him well and whom he had admired and trusted, accused him of being an apostate. The words of Shakespeare's Julius Caesar come to mind: "Et tu, Brute?"

Publication of the letter put Jefferson in an extremely difficult and embarrassing position, and minimizing the clear implications of what he wrote presented a severe challenge. Jefferson felt his published letter, as retranslated from Italian to French and back to English, misrepresented the meaning of his original letter, but he confessed to Madison that he feared that any attempt to explain what he meant would "embroil me with one whose character is still popular with 9/10ths of the country." (He could have added still popular in spite of the constant barrage of negative press in which Jefferson played a role.) Apparently, the possibility of apologizing and explaining that it was a private letter written in a moment of high passion and should not be taken as a true expression of Jefferson's feelings about the President was not seriously considered.

The most detailed critique of Jefferson and the Mazzei letter comes from the pen of Henry Lee, the controversial son of Henry "Light Horse Harry" Lee and older half brother of Robert E. Lee. Admittedly biased, *Observations on the Writings of Thomas Jefferson* is nevertheless a scathing critique of what Lee views as Jefferson's almost bottomless capacity for duplicity. He quotes from an earlier poem:

> O what a tangled web we weave
> When first we practice to deceive.

The theme is continued in a stanza of his own poem:

> But his Anas show such bias
> He must have been Ananias.

(Ananias was an infamous liar in the Bible.)

Lee sharply contrasted Washington's response to Edmund Randolph, who accused Washington of malicious treatment, with what Jefferson did. The President immediately gave Randolph his permission to make *anything* he ever wrote him public. Jefferson, on the other hand, reacted to publication of the Mazzei letter by stonewalling and asking his protégés, Madison and Monroe, to help him figure out the best tactic to minimize the political damage. To Madison he implored, "Think for me on this occasion, and advise me what to do."

To illustrate the depth of George Washington's estrangement from Thomas Jefferson, it is necessary to touch briefly on the Langhorne affair that occurred the year after the publication of the Mazzei letter. Washington received a rather innocuous letter from a John Langhorne implicitly critical of Jefferson and desiring a reply from Washington. What made the letter interesting, as John Nicholas, a staunch Federalist from Albemarle County, pointed out to Washington in several letters, was that there was no actual person by the name of Mr. Langhorne. The real author of the "Langhorne" letter was Peter Carr, the nephew and dependent of Thomas Jefferson. Nicholas, who described Jefferson as "one of the most artful, intriguing, industrious and double-faced politicians in all America," developed the argument that the letter was part of a nefarious plot to entrap Washington into writing things that could be politically useful to the Republicans.

What the author of the letter actually sought to achieve is uncertain. There is absolutely no evidence that Jefferson was in any way involved, and Carr's motives are unclear. What makes this relatively innocuous letter important is the remarkably strong response Nicholas's charges drew from the Master of Mount Vernon. It lays bare the depth of his smoldering anger at the author of the Mazzei letter, whose morals, in John Marshall's words, "could not be pure." Washington replied to Nicholas, "Nothing short of the Evidence you have adduced, corroborative of intimations which I had received long before, through another channel [Lee], could have shaken my belief in the sincerity of a friendship, which I had *conceived* was possessed for me, *by the person* to whom you allude" (emphasis in the original).

Fanning Washington's anger at Jefferson was Nicholas's assertion that Jefferson had aided his disciple, James Monroe, in the writing of Monroe's book *A View of the Conduct of the Executive in the Foreign Affairs of the United States*. Monroe had been appointed ambassador to France in 1794, but was recalled by the Washington administration in 1796 for not adequately defending the administration's decision to sign the Jay Treaty. Monroe's book was a lengthy defense of his diplomatic conduct and a strident condemnation of the Washington administration's foreign policy. Jefferson quietly helped Monroe compile his defense, and there is no doubt that he was very pleased with the final product. As he wrote Madison, "Monroe's book is considered masterly by all those who are not opposed in principle, and it is deemed unanswerable." President Washington, in contrast, viewed Monroe's attack on his foreign policy as a diatribe, full of mistakes, innuendos, and malice. In a rare display of anger, he took up his pen to jot down in the margins of the book his rejoinders to various aspects of Monroe's argument. The editors of the *Papers of George Washing-*

ton conclude, "GW's remarks on Monroe and his book, taken together, comprise the most extended, unremitting, and pointed use of taunts and jibes, sarcasm, and scathing criticism in all of his writing."

First the Mazzei letter, then support for Monroe's bitter diatribe, and now involvement in a secret plot to attempt to embarrass Washington. The important point is not that Jefferson was engaged in the Langhorne affair. The important point is that George Washington believed him to be capable of such a dirty and shabby trick. As Washington subsequently confided to his trusted nephew, Bushrod, "If he [i.e., Nicholas] could prove, indubitably, that the letter addressed to me, with the signature of Jno. Langhorne, was a forgery, no doubt would remain in the mind of any one, that it was written with a view to effect some nefarious purpose, and if the person he suspects [i.e., Jefferson], is the real Author or abettor it would be a pity not to expose him to Public execration."

Sadly, it had come to this. The mutual admiration that two of America's greatest men felt for each other had soured, at least on Washington's part, so that he believed Jefferson capable of almost any deception that might gain some political advantage. Perhaps Washington's "mortification" in having earlier misjudged Jefferson's character fueled his anger and disappointment. Further evidence of the depth of the rupture is provided by Martha Washington's response to Jefferson's election as president in 1800, the year after her husband's death. She believed it was the greatest misfortune the country had ever experienced, and she explained why. Jefferson was "one of the most detestable of mankind." In a later conversation, she apparently declared that the worst day of her life was when her husband died, and the second worst day was when President Jefferson visited Mount Vernon to pay his respects. One hears in these sharp and bitter words an echo of George Washington's own views as he shared them with his beloved wife.

Jefferson's response to the break is also revealing about his complex personality. His relationship with Washington had gone from a deferential one to one of mutual admiration and then to dire misunderstanding. Jefferson didn't want it to end on such a sour note. He and Washington should be reconciled, for Jefferson always deeply admired the "real" Washington. (Later, in 1814, Jefferson composed what was a generally favorable summary of Washington's character, and it became the most famous assessment of the man.) Since they ought to be reconciled, Jefferson, who was capable of considerable self-deception, convinced himself that they had been. In 1813, Jefferson wrote about the Mazzei letter and asserted, "I never saw him afterwards or these malignant insinuations should have been dissipated before his just judgment, as mist before the sun." Even later, he declared it was absolutely false that he was referring to Washington in the Mazzei letter. By "Samsons" and "Solomons" he had merely meant the members of the Society of Cincinnati, and he assumed Washington understood his true meaning, and contended that Washington would never "have degraded himself so far as to take to himself the imputation in that letter on the 'Samsons in combat.'" (Jefferson never said this at the time, and overlooked the fact that Washington was the president of the Society of Cincinnati.)

The two men might have been reconciled in Jefferson's fantasy, but not in reality. Indeed, the very night before he died, Washington attacked the conduct of Jefferson's disciples, Madison and Monroe. In one sense, their friendship was a casualty of the political wars of the 1790s, which was matched in intensity only by the decade of the 1850s as the Civil War loomed. As Jefferson himself noted, "Party animosities have raised a wall of separation between those who differ in political sentiments." Certainly, sharp differences in political philosophies played a major role in the two former friends becoming reluctant enemies.

Their differing personalities played an important role as well. Washington's extreme sensitivity to criticism, especially about the purity of his intentions, made him inordinately sensitive to any perceived attacks on his honor. In Jefferson's words, "I think he feels these things more than any person I ever yet met with." Jefferson's tendency to see the world as divided between "rogues" and "honest men," his tendency to use exaggerated rhetoric, combined with a dislike of direct confrontation often led him to act in ways his critics viewed (and still view) as devious and deceitful. If, in some manner, Jefferson could be asked to explain his treatment of George Washington, he would insist that he always viewed Washington with profound respect and admiration. The tragedy for their friendship is that George Washington would not believe him.

Alexander Hamilton. Portrait by John Trumbull. (Courtesy of the New-York Historical Society)

7

The Great Collaboration

The Increasingly Close Relationship between George Washington and Alexander Hamilton

In every relation, which you have borne to me, I have found that my confidence in your talents, exertions and integrity, has been well placed.—*George Washington*

ALEXANDER HAMILTON IS UNIQUE EVEN AMONG THE INNER CIR-
cle of the six most famous and renowned founding fathers. George
Washington lived until he was sixty-seven, and the others—Benjamin
Franklin, Thomas Jefferson, James Madison, and John Adams—all
lived into their eighties or beyond. (Adams was ninety.) Hamilton was
dead before his fiftieth birthday. All of the other founders were native-born Americans. Hamilton was born on the tiny British island
of Nevis in the Caribbean. None had such a stigmatized childhood to
overcome. He was the illegitimate son of Rachel Lavein (a woman im-
prisoned for "whoring" by her vengeful husband), and her paramour,
a wayward Scot of noble lineage by the name of James Hamilton. His
father later deserted the family, his mother died in early 1768, and
her vengeful husband made sure neither of her two illegitimate sons,
"born into whoredom," received a penny of inheritance.

All of the founders engendered a certain amount of controversy,
but none proved to be (or remains) as divisive a figure as Alexander
Hamilton. He was the bête noire of Thomas Jefferson, and the Jeffersonian image of Hamilton has had remarkable staying power, especially in view of the paucity of evidence to support it. In that rendering, Hamilton emerges as the dark side of the American picture: the
champion of the rich and well-born, an elitist distrustful and disdain-

ful of ordinary people, a proponent of a dangerously powerful national government threatening the rights of the states and the liberties of the people. His character was considered as dangerous as his philosophy. He was scorned as a Machiavellian intriguer with a Napoleonic complex. Perhaps the most scathing comments come from John Adams, who came to despise the man whom he called "a bastard brat of a Scotch peddler," a man who lived his life in a "delirium of Ambition." Adams thought he knew the source of Hamilton's ambition. It was from a "superabundance of secretions which he could not find whores enough to draw off." Even in the era of "shock jock" radio shows, that is hard to surpass. Adams's wife, Abigail, was not much kinder: "I have read his heart in his wicked eyes. . . . They are lasciviousness itself." How a man who generated such vituperative comments became George Washington's most significant and influential advisor is one of the most interesting and important stories in America's founding.

To historians of the early national period, the term "the great collaboration," the title of an important book by Adrienne Koch, normally refers to the remarkably productive relationship between Thomas Jefferson and James Madison, the subjects of Koch's study. Viewed as the founding fathers of the democratic movement in America, these two great men have received the lion's share of the praise and attention. As my chapter title indicates, there was another "great collaboration." Indeed, one might argue that it was an even greater collaboration than the one between Jefferson and Madison. The remarkably productive alliance between George Washington, the Father of the Country, and Alexander Hamilton, the Father of American Government (and the Father of American Capitalism), did more than anything else to bring about the modern United States of America. As George Will expressed it, if you want to see Alexander Hamilton's memorial, look around America. Their relationship was not only extremely productive and important, but it is also fascinating, with ups and downs that reveal interesting aspects of both men's character.

George Washington was old enough to be Alexander Hamilton's father. (And it was later falsely rumored that he was in fact his father.) By the time the two men first met in 1776, George Washington was the commander in chief of the Continental Army and the most famous man in America. Alexander Hamilton was a young twenty-one-year-old captain of New York artillery. (There is a controversy among historians about whether Hamilton was born in 1755 or 1757.) Considering his background, it is amazing that he was in a position of even that much influence. Hamilton had been able to escape his fate as a "groveling" clerk on the island of St. Croix, partly because of his great talents and partly because his generous employer and others recognized his talents and sent him to the mainland to obtain an education. He attended King's College (now Columbia), got caught up in the fervor of the coming of the American Revolution, and soon produced pamphlets so sophisticated that people assumed they had been written by one of the mature leaders of the protest movement, certainly not by a teenager. This vignette points to an essential fact in assessing Alexander Hamilton. One can scarcely overstate the brilliance and power of his intellect. Later, John Marshall testified that "Hamilton's reach of thought was so far beyond" his that, compared to Hamilton's, it was like a candle "before the sun at noonday." Even his adversary, Thomas Jefferson, described him as "really a colossus . . . without numbers, he is a host within himself."

Hamilton's great mental acuity was matched by a desire for fame that seems to have been every bit as great as George Washington's. Undoubtedly, Hamilton's unusually intense ambition was part of his innate personality, but it may well have been augmented by a desire to overcome his stigmatized childhood: "The real debt Hamilton owed his father he could never have acknowledged. The stain of illegitimacy and poverty that James Hamilton had left on the family name could be effaced only by illustrious achievement, and Hamilton from boyhood on was an overachiever, one who found it necessary to more than compensate for his feelings of inadequacy." This led to a capacity for productive work that has been unsurpassed by any American statesman.

Another central aspect of Hamilton's personality, again undoubtedly a combination of his innate personality and the effects of slights he endured as a child, was his extreme sensitivity involving issues of honor. In the words of his eulogist (Fisher Ames), no man, "not the Roman Cato himself, was more inflexible on every point that touched, or seemed to touch, integrity and honor." This supersensitivity to any perceived slight led Hamilton to be involved in *ten* "affairs of honor" during his life prior to his fatal encounter with Aaron Burr. It appeared that his sense of honor inclined him toward open encounters. "For all his superlative mental gifts, he was afflicted with a touchy ego that made him querulous and fatally combative." He was in a constant battle to control his own emotions, a battle he often lost.

Hamilton officially joined George Washington's "family" (as the General himself called it) early in 1777, joining a group of remarkably talented young men (ultimately becoming thirty-two in number over the course of the war), who served as His Excellency's personal aides. In so doing, Hamilton inadvertently stumbled upon the crowning enterprise of his life: the creation of a powerful new country. A born fighter, walking a high wire of self-creation, he sensed that the importance of the revolution and his connection to Washington were his ticket to fame and glory. In yet another testament to Hamilton's remarkable ability, in the space of less than a year, and despite his youth, he became, as Washington later described him, his "principal & most confidential aid."

The harried Commander in Chief wanted, in his words, "persons that can think for me, as well as execute orders," and Hamilton's affinity for the way Washington thought was unequaled. Viewing things the same way, Hamilton was soon able to compose Washington's letters for him, putting into words what Washington wanted to say—and doing it more eloquently than he could. In the words of Ron Chernow, the author of the best-selling biography, *Hamilton*, his aide was "able to project himself into Washington's mind and intuit what the general wanted to say, writing it up with instinctive tact and deft diplomatic skills. It was an inspired piece of ventriloquism: Washington gave a few general hints, and presto, out popped Hamilton's letter in record time." It is easy to understand how delighted the overburdened General would be on discovering someone with this skill.

The young aide, however, was much more than simply a superb secretary. George Washington, clearly seeing something special and understanding Hamilton's unique abilities, quickly placed him in situations where his talents could be developed and used. His Excellency sent him on very sensitive and important missions. For example, in late November of 1777 he sent Hamilton, who had been his aide for less than a year, to General Horatio Gates, the hero (whether deservedly or not) of the Saratoga campaign with orders to extract from his command a thousand soldiers needed by Washington. The errand was an indication of the Commander's great trust in Hamilton, for the task was a delicate one, requiring ingenuity, tact, and skill. He performed a similar task with General Putnam, ruffling some feathers in the process but maintaining Washington's confidence and support. The young lieutenant colonel's description of General Putnam indicates his frankness and tendency to use pungent and caustic language, a tendency he never lost: "Every part of this Gentleman's conduct is marked with blunder and negligence, and gives general disgust." Another quality that made him invaluable was Hamilton's complete fluency in French, which aided Washington's dealing with France and that ally's many generals and officers.

One might reasonably expect that Alexander Hamilton would be delighted to find himself in such an important position, but the facts do not support such an assertion. Alexander Hamilton's personality was not that of an aide, even the most important aide of the commander in chief of the American forces. His inclination ran strongly to command and to execute, not to carrying out the orders of another, and his personality insured there would be some friction between himself and his commander. There is no doubt that the relationship between the two men was strong and tenacious. What its exact nature was is much harder to say. Young Hamilton was clearly ambivalent and conflicted in his feelings about Washington, torn between his desire to defer to him and to please His Excellency (as he regularly addressed him), and his apparent need to resist being dependent on him. It would have been almost impossible for two such strong characters to be in constant contact without a certain amount of friction. Hating any sense of dependency, Hamilton tended to hold himself aloof from his commanding general. If one is willing to venture into psychohistory, it seems plausible to speculate that such a course of action would also guard against his deep-seated fear of abandonment and disappointment. Perhaps, having been abandoned by his birth father, Hamilton feared allowing himself to get too close to a substitute father lest he be abandoned again.

Then too, Hamilton's strongest desire was for military glory and fame. Youthful fantasies of performing illustrious deeds in battle still had a strong hold on him. (In his first surviving letter as a very young teenager, he wished for a war with its attendant opportunity for fame and honor.) Yearning for military glory, resenting his dependence on Washington, increasingly frustrated by the General's seeming indifference to his plight, Hamilton felt trapped. Many of his letters, especially those to his closest friend, Colonel John Laurens, show signs of depression: "I hate Congress—I hate the Army—I hate the world—I hate myself—the whole is a mass of fools and knaves." He bitterly declared that "three fourths of them [members of Congress] are mortal enemies [to talent] . . . and three fourths of the other fourth have . . . contempt [for integrity]." In the same letter, he seemed suicidal: I "am disgusted with everything in this world. I have no other wish than as soon as possible to make a brilliant exit."

Being so desirous of fame, the Little Lion (Hamilton's nickname by his fellow aides because of his short stature and commanding personality) could not avoid being jealous of all the fame General Washington garnered. As sociologist Barry Schwartz demonstrates, the crisis and collective fervor of the revolution propelled Washington's image far beyond the realm of any normal reputation, however sterling. The people desperately needed a symbol that would unite their varying and fractious regions and stand for something that all could be proud of. His Excellency filled the bill, and the result was an adoration of General Washington almost approaching idolatry. Such excessive praise did not sit well with Alexander Hamilton. "Being brilliant and coldly critical," working intimately with the General, Hamilton detected numerous flaws in Washington less visible to others. To his eye, the Commander was not what he appeared to be on first impression. Rather, Hamilton saw him as demanding and moody, with an uneven and explosive temper, and given to periodic outbursts at his aides. And Washington was selfish, keeping Hamilton chained to a desk he despised, seeming to offer release but never fulfilling his promise.

The elements for a rupture were all falling into place: "I explained to you," Hamilton wrote plaintively in 1779, "my feelings with regard to military reputation, and how much it was my object to act a conspicuous part by some enterprise that might raise my character as a soldier above mediocrity. You were so good as to say you would be glad to furnish me an occasion." But the time never seemed right to Washington. How valuable he considered Hamilton's help is clear from his reiterated efforts to keep his hold on the young prodigy. In Washington's mind, the time for Hamilton's departure was always "not yet."

The break finally came in February of 1781, hastened by two developments in 1780. The first was the execution of Major John André, the top aide of the British commander in chief, Henry Clinton, as a spy for André's role in the infamous treason of Benedict Arnold. Alexander Hamilton was completely won over by the dashing André, who demonstrated the type of character, courage, wit, and sophistication that Hamilton desired for himself. André, realizing that his fate was sealed, desired only to be shot like a soldier and not hanged like a thief. Hamilton strongly pleaded his case, but Washington would not budge, and André was hanged. Hamilton was stunned by what he took as Washington's callousness in refusing André's wish to die with honor like a soldier. (And perhaps he connected it with how Washington kept him from an honorable life as a soldier.) Never before had His Excellency appeared to Hamilton in so unfavorable a light: stern, obstinate, and insensitive to the finer feelings of a gentleman. Commenting on the event to his fiancée, Hamilton wrote, "Some people are only sensible to motives of policy, and from a narrow disposition mistake it." Washington seemed to the young colonel to almost have a heart of stone.

The second event was Alexander Hamilton's marriage in December of 1780 to Eliza Schuyler, the daughter of General Philip Schuyler, one of the wealthiest and most important men in the state of New York. Before his marriage, if Hamilton had walked away from headquarters, he would have had no support system. But now he had a powerful and enthralled father-in-law. (Despite Hamilton's shaky pedigree, General Schuyler sincerely welcomed him into the family and viewed him as a rare gem who could do no wrong.) This new security apparently made Hamilton ready to seek a break at the first opportunity.

It came on February 16, 1781, and from our perspective, seems surprisingly trivial. His Excellency met his aide at the top of the stairwell and asked to see him. Hamilton indicated he had to deliver a message to another aide but would be with Washington shortly. Meeting his friend Lafayette on the way back, Hamilton was slightly delayed (in his telling, no more than a minute or so). When he reached the General, he was met with the curt rebuke, "You have kept me waiting at the head of the stairs these ten minutes. I must tell you, sir, that you treat me with disrespect." Hamilton rejoined that he was not aware of doing so, but "since you have thought it necessary to tell me so, we part."

That was it! And within an hour, the General sent another aide and Hamilton's friend, Tench Tilghman, bearing an olive branch with instructions to smooth out the quarrel and set up an interview between the two men. Hamilton would have none of it. He asked to be excused from even discussing the incident with Washington, further requested the General not to say anything to any one about the quarrel, and promised to stay on as if nothing had happened until other aides returned and took up the slack.

Hamilton sought to justify his actions in a long, much revised, letter to his father-in-law in which he made the rather astonishing confession, "For the past three years, I have felt no friendship for him and have professed none." He further indicated that he could reveal much that was negative about the General but would hold his pen until the end of the war since he admitted Washington was useful to the cause. Hamilton succinctly expressed his view of the quarrel in a letter to another aide and friend: "The Great Man and I have come to an open rupture. . . . Without a shadow of reason and on the slightest of ground, he charged me in the most affrontive manner with treating him with disrespect . . . proposals of accommodation have been made on his part but rejected. I pledge my honor to you that he will find me inflexible. He shall for once at least repent his ill-humor." It is worth noting that although the two men agreed to keep the incident a secret, Hamilton then wrote his version of the quarrel to a number of key mutual friends. Washington, who "religiously" remained silent, was hurt when he found out that Hamilton had not done himself what he had asked Washington to do.

One might logically assume that the aftermath of the incident would write finis to the relationship between George Washington and Alexander Hamilton, much as the publication of the Mazzei letter would lead Washington to sever his relationship with Thomas Jefferson. A brash aide keeps his harried commander in chief waiting, responds to a relatively minor rebuke by quitting on the spot, refuses a genuine offer at reconciliation or even to speak to the General about it, and then shares his side of the story with friends while denying Washington the same opportunity. For such effrontery, one might expect that Washington would simply consign Hamilton to historical oblivion, keep him away from the center of power or, more importantly, from any chance to find the military glory that Hamilton so desperately sought.

Instead, Washington responded to Hamilton's request and found a military command for him and allowed him to lead the assault on Redoubt no. 10 at Yorktown, one of the climactic moments of the campaign leading to the surrender of Cornwallis and the virtual end of the war. On one level, Washington's forbearance seems almost supernatural. We will never know exactly why he acted as he did, but I think there were likely several factors at work. George Washington saw much of himself as a young warrior in the French and Indian War in the young Colonel Hamilton of the American Revolution. Both young men were brash, impulsive, quick-tempered, overly ambitious, and possessed with a burning desire for military glory. This empathy helps explain his toleration of Hamilton's antics. And, of course, Alexander Hamilton possessed many positive qualities. Washington had earlier written about him and declared that no one "is more firmly engaged in the cause, or exceeds him in probity and sterling virtue." Finally, George Washington was inherently a very fair man. He had, perhaps selfishly, perhaps unfairly (even if understandably), kept Hamilton on as an aide for longer than he should have. Hamilton had more than paid his dues and performed yeoman service for the commander in chief and for the new country. The General might well have concluded it would simply be wrong to deny him his chance for military glory. Interestingly, in accommodating Hamilton's wishes, Washington, whether with specific intent or not, left the door open for the relationship to continue into the future. It would not be quite the same kind of relationship that they had as general and aide. The break allowed for the emergence of a new one, one of a senior partner to a junior partner, but a partnership nevertheless.

During these years, General Washington was never personally close to Hamilton in the way he was to Lafayette, who really appears to be almost a surrogate son (a role Lafayette, unlike Hamilton, was eager to play). Nevertheless, one senses affection for Hamilton in addition to deep respect for his remarkable talents and contributions. As Lafayette tried to reassure Hamilton, "I know the General's friendship and gratitude for you, My Dear Hamilton, both are greater than you perhaps imagine." And, despite the harsh words written in anger, there was much in George Washington that Hamilton admired. In his words, the General was a "very honest" man, a true patriot who would "never yield to any dishonorable or disloyal plans into which he might be called; . . . he would sooner suffer himself to be cut to pieces." Shortly after watching Washington rally the Continental forces at the Battle of Monmouth, Hamilton declared, "I never saw the general to so much advantage. His coolness and firmness were admirable. . . . America owes a great deal to General Washington for this day's work." (And he was a second for his friend John Laurens in a duel with General Charles Lee when the latter criticized Washington.)

Hamilton was too cocksure and critical to ever act in a fawning manner toward Washington as Lafayette did. Yet, he knew the character of the man well enough to write Washington two months after resigning his post to request His Excellency's help in securing a military command. It was done with the expectation that Washington would in fact help him. Almost in the manner of a recalcitrant son who takes parental forbearance for granted, Hamilton apparently believed it was in character for Washington to reward fractious aides. In his case, he was correct.

There is no indication of any type of special and close relationship between the two men in the time between Yorktown and Washington's inauguration as the nation's first president. In the events leading up to the famous incident known as the Newburgh Conspiracy, Washington had been somewhat alarmed at Hamilton's willingness to use the army to pressure Congress into reform and warned him that the army was a dangerous instrument to play with. When Washington made Hamilton a brevet colonel at the end of the war, there apparently was no friendly thank-you letter from Hamilton. There is no evidence Hamilton joined the weeping officers at Fraunces Tavern in

New York City as they bid a fond farewell to their commander or that he made any effort to see the General on his visit to the city. Their correspondence in the years immediately after the war was meager and perfunctory.

If America had prospered under the Articles of Confederation, it is unlikely that Washington and Hamilton would have had any more significant contact. But it did not prosper, and the desire to preserve and strengthen the American union once again brought these men back into a working relationship. The bond between them was not so much one of personal intimacy as one of shared views and common goals for the country they both loved: "By dint of his youth, foreign birth, and cosmopolitan outlook, [Hamilton] was spared prewar entanglements in provincial state politics, making him a natural spokesman for a new American nationalism." The Constitutional Convention was the brainchild of Alexander Hamilton, as much as of any man. George Washington's reluctant decision to attend insured the gathering would be the last best effort to strengthen the central government and give it sufficient power to keep the "United States" united as one country. Hamilton's views on how to change the government were more extreme than any of his colleagues at Philadelphia, and it is interesting that he and Washington did not discuss his ideas before Hamilton left for an extended period in the middle of the convention. Washington did write that he was sorry Hamilton had left and wished he would return.

With the ratification of the Constitution in the summer of 1788 it was a foregone conclusion to everyone (with the possible exception of Washington himself) that only the man who was viewed as the savior of American liberty should be its first president. Hamilton was among those who wrote and forcefully argued that Washington, whatever his personal desires, *must* be president. Hamilton was surprisingly blunt, basically arguing that in attending the Constitutional Convention, Washington implicitly committed himself to accepting the presidency and to refuse would be going back on his unspoken pledge. Hamilton later explained why he was so outspoken: "I trust that the greatest frankness has always marked and will mark every step of my conduct towards you." Washington responded favorably. While Hamilton possessed a devastating candor that sometimes got him in trouble, his frankness appealed to Washington, who admired Hamilton's transparency and straightforward approach (which, incidentally, was quite different from the approach used by Jefferson).

After Robert Morris, the financial wizard of the American Revolution, declined the President's request to be his secretary of the treasury, Washington next asked his brilliant and financially savvy former aide to take the post. It turned out to be perhaps the most important decision that George Washington made as president of the United States. As expanded upon in chapter 3, Washington's determination to secure the union defined his presidency. The success of his administration largely hinged on the adoption of fiscal policies that would revive confidence in the fledgling nation, for the country seemed to be drowning in a debt it could not pay off. (The nation's entire income under the Articles of Confederation was less than the interest on the debt.) President Washington knew a great deal about foreign affairs and about issues involving war with Native Americans and trade, but he knew little about the intricacies of high finance. Lacking that type of financial knowledge, the President in effect told Hamilton that the Department of Treasury was his bailiwick. He left the way open, and Hamilton, always eager to seize control, quickly filled the vacuum.

It is not an exaggeration to say that Hamilton was much more than merely Washington's secretary of the treasury. Concerning himself with every phase of public policy, he was in many ways Washington's prime minister, and in at least one famous letter he attacked critics of "me and my administration." His complicated financial plans involved funding the debt, paying the full amount to whoever currently held the certificates of debt (often to great benefit of speculators and to the detriment of original holders of the certificates). His plans for the federal government to assume the war debt for all the states, for the establishment of a new powerful national bank, new excise taxes, and government encouragement of manufacturing were audacious, very controversial, and amazingly successful in putting the credit of the United States on a sound economic footing. In Ron Chernow's telling phrase, Alexander Hamilton was "a messenger from the future that we now inhabit." No one else "articulated such a clear and prescient vision of America's future political, military and economic strength."

He was an early promoter of what later was called high-tech capitalism (he set up the legal framework for capitalism) and championed
the development of a world-class military force. Basically, all of his
endeavors were directed toward establishing the United States as a
formidable nation.

His far-reaching program engendered great controversy and intense opposition. It led to the central fact of Washington's first administration: the bitter split between his two top advisors and the
beginning of what ultimately led to the creation of our modern political parties. Beginning a tendency that continues to the present day,
the opposing sides both "surveyed the political landscape as if looking
through hideously distorting spectacles, seeing grotesque and tor-
menting shapes and figures that were products of intense and deeply
felt fears." As Jefferson and Madison saw it, Hamilton was creating a
vast system of special privilege that enriched the few at the expense
of the many, encouraged an unhealthy speculative spirit among the
people, upset the balance of property in society, and corrupted the
national legislature. In the Hamiltonian insistence on a loose con-
struction of the Constitution, Jefferson espied a dangerous trend to
aggrandize the powers of the central government at the expense of
the authority of the states and the liberties of the people. Under Hamilton's diabolical leadership, the Secretary of State feared the United
States would re-create the very political and economic institutions
that hopefully had been destroyed by the American Revolution. In
1792, Jefferson explicitly warned the President that Hamilton hoped
to "change . . . the present republican form of government to that of a
monarchy."

Hamilton, of course, saw it very differently. In his words, "I assure you on my *private faith and honor* as a man that there is not . . .
a shadow of foundation of it. . . . I am *affectionately* attached to the
Republican theory. . . . The only enemy which republicanism has to
fear in this Country is the spirit of faction and anarchy," which would
not let government work effectively and thus would set the stage for
disaster (emphasis added). Ron Chernow emphasized the positive aspects of his program: "Hamilton promoted a forward looking agenda
of a modern nation-state with a market economy and an affirmative

view of central government. His meritocratic vision allowed greater scope in the economic sphere for the individual liberties that Jefferson defended so eloquently in the political sphere."

Over time, the hatred between the two departmental heads became palpable, and the President, despite his very best efforts, could not heal the breach—or even paper over the differences. Certainly, Hamilton was partly to blame. He was incapable of the forbearance His Excellency requested. A captive of his emotions, Hamilton revealed an irrepressible need to respond to attacks and never knew when to stop. That is one of the very significant differences between Washington and Hamilton. The mature Washington managed, with few exceptions, to control his emotions and passions. Alexander Hamilton never did, and while Hamilton would function brilliantly under Washington's calming influence, without it he was likely to go off the deep end and make major errors of judgment.

Jefferson's hostility toward Hamilton came out most clearly in his outburst to Washington, one Virginia planter to another, about the immigrant interloper. He declared he could no longer stand to have his reputation "beclouded by the slanders of a man whose history, from the moment at which history can stoop to notice him, is a tissue of machinations against the liberty of the country which has not only received and given him bread, but heaped its honors upon his head." In the words of one Hamilton scholar, "At bottom, Thomas Jefferson could not countenance the fact that an immigrant upstart without pedigree had dared challenge him." Landed aristocrat though he was, Washington did not allow such statements to cloud his confidence or his trust in the brilliant West Indian. Indeed, I think it is significant that Washington was obviously more impressed by Hamilton's defense of his conduct in office than by Jefferson's criticism of it. For Washington sent Jefferson's critique to Hamilton for his rejoinder (pretending the criticism came from someone else), but never communicated to Jefferson the substance of Hamilton's reply so that Jefferson might respond. In short, Hamilton's rejoinder satisfied the President.

Another incident bolsters this interpretation. On October 1, 1792, responding to Jefferson's charges that Hamilton was a monarchist, Washington lectured Jefferson that "as to the idea of transforming this government into a monarchy, he did not believe there were ten men in the United States whose opinions were worth attention who entertained such a thought." There is no record that Washington *ever* spoke or wrote to Hamilton in this curt, condescending tone. Given that Washington was the soul of tact and diplomacy, this blunt rebuke is highly revealing. It is almost as if the President is telling his secretary of state that he has fallen victim to a crackpot conspiracy theory.

Jefferson, who recorded the conversation in his personal notes, apparently interpreted the comments differently. He could never accept the fact that Washington might agree with Hamilton on the merits of the argument and looked for other explanations, such as the President's general decline due to aging and Hamilton's skill as a manipulator. Ron Chernow is on target. Alexander Hamilton "gained incomparable power under Washington because the President approved of the agenda that he promoted with such tireless brilliance." Jefferson was wrong when he charged that Hamilton manipulated the President. Despite how often the charge is made, and it is still made regularly, the idea that Washington was essentially Hamilton's puppet simply does not reflect reality. In areas he considered his province and responsibility, George Washington was, among human beings, one of those most unwilling to be led. On fundamental political matters, Washington was simply more in tune with his secretary of treasury than he was with his secretary of state. They shared an intense nationalism, belief in a strong central government, and a relentlessly realistic view of human nature. As Washington once expressed it, "the motives which predominate most in human affairs is self-love and self-interest." The basic fact is that, for better or for worse, George Washington was more of a Hamiltonian than he was a Jeffersonian.

Hamilton resigned his position in 1795 to return to private practice and to care for his growing family (he and Eliza had eight children). It should be noted that Hamilton remained a relatively poor man throughout his years of public service, despite the opportunities for achieving great wealth. He conducted his affairs at the Treasury Department with such probity that his many enemies, try as they might, could never prove any personal malfeasance in his position. (It is now clear that Jefferson was behind the failed Giles Resolutions that called for Hamilton's ouster for misappropriation of public funds.) His critics failed because he lived up to his pledge: "It shall never be said, with any color of truth, that my ambition or interest has stood in the way of the public good." Hamilton expressed his approach on the way a public official should act when a friend suggested an action which while legal might appear improper: "You remember the saying with regard to Caesar's wife. I think the spirit of it applicable to every man in the administration of finances in the country." (Caesar's wife was not only to be pure—she must *appear* to be pure as well.) As to why he worked so hard, suffered extreme criticism, and sacrificed financially for as many years as he did, Hamilton made two revealing comments: "There must be some public fools who sacrifice private to public interest." Or again, writing to his fascinating sister-in-law, Angelica Church, "You will ask why I do not quit this disagreeable trade. How can I? What is to become of my fame and glory?"

When Hamilton resigned, the President wrote a letter which indicates how closely and effectively they had worked together: "In every relation, which you have borne to me, I have found that my confidence in your talents, exertions and integrity, has been well placed. I the more freely render this testimony of my approbation because I speak from opportunities . . . w[hi]ch cannot deceive me." The treasury secretary was also impressed. He described the President as "modest and sage." Facing complicated issues, Washington "consulted much, pondered much, resolved slowly, resolved surely." Hamilton's resignation by no means ended his relationship with Washington. He remained the President's unofficial but most trusted advisor, and he played a key role in trying to win support for the controversial Jay Treaty, being stoned by an angry mob in the process. (This is expanded upon in chapter 3.) The two men, now exchanging notes marked "private," closely cooperated in producing one of the great documents in American history, "Washington's Farewell Address." While Hamilton was the major wordsmith, the ideas and the spirit were Washington's. As Richard Norton Smith concludes, "The Farewell Address became, like the administration it capped, an intellectual alliance between two like-minded nationalists."

Washington's genuine affection for Hamilton, as well as his exquisite tact, is best illustrated in the aftermath of the Maria Reynolds scandal that broke shortly after Washington left office. It was the first great sex scandal in American history, and it captivated Americans' attention then as the Monica Lewinsky scandal did in the 1990s. In briefest essence, Hamilton carried on a fairly lengthy adulterous affair with the seductive Maria Reynolds, apparently with the encouragement of her husband, James, who then blackmailed the secretary of the treasury. The tryst became public knowledge in 1797 as a result of an article by the scandalmonger James Callender, who also claimed that Hamilton had helped James Reynolds by giving him inside information from the Department of Treasury. (Ironically, Callender would later be the first to publish the charges linking Hamilton's nemesis, Jefferson, to his slave, Sally Hemings.) The charge of public malfeasance led Hamilton to do something that hurt his family, shocked his friends, and titillated the nation. He published an unprecedented ninety-seven-page confession, laying out in excruciating detail the specifics of the affair. Why did he do it? Perhaps there was some deep psychological need for self-flagellation, but the main reason was to prove that while he had been guilty of a private sin, he was not guilty of a dereliction of his trust as a public official. So important was his public image and his need for a spotless official reputation that Hamilton was willing to risk destroying his marriage and humiliating his colleagues by publicly admitting to a sordid affair which included many meetings in his own home while his wife was away.

In the midst of the crisis, but without making any reference to it, George Washington sent Hamilton a valuable wine cooler that had been on his desk when he was president "as a token of my sincere regard and friendship for you, and as a remembrance of me." In the brief letter which he began with the salutation, "My dear Sir," a salutation Washington used only with those with whom he was very friendly, he twice assured Hamilton that he was his *"sincere"* friend and also sent his wife's regards (Martha and Eliza were close friends). The letter was notable for what it did not say as well as what it did say. The most famous and revered man in the country was expressing his solidarity with a friend in a time of great personal crisis—and doing it with great sensitivity. Hamilton was moved by the gesture: "The token of your regard which it announces, is very precious to me, and will always be remembered." The wine cooler in fact became one of the family's most treasured possessions, along with a Gilbert Stuart portrait of Washington that was given as a gift at another time. Washington ended another letter that year with strong words that he rarely employed: "I would wish you to believe, that with great truth and sincerity, I am *always Your Affectionate friend*" (emphasis added).

Another example of their friendship is that, after leaving office, Washington wrote to Hamilton and asked him to aid Lafayette's son in his effort to return to France. (Both men were fond of Lafayette, which further strengthened their relationship.) Washington requested Hamilton to advance the young Lafayette $300 on his, Washington's, behalf, a request Hamilton honored. Other events dealing with France soon pulled the two men back into direct face-to-face contact. George Washington's dream of a peaceful, undisturbed retirement was shattered by the crisis with France that seemed likely to lead to war in the aftermath of the XYZ Affair in 1798, during which French officials sought bribes from American diplomats before agreeing to meet with them. Once again, in the midst of crisis, the nation turned its gaze to the Master of Mount Vernon.

The aging General, enjoying retirement, was called upon to be the commander in chief of the American forces raised to meet the impending struggle as France and America engaged in an undeclared war. Washington, while professing his typical reservations, agreed to take on the onerous responsibility, but only if Alexander Hamilton were made his second in command. In this case, second in command would be particularly important, as Washington declared he would take to the field only in the unlikely case of an actual invasion by French troops. Washington essentially forced President John Adams (who, as we have seen, despised Hamilton) to accept his choice by threatening resignation unless he did so. (One wonders how President Washington would have responded, if someone had treated him in the heavy-handed manner that he treated his successor.)

The choice of Hamilton as his second in command also temporarily ruptured the close friendship between Washington and General Henry Knox, one of the few men whom Washington declared that he "loved." Knox was deeply hurt and offended by Washington's action of ranking Hamilton, a colonel in the past war, ahead of him, who had been a major general. As a sign of just how close Washington had become with Hamilton, he confidentially shared Knox's angry letter with his second in command "as a proof of my frankness and friendship." Hamilton showed the same type of candor in sharing with Washington his negative assessment of James McHenry, the secretary of war: "My friend McHenry is wholly insufficient for his place, with the additional misfortune of not having himself the least suspicion of the fact."

Of course, the threatened war did not materialize (thanks in large part to Adams's courageous diplomacy). It was a frustrating experience for the former president, who may have become concerned with Hamilton's plans to perhaps use the crisis for causes other than the defense of the country against France. Joseph Ellis argues that Hamilton wanted to use the new army, officered completely by Federalists, to awe Virginia into better submission to the national government. For this or for some other reason or reasons, the final letters between the two men lacked the closeness and intimacy of those leading up to the war.

George Washington's sudden death on December 14, 1799, shocked the entire nation. It was a certainly a terrible blow to Hamilton on several levels. While Hamilton's correspondence focused on Washington's death primarily in political terms, he was undoubtedly touched by personal grief as well, as indicated by his comment, "Tis only for me to mingle my tears with those of my fellow soldiers." In his condolence letter to the President's widow, Hamilton referred to "the numerous and distinguished marks of confidence and friendship of which you have yourself been a witness." To a friend, he asserted, "Perhaps no friend of his has more cause to lament, on personal account, than my self." His best known—and most controversial—comment was to Washington's personal secretary Tobias Lear, "I have been much indebted to the kindness of the General, and he was an Aegis very essential to me." Critics have interpreted the term "aegis" in a very negative way. They utilize it as proof that Hamilton "used" Washington to achieve his goals. Personally, I don't believe Hamilton intended it in that fashion. Hamilton knew how much Lear loved Washington and would not have written him a letter emphasizing how he used him. Rather, in employing the word "aegis," I believe Hamilton meant to acknowledge what a "protector" Washington was as opposed to an instrument (a shield) that was to be wielded by him. There is a subtle but significant difference.

The final example of how close the men had become is revealed by Hamilton's concern as to what would happen to the many confidential letters that they had shared (we know that Hamilton had used a simple code in some of them). Lear acknowledged the problem, admitting there are "many which every public and private consideration should withhold from further inspection." Apparently, they were destroyed, as no letters from Hamilton to Washington employing any code have been found. Perhaps those letters would have enabled us to flesh out in even more detail the relationship between them, but the evidence is clear that while Washington broke with Jefferson, Madison, and Monroe (all Hamilton's opponents as well), he remained friendly and close to Hamilton until his own death. Some dispute the amount of affection between the two men, noting, for example, that Hamilton never visited Mount Vernon, but they ignore the fact that Washington sincerely invited him to come and that Hamilton rarely traveled beyond New York City and Albany.

Washington's death ended perhaps the most productive collaboration in American history. Certainly, George Washington was the senior partner and the superior man in terms of overall character. But Alexander Hamilton, despite his many flaws (even his eulogist, Gouverneur Morris, privately conceded he was vain, opinionated, and indiscreet), also had numerous admirable and likable characteristics (courage, intellect, charm, wit, personal probity, and deep patriotism) that earned the affection of Washington. George Washington is the "Indispensable Man" in the founding of America. But could he have achieved his goals for a strong and economically powerful nation without the ideas and skillful administration of his secretary of the treasury? The answer is almost certainly "no." Thus, it is fair to conclude that Alexander Hamilton was the indispensable man to the "Indispensable Man."

"The Only Unavoidable Subject of Regret"

George Washington and Slavery

[I] shall frankly declare to you that I do not like to think, much less talk of it.—*George Washington*

IN HIS NOVEL *THE HUMAN STAIN*, PHILIP ROTH NOTES THAT ONE of America's oldest communal passions is to indulge in the "ecstasy of sanctimony." We feel good and morally superior by condemning the moral failings of others, past and present. One way this is done is by pointing out the hypocrisy of the Founding Fathers in proclaiming that all men are created equal and entitled to liberty while keeping 20 percent of their own population in life-long servitude. In the late 1990s, a New Orleans school named after George Washington changed its name because of a new edict declaring that no New Orleans schools could be named after slaveholders. The Father of His Country was deemed unworthy to have a local school named after him. Indulging in the "ecstasy of sanctimony" is certainly not new. As president, Washington received a letter which read in part, "Ages to come will read with Astonishment that the man who was foremost to wrench the rights of America from the tyrannical grasp of Britain was among the last to relinquish his own oppressive hold of poor unoffending negroes. In the name of justice what can induce you thus to tarnish your own well earned celebrity and to impair the fair features of American liberty with so foul and indelible a blot." The fiery nineteenth-century abolitionist William Lloyd Garrison confidently assured his listeners that even as he spoke, George Washington was writhing in the flames of eternal damnation, his just punishment for the sin of slaveholding.

As we shall see, the story of George Washington and slavery has much material in it for those desiring to engage in the "ecstasy of sanctimony." Yet, a quote from another famous novelist, Ellen Glasgow, warns us of another, even more prevalent danger: "To take a true view, one must not believe what is pleasant over what is painful in spite of the evidence." It is "pleasant" for most contemporary readers, especially those who hold Washington in high esteem, to view him as a kind and humane slaveholder and as a man who did what he could to end the evils of slavery, ultimately freeing all of his slaves. The story of George Washington and slavery has much material in it for those desirous of holding this view. Nevertheless, the motivation to think positively about Washington on this complicated issue can easily keep us from "taking a true view." A careful examination of the record reveals that George Washington was more of a traditional Virginia planter than we might wish him to have been and was not exempt from employing the cruelty that was essential in maintaining a system based on human slavery. Can one avoid the "ecstasy of sanctimony," be sympathetic with Washington and the dilemma he faced, admire his growth on the issue, and yet record accurately his words and actions, many of which make for difficult reading and grate on the sensitivities of most modern readers? It is worth a try.

George Washington was born, reared, and lived in Virginia, where approximately *40 percent* of the population were slaves for life. Slavery was such an intricate and crucial aspect of the plantation economy and social system of the hierarchical, gentry-dominated colony that a visitor in 1757 noted that it was virtually impossible to live properly in Virginia without slaves. Approximately 99 percent of the African Americans living in Virginia were lifelong slaves, and the blacks were virtually universally viewed as degraded human beings. The Slave Code gave almost a free hand to the owners, declaring that "if any slave shall happen to die [as a result] of his or her correction, by his or her owner, no person shall undergo any prosecution for the same."

During the pre-Revolutionary years, Washington's views toward slavery were, as far as the record reveals, conventional, reflecting those of a typical Virginia planter of his time. He, like virtually every other white Virginian, took slavery for granted: "Slaves were part of the social fabric; they blended into the landscape; no self-respecting household was without them." Young George first became a slave owner at the age of eleven when he inherited 10 slaves as a result of his father's untimely death in 1743. This number would steadily increase throughout his lifetime. He purchased 13 in the year of his marriage and another 42 between 1761 and 1773. By the Revolution, there were about 150 slaves at Mount Vernon and, by the time of his death in 1799, that number had grown to over 300. Washington's early insensitivity to the evils of the institution and his rather routine acceptance of them are reflected in a letter he penned in 1766:

> Sir: With this letter comes a Negro (Tom) which I beg the favour of you to sell, in any of the Islands you may go to, for whatever he will fetch, & bring me in return for him: one hhd of best molasses, one ditto of best Rum, one barrl of Lymes—if good and Cheap, . . . And the residue, much or little, in good ole Spirits That this Fellow is both a Rogue and a Runaway . . . I shall not pretend to deny—But . . . he is exceeding healthy, strong, and good at the Hoe . . . which gives me reason to hope he may, with your good management, sell well (if kept clean and trim'd up a little when offerd for sale[)] . . . [I] must beg the favour of you (least he shoud attempt his escape) to keep him handcuffd till you get to Sea.

An uneasy mixture of *commercial, patriarchal, and paternalistic* elements shaped George Washington's dealings with his slaves. These aspects were often in conflict with one another and led to inconsistent action. On one hand, Washington tended to view slavery as a commercial enterprise. It was simply an integral part of his desire to amass a fortune from tobacco and grain cultivation and to keep debts to a minimum. In this sense, Mount Vernon slaves were his chattel, his human property. The language he used in buying them might be applicable to livestock. He wished "all of them to be strait limbed, & in every respect strong and healthy with good Teeth." As the historian John Ferling notes in his often perceptive but essentially critical study of "the first of men," "He was not moved to express hatred or love or empathy for his chattel. They were simply business propositions, and his comments regarding these unfortunate people were recorded with about as much passion as were his remarks on wheat rust or the efficacy of a new fertilizer."

The Master of Mount Vernon unquestionably assumed that his slaves would "be at their work, as soon as it was light, [and] work till it was dark." Washington's goal for his bondsmen and women was explicit: "that every laborer (male and female) does as much in 24 hours as their strength, without endangering their health or constitution, will allow." Or again: "It has always been my aim to feed & cloath them well, & be careful of them in sickness—in return, I expect such labour as they ought to render." However unfair and unreasonable such a statement might seem, it can help us understand Washington's position if we realize that he thought that he had entered into a type of "patriarchal contract" in which his slaves owed him service in return for care. Reciprocal obligations and duties between master and servant were the essence of the patriarchal system. Washington saw himself essentially as the provider (the father-figure in the household whose authority lay at the core of the hierarchical system of the early modern British American world), who would protect and care for his dependents. But it was a two-way street, and the slaves owed him something in return. Indeed, in a letter to his cousin and manager, Lund Washington, he qualified his declaration that "they [the slaves] have a just claim to their Victuals & cloaths" with the jarring proviso, "if they make enough to purchase them." When a slave complained that he could not work because his arm was in a sling, the Master of Mount Vernon showed him how and added, "If you can eat with one hand, you can work with one hand." He would give them "every thing that is proper for them" and prevent "as far as vigilance can—all irregularities and improper conduct." The patriarchal compact was potentially an austere code which justified severity to ensure that the slaves kept up their end of the "contract."

Washington often thought he, not his slaves, suffered from the arrangement. Following a fire, Washington wrote a very illuminating letter to his plantation manager: "I wish you would inform him [Isaac] that I sustain injury enough by their idleness, they need not add to it by their carelessness." It was Washington who sustained "injury" from the system of slavery. Thinking in these terms, he was eager to get as much back for his investment as possible. For example, he did a time and motion study on his four slave carpenters to discover how much timber they could hew and how much plank they could saw in a given time under his supervision and then expected them to produce a similar quantity in his absence. While in Philadelphia, he learned that the sewing women at Mount Vernon produced nine shirts each week when Martha supervised them and only six in her absence. He lamented, "Lost labour can never be regained," and urged his overseers to be constantly vigilant because "There are few Negroes who will work unless there be a constant eye on them." He reminded the overseers always to remember that the slaves were working for him. In his words, "I expect to reap the benefit of the labour myself."

Washington found, however, to his constant and growing frustration, that it was not an easy matter to reap the benefits of their labor. Typically, he complained that Peter, who was supposed to be riding the plantation checking on Washington's stock, was usually engaged "in pursuits of other objects . . . more advancise of his own pleasure than my benefit. . . . Every place where I have been there are many workmen, and little work." Washington increasingly viewed the system of slave labor as inefficient. He had a litany of complaints. Slaves feigned illness, destroyed equipment, were often idle, and regularly stole his corn, meat, apples, and liquor. He lamented that, unless watched, the slaves would get two glasses of wine for every one served in the mansion. Everything not nailed down was in danger of being stolen. And how could it be nailed down when even the nails were disappearing? "I cannot conceive how it is possible for 6,000 twelve penny nails could be used in the Corn house at River Plantation, but of one thing I have no great doubt and that is, if they can be applied to other uses, or converted into cash, rum, or other things, there will be no scruple in doing it."

Washington tried hard to thwart the thieves. Overseers were to visit slave quarters at unexpected times and lie in wait along the roads to catch anyone making off with goods from the plantation. Workers were to turn in broken and worn out tools and utensils before receiving replacements. Nails were to be rationed, and comparison made between the number issued to carpenters and the number actually hammered into beams and planks. All of the sheep from the five plantations were to be brought together into one herd and watched constantly. They were to be sheared after they were washed. "Otherwise," he worried, "I shall have a larger part of the Wool stolen if washed after it is sheared." At one point Washington even ordered that most of the dogs belonging to slaves at Mount Vernon be shot because they served as sentinels for night raids on plantation stores. He further ordered, "if any Negro [still] presumes under any pretense whatsoever, to preserve, or bring one into the family . . . he shall be severely punished, and the dog hanged."

In his effort to achieve a disciplined workforce, Washington occasionally resorted to corporal punishment, although there is no record that he ever personally administered it. There is, however, the testimony of Henrietta Liston, the perceptive wife of the British ambassador. While acknowledging the President's consistent control of his passions on public occasions, she noted that "in private and particularly with his Servants, its violence sometimes broke out." Another visitor was shocked at the way the President spoke to his slaves—"as differently as if he had been quite another man, or had been in anger." One of Washington's former slaves much later recalled that his master was "exact and strict" and might complain "in language of severity." Washington justified the occasional severity. In his words, "if the Negros will not do their duty by fair means, they must be compelled to do it." That was what the patriarchal compact was all about.

George Washington was not a cruel man, but his actions often seemed cruel. When confronted by a particularly recalcitrant bondsman, he simply directed his manager to "give him a good whipping." Occasionally, female slaves felt the whip as well. He wrote his manager, "Your treatment of Charlotte was very proper, and if She, or any other of the Servants will not do their duty by fair means, or are impertinent, correction (as the only alternative) must be administered." Regarding one runaway, "Let Abram get his deserts when taken, by way of example; but do not trust to Crow [one of the white overseers] to administer it as he is swayed more by passion than judgment in all his corrections." In another case, he advised, "As for Waggoner Jack, try further correction accompanied by admonition and advice." (Admonition and advice along with close supervision were Washington's mantra.) Apparently in this case it did not work, for Washington later wrote his plantation manager to warn a young slave named Ben that if he did not shape up, "I will ship him off as I did Waggoner Jack for the West Indies where he will have no opportunity to play such pranks." (Sending a recalcitrant slave to the West Indies was essentially a death sentence. In addition to sending Tom there in 1766, Washington did the same to the Virginia-born Will Shag, a constant runaway, five years later.)

While the Master of Mount Vernon preferred admonition and advice, the threat of punishment was often employed. He had his manager tell Muclus, "if his pride [!] is not a sufficient stimulus to excite him to industry, & admonition has no effect on him, that I have directed you to have him severely punished and placed under one of the Overseers as a common hoe negro." When the women referred to above did not produce a sufficient number of shirts while Martha was absent, Washington had his manager warn them "that what has been done, shall be done by fair or foul means" or he would send them off to be common laborers on his outlying farms. Interestingly, he recognized that with a few of his servants, severe punishment was counterproductive. About French Will he noted, "Harsh treatment will not do with him. You had better therefore let him piddle, and in this way (though I believe little trust is to be placed in him) get what you can out of him."

There is some dispute about the living conditions of the slaves at Mount Vernon as the evidence and testimony are in conflict. Certainly, they did not live well. One visitor to Mount Vernon, Julian Niemcewicz, a Polish aristocrat, was shocked by the living quarters of Washington's slaves, referring to them as "huts," adding "for one can not call them by the name of houses. They are more miserable than the most miserable of the cottages of our peasants." Washington himself seemed to acknowledge their very rudimentary condition for, when he later sought Europeans to work Mount Vernon's fields, he admitted that the slave quarters "might not be thought good enough for the workmen or day laborers" of England. Clothing and blankets were carefully rationed. A woman would receive an extra blanket if she had a child, but, if the child died, the woman would not be issued a new blanket for herself but rather was to use the one given to her child. Discussing clothing for the children, another French nobleman declared the Negro quarters "swarm with pickaninnies in rags that our beggars would scorn to wear." The slaves' rations consisted chiefly of maize, herring, and occasionally salt meat. These rations were likely minimal and Washington's slaves, on at least one occasion, took the extraordinary step of petitioning their master, claiming they received an inadequate supply of food.

Perhaps the above description of the conditions at Mount Vernon is too harsh. Certainly, others wrote in a more positive light, and Washington had a reputation as a comparatively humane and kind master. One French visitor noted that the "slaves were well fed, well clothed, and required to do only a moderate amount of work," while another Frenchman observed the approximately fifty slaves on River Farm quarters were "warmly lodged chiefly in houses of their own building." Despite some critical comments, Julian Niemcewicz noted the slaves had gardens and chickens and averred that Washington treated his slaves "far more humanely than do his fellow citizens of Virginia. Most of those gentlemen give to their Blacks only bread water and blows." If a part of Washington disliked spending money on things like clothes, blankets, medicine, and food (and he was characteristically careful how he spent money in all aspects of his life), strong paternalistic elements also influenced his outlook and actions.

While Washington never referred to his slaves as his children, he did refer to them as part of his family. (And only very rarely as "my slaves"—they were usually "my servants" or "my Negroes" or "my people" or "my black labourers.") Washington recognized that slaves, whatever their legal status as human chattel, experienced the same range of emotions as those not in bondage, and he attempted to make accommodations where possible. Although Virginia law did not do so, Washington recognized the validity of slave marriages and became increasingly concerned for slave families and their personal relationships. In time, he resolved that he would not break up families or sell slaves without their permission. In his words, "To disperse families I have an utter aversion." Or again, "It is against my inclination . . . to hurt the feelings of those unhappy people by a separation of man and wife, or of families."

Throughout his adult years, George Washington was always very concerned with his reputation as a man of honor and fairness and with how people viewed him. He was particularly thinned-skinned and sen-

Washington talking to his slaves. (Courtesy of the Mount Vernon Ladies' Association)

sitive to criticism—even to criticisms made by his African American slaves. It led him to act in ways one might not expect the lord of the plantation to act. For example, he wanted certain things given to the slaves because he did not want *his* feelings "hurt" by slave complaints which he admitted would make him "uneasy." During 1787, his need for a bricklayer led him to purchase Neptune, only to find that "he seems to a great deal disconcerted on account of a wife which he says he has. . . . This also embarrasses me, as I am unwilling to hurt the feelings of anyone." One former slave, a carpenter by the name of Sambo (who had deserted to the British but was recaptured after York-town), recalled that although George Washington was his master, he would still not borrow Sambo's small boat (interestingly, Sambo had a boat) without asking permission and would always put it back exactly on the spot from which he borrowed it, even if the President had to drag it twenty yards due to a change of tide.

Washington's orders to his farm managers make it apparent that he was eager to avoid any legitimate criticism of his conduct as a master. In writing to one plantation manager, he was crystal clear: "In the most explicit language I desire they may have plenty; for I will not . . . lye under the imputation of starving my negros and thereby driving them to the necessity of thieving to supply the deficiency." (Washington declared he would be amenable to giving more food, but if he did so, the slaves would sell it rather than consume it.) Washington was also sensitive on the issue of working slaves when they were ill, insisting, "I never wish my people to work when they are really sick." He instructed his manager, "It is foremost in my thoughts, to desire you will be particularly attentive to my Negroes in their sickness, and to order every Overseer positively to be so likewise; for I am sorry to observe that the generality of them view these poor creatures in scarcely any other light than they do a draft horse or ox, neglecting them as much when they are unable to work instead of comforting and nursing them when they lie upon a sickbed." Washington's cash accounts show considerable outlays for both black and white physicians to treat ill slaves.

Dennis Pogue, Mount Vernon's archaeologist, has studied the animal and fish remains found in the slave quarters and concludes, "Taken together, the archaeological evidence of the slave life at Mount Vernon suggests a possibly less-controlled existence than indicated by the usual stereotypical view of slavery. The diet was more diverse, and therefore probably more healthful, than previously believed. Bones of such wild fowl as quail, duck, goose and turkey, such wild animals as deer, squirrel, rabbit, and opossum and such non-schooling fish as pickerel, gar & bluegill were recovered. The slaves were able to hunt, fish, raise poultry and tend gardens to supplement their food allotment." It might surprise modern readers to learn that Washington allowed some of his slaves to own firearms, and he even provided ammunition for them, undoubtedly to hunt game for his table.

Washington's slaves not only hunted for him. He occasionally purchased their produce, such as eggs from their chickens and potatoes and melons from their gardens. Certainly, his most unusual purchase was their teeth. Thanks to the efforts of Mount Vernon's indefatigable researcher, Mary Thompson, we know that in 1784 George Washington purchased nine teeth for £6 2s (at 13 shillings and sixpence apiece) from several unnamed "Negroes." A French dentist, who specialized in tooth transplants and first treated Washington in 1783, advertised in newspapers for people to sell him teeth. It is not clear whether Washington bought his slaves' teeth to have them implanted in his mouth or to be used in his dentures. Either way, it reveals the intimate connection between master and slave in a way that is rarely thought about.

What was Washington's attitude toward his slaves in particular and blacks in general? Was he a racist? There can be no denying that Washington's observations on those held in bondage contain many unfortunate comments and would be considered "racist" from a modern perspective. One scholar summarized his views: "Blacks were ignorant and shiftless; they were careless, deceitful, and liable to act without any qualms of conscience." Describing a slave named Betty, Washington lamented that "a more lazy, deceitful & impudent huzzy" cannot be found in the United States. Of his black carpenters, he declared "there is not to be found so idle a set of Rascals." He warned about "the people who are at work with the gardener, some of whom I know to be as lazy and deceitful as any in the world (Sam particularly)." (Such negative comments are prevalent in Washington's correspondence, but it is worth noting that he also often used similar words in describing his white workers.) He recommended keys be left with a white servant because "I know of no black person about the house [who] is to be trusted." When he called for all his sheep to be herded together, he commented, "I know not the Negro among all mine, whose capacity, integrity, and attention could be relied on for such a trust as this."

George Washington was an elitist by temperament and upbringing. No doubt, he had an "engrained sense of racial superiority" and did not identify with the plight of his bondsmen and bondswomen. His first reference to blacks in his papers set the stage for many that were to follow. At midcentury, when referring to his frontier experiences, amid "a parcel of Barbarian's and an uncouth set of People," he described never taking off his clothes, sleeping in them "like a Negro." In other words, blackness, in his mind, was synonymous with uncivilized behavior. He showed little sympathy for their efforts to cope with their condition as slaves. Historians may view actions such as slowdowns, damaging equipment, feigning illness, running away, and stealing as justifiable means of resisting oppression. Washington simply saw them as evidence that the blacks as a group were lazy and untrustworthy. As a general rule, he believed that blacks were different from whites and were likely to be a bad influence on them.

Washington did recognize the power of the slaves to influence the whites around them. He complained about an early farm manager, Anthony Whitting, who "finding it troublesome to instruct the Negros, and to compel them to the practice of his modes . . . slided into theirs." He declared that Thomas Green, overseer for carpenters, was "too much upon a level with Negroes" to exert authority. While encouraging Arthur Young in Great Britain to send English workers to Mount Vernon, he added a cautionary note, "but it deserves consideration how far the mixing of whites and blacks together is advisable; especially where the former, are entirely unacquainted with the latter." The racial implications of the advice are made clearer in another letter in which Washington stated that he wanted to keep poor whites "as separate, and as distinct as possible from the Negroes, who want no encouragement to mix with, and become too familiar (for no good purpose) with these kinds of people." He warned Sally Green, Thomas Green's daughter, not to open a store if she wanted continuing support from him, as he feared it "would be no more than a receptacle for stolen produce, by the Negros."

This essentially negative and unsympathetic view of his African American slaves helps explain some of Washington's ambivalence toward abolishing slavery. While slavery was an evil, Washington was in no great hurry to end it. In a conversation with the British actor John Bernard, Washington came close to explicitly racist language in justifying fighting for freedom while also maintaining slavery: "This may seem a contradiction, but . . . it is neither a crime nor an absurdity. When we profess, as our fundamental principle, that liberty is the inalienable right of every man, we do not include madmen or idiots; liberty in their hands would become a scourge. Till the mind of the slave has been educated to perceive what are the obligations of a state of freedom, the gift would insure its abuse."

Nevertheless, in spite of such racially charged quotes, it is important to emphasize that George Washington's prejudices were not hard and fixed, and his sense of ingrained racial superiority did not lead

him to negrophobia. In the vast record of his correspondence there
are no explicit statements by Washington that blacks were innately
inferior to whites. Even in Washington's racially disparaging remarks
to the actor John Bernard, he did not doubt that the mind of the slave
could be educated to receive the gift of freedom. Similarly, he believed
whites could lose the gift. Before the war, he had warned that if the
Americans did not resist British tyranny, they would become "as tame
and abject slaves as the blacks we rule over with such arbitrary sway."
In other words, whites and blacks could both become equally abject
slaves or both could equally enjoy liberty. In short, although Washington never had a high opinion of blacks, he did not seem to believe they were inherently inferior. As Joseph Ellis notes, Washington
"tended to regard the condition of the black population as a product
of *nurture* rather than *nature*"—that is, he saw slavery as the culprit,
"preventing the diligence and responsibility that would emerge gradually and naturally after emancipation." Perhaps that explains why
Washington never championed colonization of freed blacks. (Phil
Morgan makes the interesting observation that ultimately, despite his
concerns, Washington had a more optimistic view of a post-slavery
future than did Jefferson. In an irony of ironies, the rock-solid realist
of Mount Vernon was more visionary than the idealistic dreamer of
Monticello.)

George Washington respected individual blacks and had affection
for them. His affection and gratitude to his personal body servant,
Billy Lee, was obvious from his comments in his will (in which he gave
Billy his immediate freedom and an annual annuity) and elsewhere.
He bemoaned the loss of his slave, Paris, and referred to the death of
"trusty old negro Jack." He thought highly enough of Christopher
Sheels that he paid a large amount of money to treat him when he was
bitten by a mad dog, and kept him as his personal body servant even
after Christopher sought to escape from Mount Vernon. He regularly
employed black physicians and often used black overseers on his plantation farms. In 1766, Washington appointed a slave named Morris
to the post of overseer at Dogue Run Farm and, beginning in 1767,
made annual, sometimes biannual, payments to Morris as a reward
for his efforts. Another successful black overseer, Davy, a mulatto
slave trained as a cooper, managed Washington's Muddy Hole farm

for many years. Washington considered him a capable overseer, and declared that Davy "carries on his business as well as the white Overseers, and with more quietness than any of them." Although he distrusted Davy's honesty regarding livestock, Washington was willing to overlook that shortcoming because of Davy's other contributions. For his efforts as overseer, Davy was rewarded with special quarters, two or three hogs at killing time, and other privileges. At one time, Washington even seriously considered employing white laborers to the task of raking and binding, which would have placed the whites in subservient positions to a set of specialized black mowers.

Other examples also reveal that Washington's mind was not closed when it came to recognizing talent among the blacks. When he was in need of good workmen, Washington made clear he believed they could be of any race or religion: "I am a good deal in want of a House Joiner and Bricklayer, (who really understand their profession). . . . If they are good workmen, they may be of Asia, *Africa*, or Europe. They may be Mahometans, Jews or Christian of any Sect, or they may be Athiests" (emphasis added). Perhaps the best example of General Washington's recognition of black talent is contained in his response when the black poetess, Phillis Wheatley, sent him a flattering poem. Thanking her for the "elegant Lines," he added he would "be happy to see a person so favoured by the Muses, and to whom *nature has been so liberal and beneficent in her dispensations*" (emphasis added). She apparently did meet him later at his headquarters, but no record of their exchange has survived.

There is no question that over time George Washington became increasingly antislavery, and one can find numerous quotes from Washington's writings to support such an assertion: "I can only say that there is not a man living who wishes more sincerely than I do, to see a plan adopted for this abolition of [slavery]." "It [is] among my first wishes to see some plan adopted, by which slavery in this country may be abolished by slow, sure, and imperceptible degrees." "I wish from my soul that the legislature of this state could see the policy of a gradual abolition of slavery. It would prevent much mischief." He worried, "I shall be happily mistaken, if they are not found to be a very troublesome species of property 'ere many years pass." "No man desires more heartily than I do [the end of slavery]. Not only do I pray for it on the score of human dignity, but I can clearly foresee that nothing but the rooting out of slavery can perpetuate the existence of our union." (And by the way, while president, Washington made clear that if slavery caused a breakup of the union, he would cast his lot with the North.) He wished "to liberate a certain specie of property . . . which I possess very repugnantly to my own feelings." And "The unfortunate condition of the persons whose labour in part I employed, has been the only unavoidable subject of regret. To make the Adults among them as easy & comfortable in their circumstances as their actual state of ignorance and improvidence would admit; and to lay a foundation to prepare the rising generation for a destiny different from that in which they were born, afforded some satisfaction to my mind, and could not I hoped be displeasing to the justice of the Creator."

Tracing the process and progress of Washington's developing convictions that will ultimately end in the manumission of his slaves is extremely difficult. Given the plethora of antislavery quotes from his pen, it is easy for a sympathetic biographer to make Washington into more of an antislavery advocate than he was in reality. Henry Wiencek, the author of the most comprehensive treatment of Washington and slavery, occasionally falls into this pitfall. Wiencek is so personally outraged at some of the evils of slavery, such as the raffling off of slave families, that he convinces himself that Washington, whom he admires, must have been equally outraged. Washington "shrank in repugnance from the memory of what he had seen and what he himself had done there—an act so morally corrupt and of such stupefying cruelty that he vowed never to repeat it." Yet this appears to be a case of believing what is pleasant in spite of the evidence, for there isn't any concrete data to support his assertion.

Phil Morgan is correct in describing the process of Washington's evolution on the slavery issue as "tortuously gradual." Joseph Ellis concurs: "Morgan and I tend to disagree with Wiencek about how Washington's mind worked on this tortured subject, concluding that moral considerations were always mixed with economic assessments, and that there were no dramatic epiphanies, but rather a gradual and always contested thought process." While the President might wish for the end of slavery in the long run, in the short run he was quick to protect his interests if he felt them threatened. He actively pursued the two runaways, Ona Judge, and his cook, Hercules, who left him for freedom in the North. In one of the most troublesome incidents of his presidency, he secretly ordered his secretary, Tobias Lear, to use subterfuge to take some of his slaves back to Virginia for a brief time so that they would not be eligible to claim their freedom under a Pennsylvania law freeing slaves after six months' residence in that state: "I wish to have it accomplished under pretext that may decieve both them and the Public." In this same troubling letter, Washington doubted, if the slaves were in fact freed, "they would be benefitted by the change," but condescendingly admitted, "the idea of freedom might be too great a temptation for them to resist."

Washington often appeared to have trouble appreciating the desire for freedom among slaves, especially if they were comparatively well treated. Part of his anger against Ona for "absconding" stemmed from the fact that she showed "ingratitude." She had received favored treatment in the past and in Washington's mind she was treated more like a member of the family than as a servant. He was angered at the Quakers' antislavery activities for a number of reasons, but one was because he felt they were stirring up unnecessary trouble between owners and slaves. In words that later pro-slavery champions like Thomas Roderick Dew might use, Washington complained, "But when slaves [who] are happy and contented with their present masters, are tampered with and seduced to leave them; when masters are taken unawares by these practices, when a conduct of this sort begets discontent on one side and resentment on the other . . . it is oppression in such a case, and not humanity in any, because it introduces more evils than it can cure."

Countering these examples, a "true view" must include reference to the fact that when Washington left the presidency, he in fact allowed a few of his slaves to remain in the city, where they would be able to claim freedom under Pennsylvania law. More importantly, his correspondence with the English reformer Arthur Young demonstrates that, while president, Washington seriously explored a way of freeing his slaves, even though it would have meant a major change for him as the Master of Mount Vernon. To the authors of the major study on Washington and Mount Vernon, the proposal was remarkable: "Renting out four fifths of Mount Vernon to free the slaves! To let go what he had spent a lifetime acquiring, building, and improving was for Washington a radical step." His feelings about slavery had brought him to that point. He wanted to simplify Mount Vernon's management and eliminate what he had come to see as a great blight upon it, the presence of slavery. Nothing came of the effort, but it is indicative of Washington's growing desire to liberate the slaves that, in his words, "I possess very repugnantly to my own feelings."

What brought Washington to feel this repugnance? I think part of it was because he increasingly realized that slavery was an impractical and inefficient system, and he viewed the separation of families as a "frightful cruelty." Additionally, there seems little doubt that he was influenced by the rhetoric of the American Revolution and by constant contact with antislavery men he admired such as John Laurens, Alexander Hamilton, David Humphreys, and Lafayette. I think Lafayette, whom Washington loved as a son, was particularly influential, as he was a very strong advocate for the abolishment of slavery and exchanged several letters with Washington on the subject. Then too, the General may well have been impressed and moved by the courage and dedication of black troops in the American army. As he came to recognize their value to the American cause, he became more sympathetic with the idea of freedom for them.

For whatever combination of reasons, he became increasingly eager to see slavery put on the path toward ultimate extinction, although he cautioned it must be done gradually. "Time, patience, and education" were needed in the struggle. George Washington was the most cautious and lukewarm abolitionist that one might imagine. He wanted an end to slavery, but only under certain circumstances. It was never a top priority. It is important to note that all of his antislavery quotes were expressed in *private* correspondence or conversations. During his lifetime, the President never took a public stance against slavery or called for its end. This was a calculated decision on his part. It was a matter of priorities. A critic might write, "the only true policy is justice; and he who regards the consequences of an act rather than the justice of it gives no very exalted proof of the greatness of his character," but George Washington knew it was not that simple. In the vivid analogy of one scholar, Washington was "politically shackled by the grating chain [of racism and slavery] that snaked through the new republic and diminished every life it touched."

The President made the creation and unity of the new nation a higher priority than attacking slavery. Indeed, in his mind there was never any contest. While he was convinced slavery must eventually be eradicated, he was equally convinced that an early attack upon it would undermine and destroy his beloved union before it could be properly established. While we can't run the film through to see what would have happened if a major effort had been mounted against slavery by Washington in the early years of the republic, virtually all of the founders—and most historians—agree it would have led to the breakup of the union. Joseph Ellis, in his work *Founding Brothers*, makes clear that no one in authority in the new federal government was thinking about doing that and all believed any effort to do so was diametrically opposed to remaining a united nation. George Washington was a "rock-ribbed realist." The establishment of a permanent union under the new Constitution was extremely challenging and difficult but possible.

The President well understood that the remarkably profound affection his countrymen held for him was crucial to attaining that goal. To dissipate that affection on a quixotic crusade attacking slavery held no appeal for the Master of Mount Vernon. He felt the best way to deal with slavery on the national level was, if possible, simply to ignore it. The issue was just too divisive. That is why he confessed, I "shall frankly declare to you that I do not like to think, much less talk of it." He rejoiced that the Quaker petition against slavery, which he described as "very mal-apropos," had been put aside. The issue, he hoped, had "at length been put to sleep and will scarcely awake before the year 1808." In his justly famous Farewell Address, where Washington laid out the various crises facing the new nation and the best course of action to follow, he never even mentioned slavery. One could read the entire document and not even know that slavery existed in the United States.

Of course it did, and Washington recognized that his ownership of slaves posed a potential threat to his honor and to his historical reputation, matters of the utmost importance to him. I don't doubt that Washington ultimately came to sincerely believe that slavery was wrong, not only for practical reasons (it was inefficient) but also for philosophical reasons (human beings should not be treated as property, and slavery violated the basic tenets of the American Revolution). But perhaps the most salient force motivating him was that George Washington wanted to be on the right side of history. No man had a greater desire for secular immortality, and he understood that his place in history would be tarnished by his ownership of slaves. To free them would be "the last and greatest debt he owed to his honor."

Washington faced this issue head on in his remarkable last will and testament, which he composed completely by himself during the summer before his death. Very significantly, in what was essentially his last act and his final pronouncement on slavery, he freed all of his personal slaves. (By law, he could not free those belonging to his wife and the Custis estate.) He provided for those slaves too elderly or too young to support themselves by calling for "a regular and permanent fund" to ensure that they were clothed and fed. (The estate made the last payment in 1832 for a "Coffin for Myrtila . . . $2.") Orphan children, or those whose parents were unable or unwilling to provide for them, would be bound as apprentices until age twenty-five. Their masters and mistresses were to teach them to read and write. Pushing education for his former slaves, at a time when it was frowned upon, sent a strong statement to his countrymen, present and future. To stress the importance he placed on his decision, Washington particularly enjoined his executors "to see that this clause respecting Slaves, and *every* part thereof be *religiously* fulfilled" (emphasis added).

Washington added one qualifying clause to his emancipation proclamation. Since many of his slaves had intermarried with the Custis slaves, he postponed the date of their emancipation until after Martha's death. (By law, Martha could not free the Custis slaves even if she had wished to. They were for her use during her lifetime but were to be passed on to the Custis heirs upon her death.) Washington did this to avoid what he called "the most painful sensations," namely that some family members would be freed while others would not. Of course, this delay in emancipation was strictly for Martha's benefit. Those "painful sensations" would happen eventually when the emancipation of Washington's slaves was effected. Martha would simply not have to witness them. Nevertheless, Martha freed Washington's slaves at the end of 1800, well before her own death in 1802. The reason she did so is telling; she confessed to Abigail Adams that "she did not feel as tho her Life were safe in their Hands."

If one needs a single, brief vignette to illustrate the near-intractability of the problem of freeing the slaves, this is it. George Washington, one of the most thoughtful and far-seeing statesmen imaginable, came up with a solution for freeing his slaves that his beloved wife ultimately came to believe endangered her very life. For those who are tempted to criticize Washington for not instituting an emancipation policy for the entire country, it is instructive to see that he could not even effectively free 124 men, women, and children on his own plantation at Mount Vernon. Washington's personal struggle to try and resolve the dilemma of slavery exposes the tragic fact that there was no realistic solution that would not involve greater cost and turmoil than the young nation could afford to bear.

Clearly, there is much grist for the critic's mill in this chapter. Washington was a lifelong slaveholder despite his belief in liberty; he countenanced acts of cruelty against fellow human beings; his actions often fell short of his words; he made racist statements and showed a lack of sympathy for the oppressed; he lived with slavery and off of slavery all his life, and only freed his slaves at his death when he no longer needed them. At one level, it seems logical to conclude that there "is substance for the argument that George Washington's life-long commitment to slavery diminishes his character." But just as clearly, that is not the entire story. In this area, as in so many others, one is impressed by the growth of the man. Roger Wilkins, an African American scholar and civil rights activist, makes an important point: "Surely I cannot on the one hand argue that cultural forces can injure [blacks] and on the other refuse to recognize and make allowances for just such cultural injuries in the lives of the founders."

Considering the time and place in which he found himself, Washington's growth on the question of slavery and race is impressive, and he must be judged against the standards of his day, not ours. He moved to allow blacks to serve in the Continental Army and acknowledged their contribution; he refused to sell slaves without their permission or to break up families, even though it meant the presence of a great many more slaves at Mount Vernon than he could effectively utilize. And, of all of the founding fathers, only George Washington actually freed his slaves. Not only did he free them, but he also rejected explicit racist language concerning innate inferiority of blacks and did not dismiss the idea of free blacks living in the United States in harmony with whites. Interestingly, his views were in contrast to those of Thomas Jefferson on all three points. A fourth point of contrast might be mentioned. There has never been a credible tale of George Washington taking advantage of a slave sexually. (West Ford is undoubtedly a descendant of the Washington family, but there is no substance to the claim that his father was George Washington.)

For reasons of state, Washington chose not to use his great prestige to publicly attack the institution of slavery, but he used that same prestige to firmly establish a permanent union for the United States based on a government dedicated to human freedom. He was not able to complete everything he might have wished to do (slavery was the one "unavoidable subject of regret"), but he worked tirelessly to make America a united nation with the tools to do so at a later date. Given the real-world situation he faced, and the crippling impact of slavery and racism on individuals as well as nations, George Washington's example of at least partially outgrowing the racist society that produced him can still inspire and encourage.

Lithograph of Washington praying at Valley Forge. (Courtesy of the
Mount Vernon Ladies' Association)

9

A Few Simple Beliefs

George Washington and Religion

> In religion my tenets are few and simple.
> —*George Washington*

IF THERE IS A TOPIC THAT IS MORE SENSITIVE AND CONTROVER-
sial than that of George Washington and slavery, it is the topic of
George Washington and religion, especially the question of Washington's Christian faith. (This was brought home to me personally
when the sponsor of my lectures at Gadsby's Tavern, to demonstrate
his chagrin at my position, angrily walked out in the midst of my lecture on the topic.) Richard Brookhiser's insightful observation helps
explain why such events occur: "Washington has been a screen on
which Americans have projected their religious wishes and aversions."
Everyone wants to claim George Washington in support of whatever
positions that they hold dear, as if his agreement would somehow val-
idate the truth of their own beliefs. In the nineteenth century, Roman
Catholics claimed that Washington secretly converted to their faith
before his death. (Some Mormons go one better and even claim that
Washington made a posthumous conversion to their faith!) Presby-
terians claimed he took communion with them; Baptists claimed him
as one of their champions. And so did Freethinkers. In the late nineteenth century, John Remsburg, in one of the most oft quoted articles
on the subject, described Washington as "an infidel."

Currently, no group is more eager to claim George Washington
as one of their own than evangelical Christians. Born-again Chris-

tians hand out copies of William Johnson's book *George Washington the Christian,* one of over thirty books of a similar title listed in the catalog of the Library of Congress. In one of his sermons, the popular televangelist the Reverend Dr. James Kennedy urged his listeners to follow the example of the first president and accept Jesus Christ as their personal savior: "George Washington came to a living faith in the Divine Savior. He came to trust in the shed blood of Christ, the perfect life of Jesus Christ, in which he was robed and in which he stood before God. . . . He prayed that the blood of Christ would cleanse him from all of his sins; that he might be accepted because of the merits, the perfect character of Jesus Christ, and not himself." Tim LaHaye, one of the most famous evangelists in America and coauthor of the remarkably popular series of novels, *Left Behind,* writes, "That President George Washington was a devout believer in Jesus Christ and had accepted Him as his Lord and Saviour is easily demonstrated by a reading of his personal prayer book, written in his own handwriting. . . . An objective reading of these beautiful prayers verifies that were George Washington living today, he would freely identify with the Bible-believing branch of evangelical Christianity that is having such a positive influence on our nation."

In my view, such claims so distort George Washington's religious beliefs that one must question either the scholarship or candor of those making them. As the renowned Washington scholar Marcus Cunliffe noted over fifty years ago, "A prodigious amount of nonsense has been written about Washington in the 200 years since his death, and much of this nonsense has had to do with religion." Nevertheless, while this is true, the task of accurately summarizing Washington's religious beliefs is not an easy one.

Frankly, part of the problem of accurately stating Washington's religious philosophy stems from his reluctance to express his views. A British diplomat observed that the President "possesses the two great requisites of a statesman, the faculty of concealing his own sentiments, and of discovering those of other men." John Adams envied what he referred to as Washington's "gift of silence." The wife of the British ambassador noted, "Most people say too much. Washington, partly from constitutional taciturnity, but still more from natural sagacity and careful observation, never fell into this common error."

Dorothy Twohig, a senior editor of the *Papers of George Washington*, observed that because of his caution and reserve he was an editor's nightmare, and it took her more than twelve years to get a good sense of the man. Yet she noted it showed how politically astute he was because he learned early on that what you don't say publicly you don't have to explain or deny. The last point is particularly relevant for his religious views. A contemporary, the Reverend Samuel Miller, noted that Washington habitually displayed an "unusual but uniform reticence on the subject of religion." Paul Boller, in his valuable study *George Washington and Religion*, concluded, "When it came to religion, George Washington was, if anything, more reserved than he was about anything else pertaining to his life." He seemed to adhere to the position of the British Lord Beaconsfield, who, in response to a question about his religious views, declared it was "the religion of wise men." Thereupon, his interviewer asked, what religion is that, and Lord Beaconsfield smiled and answered, "Wise men never tell." Washington was a wise man and never told. His faith was as aloof as he often appeared to be.

Although he never explicitly summarized his religious beliefs, he left many hints in the vast corpus of his correspondence over a lifetime. In an offhanded but revealing quote, Washington declared, "In religion my tenets are few and simple." His religious tenets were in fact "few and simple" because George Washington was "neither religiously fervent nor theologically learned." Over the length of his lifetime as an adult, Washington's beliefs, which were neither particularly profound nor completely consistent, changed very little. Nevertheless, combined with his stoicism, they served him well in dealing with the various crises he faced during his life.

At the core of his belief system was his conviction that there was an unseen but beneficent power that directed the universe and human affairs. Over and over again, in both public and private correspondence, he made this point, but probably nowhere more succinctly than in a letter to his good friend, General Henry Knox: "his ways are *wise*, they are *inscrutable*, and *irresistible*" (emphasis added). In Washington's view, these are the three central traits of the "Supreme Being" that controls human destiny. Washington's most consistent name for this force is Providence, but he often referred to the force as God or by a host of other descriptive phrases such as "the supreme disposer of all events," "the Almighty Ruler of the Universe," the "Great Architect of the Universe," the "Great Disposer of Events," and dozens of others. This supernatural force is the giver of life and actively intervenes in human affairs. Washington has often been described as a deist, but this is not an accurate description unless you categorize him as what Edwin Gaustad has called a "warm deist." The traditional deistic image of the great "watch maker" who creates the world but does not intervene in it does not comport with Washington's ideas.

Over time, although with absolutely no messianic overtones, Washington came to see himself as an agent for this ultimate power and to believe that Providence was guiding and protecting both him and America. As he looked back at his many close brushes with death in the French and Indian War and his life since, he was grateful to "that Providence which has heretofore preserved & been bountiful to me." Historian Fred Anderson finds it significant that Washington, in 1786 when it appeared that the American experiment in republicanism was failing in the troubled aftermath following her winning of independence, revisited in some detail his Providential delivery in the French and Indian War, when he nearly lost his life several times. Anderson argues the comfort that Washington derived from his faith in the ordering power of Providence rested in the reassuring knowledge that a wisdom beyond human understanding lay behind everything that happened in the world: "No matter how violent, bleak, or forbidding present circumstances seemed, everything would unfold according to a plan that human beings could only glimpse in part, but which was ultimately for the best." Providential deliverance in past crises provided Washington with hope for a similar deliverance in the present crisis.

The General regularly gave thanks to Providence for America's successes in the Revolutionary War. To Lafayette, he declared that recent progress in the war demonstrated "as visibly the finger of Providence, as any possible event in the course of human affairs can ever designate." To another correspondent, he insisted, "The hand of Providence has been so conspicuous in all this, that he must be worse than an infidel that lacks faith, and more than wicked, that has not gratitude enough to acknowledge his obligations." Sensing the preacher-like quality of his words, he jokingly added, "it will be time enough for me to turn preacher, when my present appointment ceases; and therefore, I shall add no more on the Doctrine of Providence."

If Washington often stressed the wise and beneficent quality of Providence, he almost as frequently emphasized that it was inscrutable. Washington's God did not clearly reveal Himself to mere mortals, and, from a human perspective, Providence often appeared to be capricious or unkind. In a rare philosophical mood, Washington wondered to his dear friend, Lafayette, about the curse of war which seemed to plague mankind and questioned why Providence allowed such things to happen: "To have viewed the several fields of Battle over which you passed, could not, among other sensations, have failed to excite this thought—here have fallen thousands of gallant spirits to satisfy the ambition of, or to support their sovereigns perhaps in acts of oppression or injustice!—melancholy reflection! For what wise purposes does Providence permit this? Is it as a scourge for mankind, or is it to prevent them from becoming too populous? If the latter, would not the fertile plains of the Western world receive the redundancy of the old."

Since Providence is often inscrutable, its actions can't be understood from our human perspective. We "can only form conjectures agreeable to the small extent of our knowledge and ignorant of the comprehensive schemes intended." It is best to trust Providence "without perplexing ourselves to seek for that which is beyond human ken." At one point, Washington went so far as to declare, "I will not lament or repine at any Act of Providence because I am in a great measure a convert to Mr Popes opinion that whatever is, is right." In the face of tragedies such as death or great suffering, Washington ultimately fell back on the position that "He that gave has a right to take away." Writing to his nephew, George Augustine Washington, slowly dying from tuberculosis, he opined, "The will of Heaven is not to be controverted or scrutinized by the children of this world. It therefore becomes the Creatures of it to submit with patience and resignation to the will of the Creator whether it be to prolong, or to shorten the number of our days. To bless them with health, or afflict them with pain." The will of Heaven was not to be controverted because it was beyond any human power to prevent events from happening if the Supreme Being wanted them to occur—His will was irresistible. At age twenty-six, the Virginia colonel asserted what he claimed he had already long believed: "There is a Destiny, which has Sovereign control of our Actions—not to be resisted by the strongest efforts of Human Nature." He never changed those views.

If such a view had implications that would downplay the role of human agency and discourage action by men and women, Washington never picked up on them, and he conducted his life with the conviction that action was necessary to ensure a better future. Perhaps everything was finally in God's hands, but George Washington essentially followed the advice offered by the famous words of Algernon Sydney, "God helps those who help themselves." He came close to quoting them when he wrote a colleague during the War for Independence that while one should trust in Providence, "Nothing, however, on our part ought to be left undone." Washington's philosophy justifying intense human action, while recognizing Providence's power, is perhaps most eloquently and succinctly summarized in words from Joseph Addison's play *Cato:* "'Tis not in mortals to command [guarantee] success. But we'll do more, Sempronius, we'll deserve it." (As noted earlier, *Cato* was Washington's favorite play, and he often quoted from it. He used these words in several letters, including one to Benedict Arnold when Arnold was still a promising general in the Continental Army.)

Believing a Supreme Power controlled human destiny, Washington knew it was not in his power to "command success," but that did not mean he would not do everything in his power to insure it and deserve it. (Indeed, despite his stated beliefs, George Washington, throughout his life, was something of a control freak and did everything in his power to avoid being dependent on anything beyond himself.) His view is well expressed in a letter to then governor of Virginia, Thomas Nelson, on the proper course to follow during a critical period of the war: "Unanimity in our Councils, disinterestedness in our pursuits, and steady perseverance in our national duty, are the only means to avoid misfortunes; if they come upon us after these we shall have the consolation of knowing that we have done our best, the rest is with the Gods." He expressed a similar point in another letter, "What may be in the Womb of Fate is very uncertain." Washington's use of phrases such as "Fate" and "with the Gods" illustrate how casually he employed various terms in discussing aspects of divine power. James Flexner noted, "How little he visualized Providence in personal form is shown by the fact that he interchangeably applied to that force all three possible pronouns: he, she, and it."

George Washington's God was beneficent, wise, inscrutable, and all powerful. Was He the God of orthodox Christians? Is it accurate or inaccurate to call George Washington a Christian? To even raise the issue of whether Washington was a Christian is in the minds of many people the height of insolence, if it does not go even further and approach blasphemy. When the controversial freethinker Fanny Wright informed her audiences in the late 1820s that George Washington was not a Christian, pandemonium ensued. People shouted, waved their fists, and threw things at the heretic.

Nelly Custis Lewis, the Washingtons' beloved granddaughter who was raised as their child at Mount Vernon, wrote the first editor of a collection of Washington papers, Jared Sparks, in the face of such controversy over Washington's religious beliefs: "I should have thought it the greatest heresy to doubt his firm belief in Christianity. His life, his writings, prove that he was a Christian. . . . Is it necessary that any one should certify, General Washington avowed himself to *me* to be a believer in Christianity? We may as well question his patriotism, his heroic, disinterested devotion to his country." Sparks, himself a devout Christian, agreed: "To say that he was not a Christian, or at least that he did not believe himself to be a Christian, would be to impeach his sincerity and honesty."

The answer to the question, was George Washington a Christian, ultimately depends on how one defines the term "Christian." Supporters of the argument that Washington was a Christian can certainly present a great deal of factual information to bolster their contention. Washington was a lifelong member of the Anglican Church and was baptized, married, and buried according to the rituals of the church. While he was not a regular attendant of church services, he was a consistent one. He gave money to the church and religious organizations, spending more money on his pew at Christ Church in Alexandria than any other member of the congregation. He consistently gave money and goods to the less fortunate. More significantly, he was a vestryman for Truro Parish and the godfather to a number of children, both roles requiring vows of belief in Christian teaching. On a few occasions, Washington referred to himself as a Christian, and he certainly never explicitly said he was not one. Individuals such as Eliza Powel, William Thornton, and John Marshall, all of whom knew Washington quite well, referred to him as a Christian. The vast majority of the Christian clergy supported and admired him.

In view of such evidence, and defining the term "Christian" in the broad way that the majority of Americans use the term, I believe it is accurate to say that Washington was a Christian. (Washington was a Christian in the way most eighteenth-century Virginia planters were Christian.) Ironically, however, the people who argue most vehemently that George Washington was a Christian would insist that it takes more than the points listed in the previous paragraph to make one a true Christian. It is hard to be a Christian without belief in Jesus Christ and in the redemptive power of Christ's love and his sacrifice on the cross in order to insure the forgiveness of one's sins and the hope of life everlasting. It is my contention that if one defines "Christian" as the evangelicals and other orthodox believers do, George Washington cannot properly be referred to as a Christian. In fact, Washington's "practice of Christianity was limited and superficial," and, contrary to the claims of Tim LaHaye and others, Washington would not be a supporter of "the Bible-believing branch of evangelical Christianity." Let's examine the case for making such an assertion.

A striking fact emerges from a study of George Washington's private correspondence. Not once in the myriad of letters that he wrote does he ever use the words "Jesus," "Christ," "Jesus Christ," or any synonyms for him such as "savior" or "redeemer." The exclusion is so total that it seems likely to have been the result of a conscious decision, almost as if the name, Jesus Christ, was taboo. Washington does not even refer to Jesus as a great moral teacher or prophet. There is simply no reference at all to the person, Jesus. I agree with the assessment of the evangelical scholar Gregg Frazer when he asserts, "It is almost inconceivable that a sincere believer in the deity of Jesus who accepted him as the Christ would never mention anything about such a belief to friends or family in correspondence."

Admittedly, there are a few references to Christ, either implicit or explicit, in Washington's *public* papers, although even these are few and far between. Perhaps the most explicit is in a letter to the chiefs of the Delaware Indians: "You would do well to wish to learn our arts and ways of life, and above all, the religion of Jesus Christ. These will make you a greater and happier people than you are." It should be noted that this type of rare reference to Jesus is, without exception, *not* in Washington's handwriting, but rather in that of an aide. As Douglas Southall Freeman reminds us, "the warmth of the faith was more definitely that of the aide than that of the Commander-in-Chief." Without doubt, the most religious words that Washington ever penned were in his Circular Letters to the thirteen states in 1783. He prayed that God would "most graciously be pleased to dispose us all, to do Justice, to love mercy, and to demean ourselves with that Charity, humility and pacific temper of mind, which were the characteristics of the Divine Author of our blessed Religion, and without an humble imitation of whose example in these things, we can never hope to be a happy Nation." This is commonly known as "Washington's Prayer," although the printed version includes additions like "Almighty" before God and "Grant our supplication, we beseech thee, through Jesus Christ our Lord. Amen," words that are not included in the original text. The prayer is based on the words from the book of Micah in the Old Testament: "What does the Lord require of you but to do justice, and to love kindness, and to walk humbly with your God." The phrase "Divine Author of our blessed Religion" might well refer to Jesus, but may be a reference to Jehovah.

There are many other points, besides lack of any reference to Christ, that conflict with the image of Washington as an orthodox Christian and demonstrate that Washington's interest in religion always appears to have been limited and perfunctory. For example, he did not, on average, go to church more than once a month, and he attended divine services only once during the last two years of his life. He could joke with his good friend and brother-in-law, Burwell Bassett, about church attendance and Scripture. Noting that Bassett had written him on a Sunday, "when you ought to have been at Church," Washington teased, "could you but behold with what religious zeal I hye me [go] to Church on every Lords day, it would do your heart good." In the same jocular epistle, Washington complained about assaults on his tobacco "by every villainous worm that has had an existence since the days of Noah (how unkind it was of Noah now I have mentioned his name to suffer such a brood of vermin to get a birth in the Ark)."

Another sign of Washington's unorthodox views was his refusal to take Holy Communion despite considerable pressure to do so, including implied criticism of him by the minister of the church he attended as president. The evangelical scholar Gregg Frazer raises a valid point: "Why would one who believed in the person and sacrifice of Jesus Christ so adamantly refuse to engage in the celebration of that event as instituted and commanded by Jesus? The simple answer is: one would not." Both by inclination and principle, Washington shied away from demonstrations of piety, and he demonstrated character by not performing religious rituals that he did not believe in simply in order to gain popularity. The General most likely never prayed on his knees, and almost certainly did not do so at Valley Forge. Parson Weems's famous story of Washington praying on his knees in the snow at Valley Forge is out of character for the historical George Washington and has no more historical credence than does Weems's even more famous account of young George chopping down his father's cherry tree. (Isaac Pott, the Quaker farmer who supposedly witnessed Washington on his knees had not yet purchased the farm where the incident allegedly occurred.) As Paul Boller points out, "All the legends about Washington in a pietistic posture" have stubbornly resisted all efforts to track down evidence establishing their authenticity.

Another example of General Washington's lack of doctrinaire approach was his confirming the appointment of John Murray, a universalist who denied the existence of hell, as an army chaplain despite the fact that the other chaplains petitioned for his dismissal. Additionally, there is no evidence that Washington provided any religious education for his slaves. Ona Judge, Martha's seamstress who successfully ran away from the Washingtons in the 1790s, averred in an interview in the 1840s that there was none: "She never received the least mental or moral instruction of any kind while she remained in Washington's family. . . . The stories of Washington's piety and prayers, so far as she ever saw or heard while she was his slave, have no foundation. Card-playing and wine-drinking were the business at his parties, and he had more of such company Sundays than on any other day."

George Washington's last will and testament contains no money for any religious purposes and shows no concern with any aspect of theology after the traditional opening phrase, "In the name of God, amen." A nineteenth-century clergyman, Moncure Conway, noted, "In his many letters to his adopted nephew and young relatives, he admonishes them about their morals, but in no case have I been able to discover any suggestion that they should read the Bible, keep the Sabbath, or go to church." (Washington did urge his nephew, Bushrod, "to do your duty to God and man.") Several clergymen who knew him admitted his Christian beliefs were not all they wished them to be. The Reverend Dr. Bird Wilson averred that George Washington "was esteemed by the whole world as a great and good man; but he was not a professing Christian." Washington's clergyman at one time, Bishop William White admitted, "I do not believe that any degree of recollection will bring to my mind any fact which would prove General Washington to have been a believer in the Christian revelation."

Washington's correspondence gives credence to this assertion. Nowhere is Washington franker in expressing his beliefs than in his letters to Lafayette, whose love and admiration for the General were boundless. They seemed to have shared a traditional skepticism about certain religious activities. In a little-known reference, Lafayette, a deist in belief, reminisced with the General at how they laughed together at a man who claimed that he could communicate with the Devil. In a particularly revealing letter to Lafayette, Washington wrote about Christianity as if he was an outsider to the faith: "Being no bigot myself to any mode or worship, I am disposed to indulge professors of Christianity . . . that road to Heaven, which to them shall seem the most direct plainest easiest and least liable to exception." Washington's views about "Heaven" and the afterlife also put him squarely at odds with evangelical Christianity.

The extant evidence is admittedly fragmentary and inconsistent, but a careful reading of what Washington said—and did not say—indicates that while Washington believed in some type of afterlife, his views are only superficially connected to Christianity. (Interestingly, a word search of the Fitzpatrick edition of Washington's papers indicates that Washington never used words and phrases such as "eternal life," "afterlife," "Paradise," "Angels," and "Saints.") The record is clear from numerous references that he did believe in some type of life after death. (He was a member of the Freemasons, and one of their tenets is a belief in an afterlife.) For example, Washington at least twice made reference to going "to the world of spirits." The image of "going" implies some kind of continuation of existing. On his deathbed, he declared, "I am about to change the scene." It is apparent that Washington had difficulty accepting or conceiving of the idea of nothingness. He did not believe that a person simply ceased to exist upon his death but, while life after death goes on in some fashion, Washington was ambivalent as to what type of life it would be. Though one can quote the occasional positive reference focusing on a happy afterlife, Washington more commonly painted a generally gloomy picture of the next world.

Rather than viewing death as the gateway to a better world, Washington often described death with emotive words such as a "stroke," "a severe stroke," a "blow," a "trial," a "test," "an afflictive trial," a "debt" we must all pay. When people died, he spoke of them as "poor Patcy," "poor Greene," "poor Laurens," "poor Mr. Custis," or "poor Colo. Harrison." He wrote of his own "approaching decay," and of his death as going "to the shades of darkness," "to sleep with my fathers," "to the shades below," to "the country from whence no Traveller returns," "to the tomb of my ancestors," to the "abyss, from whence no traveller is permitted to return," "to the dreary mansions of my fathers." Taken together, the overall image projected is not a bright one, certainly not a traditionally Christian one.

The most arresting aspect of Washington's view of life after death is shown in what he did not say. Not once in all of his authentic, extant correspondence did he explicitly indicate his belief in the reunion of loved ones in heaven. Certainly one of the greatest comforts of religion in general, and of Christianity in particular, is this hope. Washington may have urged those in grief to find consolation in religion, but in all the letters of condolence he wrote he never gave his recipients the comfort of his assurance that he believed they would meet again with their loved ones. Neither did Washington comfort himself with such a vision. Indeed, to the degree that he wrote about death, the emphasis was on separation. After his brother Jack's death, he lamented that he had "just bid an *eternal* farewell to a much loved

Brother who was the intimate companion of my youth and the most affectionate friend of my ripened age." Shortly before his mother died, Washington visited her in Fredericksburg. "I took a final leave of my Mother, *never* expecting to see her more." Parting from his beloved Lafayette, following the end of the war, Washington pined, "I often asked myself, as our Carriages distended, whether that was the *last sight*, I ever should have of you? And tho' I wished to say no—my fears answered yes." (Emphasis added in all three cases.) These assertions were not moderated with such words as "in this world" or the like.

In Washington's final hours, as recounted almost immediately after the fact by his faithful private secretary, Tobias Lear, the lack of religious context is striking. There are no references to any religious words or prayers, no request for forgiveness, no fear of divine judgment, no call for a minister (although ample time existed to call one if desired), no deathbed farewell, no promise or hope of meeting again in heaven. The query of a contemporary clergyman, the Reverend Samuel Miller, is pertinent: "How was it possible," he asked, "for a true Christian, in the full exercise of his mental faculties, to die without one expression of distinctive belief, or Christian hope?" It is significant that Lear ends his diary account with the explicit hope that he will meet Washington in heaven, but his sense of fidelity to a true record kept him from putting such words in Washington's mouth. Perhaps Washington did not take special leave of any of the family because "he had frequently disapproved of the afflicting farewells which aggravated sorrows on those melancholy occasions," but words of hope for a future reunion, if honestly voiced, would surely have given comfort to those left behind, especially to his wife, Martha, who was a firm believer in the Christian faith.

Evidence that George and Martha Washington viewed the concept of an afterlife differently is further supported by examining the letters written to each by Jacky Custis on learning of the sudden death of his sister, Patsy, from epileptic seizures. In his letter to his mother, Jacky urged her to "remember you are a Christian." Patsy's "case is more to be envied than pitied, for if we mortals can distinguish between those who are deserving of grace & those who are not, I am confident she enjoys that Bliss prepar'd only for the good & virtuous, let these considerations, My dear Mother have their due weight with you and comfort yourself with reflecting that she now enjoys in substance what we in this world enjoy in imagination." His letter to his stepfather is completely void of such sentiments as if they would not have given solace to Washington. The Christian image of eternal life for the faithful finds no resonance in any of Washington's known writings.

Washington's focus was not on achieving immortality and living blissfully in heaven. Rather, he appears to have been more interested in acquiring a different type of immortality, the secular immortality of fame across the ages. This quest for historical immortality was his driving passion. In yet another interesting letter to Lafayette, Washington talked about the "Bards," those poets "who hold the keys of the gate by which Patriots, Sages and Heroes are admitted to immortality!" The ancient bards are called "both the priest and the door-keepers to the temple of fame." Washington sent this letter to Lafayette via the famous American poet Joel Barlow, and, drawing on several examples from history, made the interesting observation that "heroes have made poets, and poets heroes." David Humphreys, his aide and would-be biographer, well understood his subject on this point: "Indeed, my dear General, it must be a pleasing reflection to you amid the tranquil walks of private life to find that history, poetry, painting, & sculpture will vye with each other in consigning your name to immortality." Washington's intense desire for fame was inconsistent with the traditional Christian emphasis upon the utter insignificance of this world when set against the tremendous importance of the eternal afterlife.

At this point, a reader may well ask, how is it possible that evangelical leaders like Dr. Kennedy and Mr. LaHaye could possibly teach their followers that George Washington was an evangelical Christian? They must have some evidence on their side! Most of their assertions are based on the contents of what is known as the Washington Prayer Book. It was discovered in 1891 in a trunk found at Mount Vernon, where it had been placed at some time previously. Proponents assert that the prayers are in the handwriting of the young George Washington. Extrapolating from this assertion, supporters argue that these prayers, written when he was a young man, express Washington's mature faith, and this claim allows them to assert Washington's evangelical faith. The argument is simply untenable. In the first place, it is virtually certain that the so-called Washington Prayer Book has nothing whatsoever to do with George Washington. The handwriting is not his, as confirmed by numerous Washington scholars, and the Smithsonian Institution examined the book in 1913 and refused to accept it. As one of the editors of the *Papers of George Washington* expressed it, "Even a cursory comparison of the prayer book with a genuine Washington manuscript reveals that they are not in the same handwriting." (It is probably the production of a later Washington family descendant.) George Washington's handwriting did change over his lifetime, but comparing samples of his handwriting from different periods demonstrates that the writing in the Prayer Book does not comport with any of them. To cite one example, Washington always wrote the letters "th" at the beginning of a word in a distinctive manner at all phases of his life, but the "th" of the Prayer Book is written differently.

Of course, even if one were to grant the authenticity of the Prayer Book, it is an unjustified leap to argue that something someone copied as a youngster reflects his views as an adult, especially when there is a plethora of evidence contradicting it. If Washington in fact wrote and believed in the theology of the prayers as a young man, it would only demonstrate that he was an apostate, for he did not believe in the theology of the prayers as a mature man.

Rather than viewing Washington as an evangelical Christian, it is more useful to recognize that his ethics are more Stoical than Christian, although the two systems have many points in common. Instead of being a man of "The Book," Washington tried to live by three books: *The Rules of Civility; Seneca's Morals;* and Joseph Addison's tragedy, *Cato.* He is better understood as a man of honor than as a man of religion. What is the main difference? As classical scholar Carl Richard summarized it, "The man of religion considers vice as offensive to the Divine being; the man of honor views it as something beneath him." The author of *Cato* stated it slightly differently: "The religious man fears to do evil, the man of honor scorns to do evil." George Washington's special brand of self-respect required him to respect others no less than himself. Washington "was just because justice was right and because lack of it would cost him some of his self-respect. He could not be fair to himself if he were unjust to others."

How did Washington know what was right and just? Since Providence is "inscrutable," it was not possible to confidently receive any revealed truths about it from ministers, priests, prophets, or holy books. Since the truth is not revealed in a manner beyond dispute, the key for Washington was to act in concert with your conscience, which had more power for him than revealed religion. The final admonition of the *Rules of Civility* is "Labour to keep alive in your Breast that Little Spark of Celestial fire Called Conscience." This he did. George Washington was confident he knew what was "just" and "right," and he did not rely on some kind of revealed religion or Holy Book to tell him so. His approach may seem overly simplistic in our post-Darwin, post-Freud, post-Einstein age, but it worked well for Washington in the early years of the Age of Enlightenment with its confidence in human reason.

Since Providence directs the great drama, much of it "beyond human ken," Washington declared that all we can do is to take "care to perform the parts assigned us, in a way that reason and our own consciences approve." We are to act "with the internal consciousness of rectitude in our intentions" and combine that with a "humble hope of approbation from the supreme disposer of all things." In determining the correct course, Washington confessed he had "found no better guide hitherto than upright intentions, and close investigation." His actions were guided by reason rather than by faith. In his words, one should "scorn" to expect to find "truth thro' any channel but that of a temperate and well-informed investigation."

If religion played a fairly peripheral role in Washington's own personal life, there is no denying that he perceived religion as playing a vital role in society. He had no reservations about publicly acknowledging the importance of religious faith for the nation's destiny. His reasoning (like that of many of the Founders) went basically as follows: Virtue and morality are necessary for free republican government; religion is necessary for virtue and morality; ergo, religion is necessary for republican government. His clearest statement of the need for religion is in his Farewell Address: "Religion and morality are indispensable supports.—In vain would the man claim the tribute of Patriotism, who should labour to subvert these great Pillars of human happiness, these firmest props of the duties on Men and citizens. . . . reason and experience both forbid us to expect that national morality can prevail in exclusion of religious principle." (Interestingly, Washington refused in his Address to place secular humanists beyond the pale of the moral life. He acknowledged that the "influence of refined education on minds of peculiar structure" might make a moral life unsupported by religion possible for select individuals, but a nation as a whole needed religion.)

Washington's attitude on this issue is clearly conservative. The church is to be a conserving rather than a reforming force in society. He looked at it as a bulwark of American stability and political order. As Paul Boller points out, these views on the social uses of institutional religion were conventional enough to satisfy most religionists even though they may have had doubts about Washington's adherence to the basic tenets of Christianity. Thomas Jefferson relates an interesting story that reveals how deftly Washington was able to handle a potentially divisive issue: "Dr. Rush tells me that he had it from Asa Green that when the clergy addressed General Washington on his departure from the Government, it was observed in their consultation that he had never on any occasion said a word to the public which showed a belief in the Christian religion and they thought they should so pen their address as to force him at length to declare publicly whether he was a Christian or not. They did so. However, he observed, the old fox was too cunning for them. He answered every article in their address particularly except that, which he passed over without notice." (Jefferson also declared that Washington constantly kept ministers about him for appearance' sake but was "an unbeliever.")

For reasons of state, George Washington, without compromising his beliefs, worked hard to cooperate with religious leaders and to project an image of himself that would be acceptable to them. (To antagonize the clergy would have undermined his goal of unifying the nation.) It is a sign of Washington's remarkable political astuteness that he could achieve widespread support among the religious leaders while someone like Thomas Jefferson could not. Jefferson was rather widely viewed as the avowed enemy of Christianity, although in many ways he was more religious than Washington. (The image of a sly fox has its merits.) Nevertheless, Washington, like Jefferson, was a man of the Enlightenment, and while he perceived value in organized religion, he was very sensitive to the dangers of sectarian conflict for the peace and safety of society.

Washington knew enough history to be concerned. As he expressed it, "Religious controversies are always productive of more acrimony and irreconcilable hatreds than those which spring from any other cause." Writing almost as an outsider, he expressed his concerns to an Irish reformer: "Of all the animosities which have existed among mankind, those which are caused by a difference of sentiments in religion appear to be the most inveterate and distressing, and ought most to be deprecated. I was in hopes, that the enlightened and liberal policy, which has marked the present age, would at least have reconciled Christians of every denomination so far, that we should never again see their religious disputes carried to such a pitch as to endanger the peace of Society."

The tension Washington felt between the value and danger of organized religion, reinforced by his own Enlightenment views, allowed him to be a surprisingly eloquent champion of religious liberty and freedom of conscience. As he wrote to George Mason, "No man's sentiment are more opposed to any kind of restraint upon religious principles than mine are." During the debate over ratifying the Constitution, Baptists were concerned that the separation of state and church might be compromised. Washington made his position crystal clear: "If I could have entertained the slightest apprehension that the Constitution framed in the convention, where I had the honor to preside, might possibly endanger the religious rights of any religious society, certainly I would never have placed my signature to it; and, if I could now conceive that the general government might ever be administered as to render liberty of conscience insecure, I beg you will be persuaded that no one would be more zealous than myself *to establish effectual barriers against the horrors of spiritual tyranny*, and every species of religious persecution" (emphasis added).

I don't know if Washington would have agreed with John Adams's assertion that, if they had the opportunity, "evangelicals would whip and crop, and pillory and roast" in America as they did in Europe, but he was aware of "the horrors of spiritual tyranny." He urged his soldiers, "While we are contending for our own Liberty, we should be very cautious of violating the Rights of Conscience in others, ever considering that God alone is the Judge of the Hearts of Men, and to him only in this Case, they are answerable." He was pleased at how the new constitution set up a system which maximized the chances for genuine freedom of religion. He boasted, "We have abundant reason to rejoice that in this Land the light of truth and reason has triumphed over the power of bigotry and superstition." His justly famous letter to the Hebrew Congregation in Newport, Rhode Island, best expresses his assessment of the religious rights of all citizens of the United States: "All possess alike liberty of conscience and immunities of citizenship. It is now no more that toleration is spoken of, as if it was by the indulgence of one class of people, that another enjoyed the exercise of their inherent natural rights. For happily the Government of the United States, which gives to bigotry no sanction, to persecution no assistance, requires only that they who live under its protection should demean themselves as good citizens." The address concludes utilizing the President's most often quoted verse of Scripture. (Washington quotes from the Bible with more frequency than is generally recognized.) "Every one shall sit in safety under his own vine and fig tree and there shall be none to make him afraid." This was George Washington's fervent wish both for himself and for the nation he founded and loved.

Inevitably, because of Washington's reticence and the desire of people of all shades of belief to claim him as one of their own, the question of George Washington's personal religious beliefs will remain subject to differing interpretations. If one were forced to place a label on Washington's religious belief, he might more accurately be described as a "theistic rationalist" rather than either as a "Christian" or as a "deist." Theistic rationalism refers to a hybrid belief system mixing elements of natural religion, Christianity, and rationalism, with rationalism being the predominant element. My own conclusion is that George Washington was an urbane and sophisticated man of the eighteenth century, an apostle for human reason, a champion of religious liberty, and one of the finest products of the Enlightenment.

G. WASHINGTON in his last Illness attended by Doct.^s Craik and Brown

Americans behold & shed a grateful Tear *And now is departing unto the realms above*
For a man who has gained y.^r freedom most dear. *Where he may ever rest in lasting peace & love*

Early engraving of the death of Washington. (Courtesy of the Mount
Vernon Ladies' Association)

10

He Died as He Lived

The Death of George Washington

> When the summons comes I shall endeavour to obey it
> with a good grace.—*George Washington*

I<small>T WAS NOT ONLY VERY IMPORTANT TO</small> G<small>EORGE</small> W<small>ASHINGTON TO</small>
live his life with honor. It was also very important to him that he end
his life with honor. To paraphrase the author of *The Lion in Winter*, it mattered a great deal to him how he fell, especially when that
was the only remaining action left to complete. The idea of a heroic
death held a certain fascination for Washington ever since his days as
a young colonel in the French and Indian War, when he mused about
the untimely death of a British officer. Rather than mourning the loss,
Washington declared, "Who is there that does not rather Envy, than
regret a Death that gives birth to honour and Glorious memory."
True, the man's life on earth was over, but his reputation and fame
would live on, and that was something to envy and desire. Later, an
orator during the American Revolution made the same point: "Who,
that hath worth and merit, would not quit a present uncertain life
to live eternally in the memory of present and future ages?" Washington's favorite play, *Cato*, also developed the theme of heroic death:
"How beautiful is death, when earn'd by virtue! . . . what pity is it that
we can die but once for our country." Several paintings that hung in
Mount Vernon's two dining rooms dealt with this theme of heroic
death: the death of Richard Montgomery, the Battle of Bunker Hill,
the death of James Wolfe, and the death of the earl of Chatham. Some

of these paintings were gifts, but some were acquired by Washington through purchase.

As far as one can judge from the extant records, Washington always confronted the prospect of his own death with remarkable equanimity and composure. Stoicism, perhaps acquired from his close relationship with Colonel William Fairfax, appears to have influenced his thinking. By age seventeen, Washington owned an outline in English of the *Principle Dialogues of Seneca the Younger*, and the young Washington mastered the advice in one of the chapter heads, "The contempt of death makes all the Miseries of Life Easy to Us." Seneca also wrote, "He is the brave man . . . that can look death in the face without trouble or surprise." As the Stoic Epictetus expressed it, "Will you realize once and for all that it is not death that is the source of a mean and cowardly spirit but rather the fear of death? Against this fear then I would have you discipline yourself." George Washington was one of those rare men for whom death held no terror. He fit the description of the valiant man described by Euripides who bears unflinchingly what heaven sends or by William Shakespeare in *Julius Caesar:* "Cowards die many times before their death; the valiant never taste of death but once."

Washington's stoicism, strengthened by a belief in a benign and irresistible Providence, empowered him with a calmness and courage in the face of danger that was awe-inspiring to his contemporaries. His response to his baptism by fire—"I heard Bulletts whistle and believe me, there is something charming in the sound"—drew a reaction even from King George II in England. ("He would not say so, if he had been used to hear many.") During the French and Indian War, Washington ignored the threats from angry frontiersmen "to blow out my brains," put his life at extreme risk by going between his soldiers and knocking up their guns with his sword when they accidentally fired on each other, and offered to "die by inches" a horrible death if it would stop the suffering along the frontier he was sworn to protect. He wrote truthfully, if with a touch of bravado, "I [have] . . . the resolution to Face what any Man durst."

His legendary courage as commander in chief of the Continental Army might have worried his aides but it inspired his men. His actions at Princeton and Monmouth and his response to the falling shells at

Yorktown—"cool like a bishop at prayer"—demonstrated a character seemingly immune from normal fear in the presence of death. In Jefferson's words, "He was incapable of fear, meeting personal dangers with the calmest unconcern." So great was his courage that not even his harshest critics ever brought it into question. So extreme was it that one biographer wrote, "There is a streak of something close to a mad nature in a man whose instinctive reaction to near death is sheer exhilaration, who finds the whine of bullets 'charming,' and to whom the swirl of violence is a fine tonic that calms his nerves remarkably and serves to clear his head."

The General who faced death so bravely in war had additional opportunities to demonstrate the same type of remarkable equanimity after he became president. Shortly after his inauguration as president in 1789, Washington developed a malignant carbuncle on his thigh which soon threatened his life, and the following year he developed a severe case of pneumonia that caused his physicians and friends to despair for his life. In both cases, Washington's recorded responses were stoical in the extreme. He declared to his aide, David Humphreys, "I know it is very doubtful whether ever I shall arise from this bed and God knows it is perfectly indifferent to me whether I do or not." His physician in the 1789 crisis, Dr. Samuel Bard, recalled Washington's reaction to his illness: "Do not flatter me with vain hopes. I am not afraid to die, and therefore can hear the worst. Whether tonight, or twenty years hence, makes no difference. I know that I am in the hands of a good Providence." During his brush with death in 1790, when all around him were in tears, his wife, Martha, noted that her husband "seemed less concerned himself as to the result than perhaps almost any other person in the United States."

If the burdens of his office seemed to be hastening Washington to his grave, it was a price he was willing to pay. In the words of Cato, "Your life is not your own when Rome demands it." George Washington lived by that creed. As he wrote his dear Lafayette, "But to one, who engages in hazardous enterprises for the good of his country, . . . life is but a secondary consideration." To his physician, he predicted, "The want of regular exercise, with the cares of office will I have no doubt hasten my departure for that country from whence no Traveller returns; but a faithful discharge of whatever trust I accept, as it ever has, so it always will be the primary consideration in every transaction of my life be the consequences what they may."

Washington's fascination with a heroic death should not be interpreted that Washington desired to die. His concern about dying was genuine but in no way kept him from focusing on life. On rare occasions, he could even banter and make light of death. After retiring from the presidency in 1797, he informed his favorite female correspondent, Eliza Powel, of a rather unusual pact he had made. He had "entered into an engagement with Mr [Robert] Morris and several other Gentlemen not to quit the theatre of this world before the year 1800." If Washington broke the contract, he trusted he would be forgiven, for he promised to keep his end of the bargain "unless dire necessity should bring it about maugre [in spite of] all his exertions to the contrary."

More commonly, while at one level Washington was philosophically reconciled to death and not afraid of it, a careful reading of Washington's correspondence indicates that, at another level, Washington saw death as the end of the life he loved and sought to master. In that sense, death was the enemy, "the Grim King," who often "snatched" his victims from life. One oft-repeated theme in Washington's correspondence after he left the presidency was his expectation that his final retirement would be relatively brief. He was acutely conscious that he was from a "short-lived" family. His father died at age forty-nine; his paternal grandfather at thirty-seven; his half brothers had both died early, and none of his natural siblings lived to sixty-five. While not "haunted" or "obsessed" with death, Washington, in a surprisingly large number of letters, made some type of reference to his impending demise. He was fast approaching the biblical life span of "three score and ten." His days "cannot be many"; his "thread was nearly spun"; his life was "hastening to an end"; he was "descending the hill"; he was near the "bottom on the hill"; he was "approaching the shades below"; he had only a "short time" to remain in this "theatre"; he was near the end of the "stream of life." He spoke of the "few remaining years of my life," or of a "remnant of a life journeying fast to the mansions of my ancestors." He hoped to spend the remainder of his life "nearly worn" in agriculture "while I am spared (which in the course of things cannot be long)." He speculated about "if I am alive" next year.

He refused a wedding invitation because he was "going out of life."

These references should not be viewed in a morbid fashion but rather as examples of Washington's recognition that death was an inevitable part of life. In the words of the Stoic philosopher, Marcus Aurelius, whose works he possessed, "It is the duty of a thinking man to be neither superficial, nor impatient, nor yet contemptuous in his attitude towards death, but to await it as one of the operations of Nature which he will have to undergo." Death is a debt—a debt to nature—that everyone must pay: "All must die," and "There is a time, and a season for all things," including a time to die as well as a time to live. Washington clearly viewed the deaths of both an old white servant and an old black servant as essentially positive events because of the circumstances involved: "Altho' Bishop [a white servant who had been with Washington for over thirty years] should never have wanted victuals or cloaths while he lived, yet his death cannot because of regret, even to his daughter; to whom from the imbecility of age, if not when he died, he soon must have become very troublesome to her, and a burthen to all around him." And "It is happy for old Betty, and her children and friends, that she is taken off the stage. Her life must have been miserable to herself and troublesome to all those around her."

Washington expressed a detached and philosophical view about his health, his increasing age, and his own eventual death: "Having, through life, been blessed with a competent share of it [health], without using preventatives against sickness, and as little medicine as possible when sick; I can have no inducement now to change my practice. Against the effect of time, and age, no remedy has ever yet been discovered; and like the rest of my fellow mortals, I must (if life is prolonged) submit, & be reconciled, to a gradual decline." When his sole surviving brother, Charles, died in September of 1799, Washington again contemplated his own approaching demise: "I was the *first*, and am now the *last*, of my fathers Children by the second marriage who remain. when I shall be called upon to follow them, is known only to the giver of life. When the summons comes I shall endeavour to obey it with a good grace" (emphasis in the original). He hoped that in facing death he would do nothing to sully the reputation he had spent a lifetime building. He fully expected that he would meet the final summons "with a good grace." Little did he imagine just how difficult the final challenge would be.

Death was not likely to have been on George Washington's mind as he went out to check on his various farms during the day of Thursday, December 12, 1799. His recent health had never been better, and he was actively composing detailed and comprehensive plans for the future of Mount Vernon. (The day before his death he sent his farm manager, James Anderson, exhaustive plans for his various farms that take up over seventeen printed pages in the Retirement Series of the *Papers of George Washington*.) Washington remained outside for approximately five hours despite the fact that "the weather was very disagreeable, a constant fall of rain, snow and hail with a high wind." George Washington's remarkably hardy constitution in this case may have actually worked to his detriment. The day after his death, a relative wrote, "Alas! He relied upon it too much and exposed himself without common caution to the heat in summer and cold in winter." Despite being wet and chilled, with snow still clinging to his hair and coat, Washington opted not to change his clothes before dinner on the 12th. While presenting symptoms of a cold and sore throat the following morning, and despite continued bad weather that included sleet, Washington went outside briefly in the afternoon to mark some trees he wished to have cut down. By evening, he was very hoarse but still in good spirits. He insisted on reading sections of the newspaper out loud to Tobias Lear, expressing his annoyance at the actions of Thomas Jefferson's two top lieutenants, James Madison and James Monroe. He made what would be his last entry in his diary. Fittingly for a compulsive record keeper, his final words, "Mer[cury] 28 at night," were a measurement.

Detailed research into George Washington's death produced surprises in three areas. First, his last day on earth was excruciatingly painful. Second, key aspects of his character were vividly highlighted by his actions during his final illness. Lastly, traditional orthodox Christian beliefs had little or no influence on his actions during his final struggle.

Accounts of George Washington's death uniformly downplay the horrific nature of the illness and the amount of suffering he had to endure. While recognizing that he "suffered intensely," Tobias Lear,

Washington's talented and devoted personal secretary (to whom we are eternally indebted for a detailed, eyewitness account of Washington's death), contributed to this development. Lear's words, "he expired without a struggle or a sigh," were quickly seized upon by the myriad of Washington's admirers who did not want to picture him suffering. In the words of one of those admirers, "It is a pleasing consideration to all who loved him that he went off with so little pain." The view that Washington experienced a peaceful, indeed a "beautiful death," was soon widely held. Parson Weems, Washington's first biographer and the man responsible for many commonly held myths about him, informed his readers of George Washington's actions as he felt that his spirit was ready to leave his body. Washington "closes his eyes for the *last* time, with his own hands—folds his arms decently on his breast, then breathing out *"Father of mercies! take me to thyself,"*—he fell asleep" (emphasis in the original). The headline of a story in the *Alexandria Gazette* in 1931 proclaimed, "The Beautiful Death of the Great Washington, Met End Serenely, Surrounded by Loved Ones." Such views are widely held today. Even Mount Vernon's highly effective and moving multimedia presentation of George Washington's death presented in 1999 during the bicentennial celebration of his death completely ignored the intense suffering endured by the General. In an article celebrating the same event, a prolific student of Washington commented, "It is hard to find anywhere else in history . . . a more serene death scene." The truth is very different.

Bryan Fairfax, one of Washington's closest friends and his last dinner guest at Mount Vernon, understood the import of Washington's declaration "I die hard." Fairfax noted this was "a great thing from him, because he was one of the last Men to complain. One Expression of that sort from him, to me shews more Suffering than 100 Groans from almost any other Man." Washington fit the image of the stoical man described by the ancient philosopher, Seneca, as one "who, if his body were to be broken upon the wheel or melted lead poured down his throat, would be less concerned for the pain itself than for the dignity of bearing it." While seemingly hard to credit, in some ways, Washington faced a worse torment.

It is, of course, impossible at this late date to assert with certainty exactly what malady struck the General, but the latest and most convincing medical studies indicate that George Washington died from acute epiglottitis caused by a virulent bacteria. The epiglottis is a structure composed of cartilage located just below the base of the tongue and at the entrance to the larynx (voice box). It is positioned high in the throat at the very entrance to the airway that goes through the larynx to the trachea, commonly called the windpipe, and then into the lungs. Washington exhibited many symptoms consistent with classic acute epiglottitis: rapid onset of the disease, high fever, an extremely sore throat, drooling, great difficulty in swallowing, great difficulty in speaking without true hoarseness, increased airway obstruction, especially when leaning backward, a desire to assume a sitting position in spite of weakness, persistent restlessness, and finally an apparent improvement shortly before death. It was a "textbook" case of this extremely painful and frightening disease.

The pain associated with acute epiglottitis is intense. Having an inflamed and swollen epiglottis, which would be bright red and about the size of a plum, is similar to having a raw sore located in a very sensitive spot. As the stoical Washington described his throat to Lear, "tis *very* sore" (emphasis added). While the pain is intense, the truly frightening aspect of acute epiglottitis is the obstruction of the larynx that makes both breathing and swallowing extremely difficult. The first thing an infant masters is to breathe and the second is to swallow. To have these two absolutely basic functions dramatically impaired is very frightening to anyone, no matter how brave and courageous he or she might be. Like any mortal, Washington had to face the terror of air hunger, of smothering and gasping for each breath, and his constant restlessness and changing of positions throughout the day was part of his endless effort to meet this most basic of needs. Essentially, Washington slowly and painfully suffocated to death over many hours.

There was not one thing done either for or to George Washington during his illness that was not done in love and with the very best of intentions. By the early hours of Saturday morning, the 14th, the disease had progressed so rapidly that Washington awoke feverish, in significant discomfort, and with labored breathing. As soon as Lear learned of Washington's distress later that morning, he immediately dispatched a slave to Alexandria to summon Dr. James Craik, Washington's physician and very dear friend of over forty years. Washington's confidence in Craik was complete: "The habits of intimacy and friendship, in which I have long lived with Dr. Craik, and the opinion I have of his professional knowledge, would most certainly point him out as the man of my choice in all cases of sickness. I am convinced of his sincere attachment to me, and *I should with cheerfulness trust my life in his hands*" (emphasis added). Craik's forty years of experience helped him realize that his old friend's illness was likely terminal. Martha Washington, following Craik's standing advice on what to do in an emergency, had already asked Tobias Lear to send word to Dr. Gustavus Brown in Port Tobacco to come to Mount Vernon as quickly as possible. Brown was a wealthy Edinburgh-trained physician and horticulturist who in 1799 had been busy cofounding the medical and chirurgical (surgical) faculty of Maryland. Fearful that Brown might not arrive in time, Dr. Craik quickly decided to summon his fellow physician and Mason, Dr. Elisha Cullen Dick, of Alexandria. Craik understandably did not want to face the responsibility of caring for America's greatest hero all by himself and welcomed the help of the younger but very highly regarded Dr. Dick, a graduate of the University of Pennsylvania and a student of the renowned Dr. Benjamin Rush.

Thus, George Washington received excellent medical treatment according to the best light of eighteenth-century medicine. Nevertheless, tragically, virtually every single procedure in fact compounded his suffering and perhaps hastened his demise. Even simple ministrations almost proved fatal. Lear recounted, "A mixture of Molasses, Vinegar & butter was prepared to try its effects in the throat; but he could not swallow a drop. Whenever he attempted it he appeared to be distressed, convulsed and almost suffocated." This reaction was caused by the swollen epiglottis that blocked the mixture from going into the esophagus and caused some to go into the windpipe, triggering what physicians call a laryngospasm. When food or water goes "down the wrong pipe," one chokes and coughs because the larynx immediately goes into a sustained spasmodic closure to prevent inhalation of foreign substances into the lungs. During this laryngospasm, air can neither enter nor exit the lungs. This is uncomfortable under normal circumstances, but it can be fatal when the airway is already partially compromised and breathing and swallowing are impaired.

Over the course of approximately ten hours, George Washington was bled four different times, losing approximately five pints, or over eighty ounces, of blood. This was between one-third and one-half his total blood volume. The theory behind phlebotomy was to remove the diseased matter from the body, and practitioners believed that the blood would be restored within hours. In fact, such excessive blood-letting severely weakened the General. In addition to weakening him, the aggressive treatment compromised his circulation. In acute epi-glottitis, it is difficult to inhale and receive sufficient oxygen. As a result, the patient suffers from hypoxia, deficient oxygenation of the blood. The very significant loss of blood further reduced his oxygen-carrying capacity as the hemoglobin in the blood carries the oxygen, and his blood supply was dramatically reduced.

The use of purgatives, also part of the treatment, significantly re-duced his bodily fluids and exacerbated the situation by even further compromising his circulation. Not only did the purgatives compro-mise circulation, they inflicted significant additional suffering on the patient. Repeated doses of emetic tartar were given to him to induce vomiting. Large amounts of calomel (a white tasteless medicine with mercurial properties used as a purgative) and an injection were also administered. The result was a "copious discharge of the bowels." How much discomfort these ministrations would have caused Washington, a man struggling for each and every breath, is easier to imagine than to describe. Certainly, his bedroom must have reeked of "blood and stench and sweat." Additionally, cantharides were wrapped around the patient's neck. Cantharides are dried Spanish flies ground into a powder and applied to the skin to cause blistering. While this ministration added to Washington's discomfort, it did nothing to alleviate his ailment.

The extreme difficulty in speaking and in making his wishes known significantly added to Washington's agony. Drs. Dick and Craik reported, "Speaking which was painful from the beginning, now became almost impracticable." Lear later informed Alexander Ham-ilton that Washington's condition kept him from verbalizing many of the things that were clearly on his mind. Nevertheless, although speaking was very difficult, it was not impossible, and George Wash-ington somehow managed, through a remarkable display of willpower and self-control, to summon up the strength to communicate his most pressing thoughts and wishes to those around him. His communication that fateful day, both by word and action, reveals a great deal about the man and his character. In the words of his secretary, Tobias Lear, "He died as he lived."

One of Washington's most endearing traits is that he combined a sense of power with diffidence. George Washington was a remarkable man, knew he was a remarkable man, and was feted, praised, honored, and almost worshipped in a way no other American ever has been. Yet, in Robert Frost's words, "George Washington was one of the few in the whole history of the world who was not carried away by power." His diffidence and modesty allowed him to keep a healthy psyche and not let the constant adulation go to his head. He was always respectful to ordinary people, whose greetings he never failed to return. His basic respect and concern for others, combined with his charisma and power, were keys to his success as a leader.

His concern for and sensitivity to others was not a thin veneer, an act put on either to please or to deceive people. It was an essential part of Washington's persona, so integral to his character that even in the midst of a mortal and very painful illness he demonstrated it on a number of different occasions. His concern for his wife Martha's welfare, even at the potential cost of his own, led him to refuse Martha's request to go out into the middle of the cold winter night to summon aid for fear she would aggravate her own illness from which she had only recently recuperated. When his overseer, summoned to bleed the General, manifested nervousness and anxiety about performing such an operation on his illustrious employer, Washington reassured him, "Don't be afraid."

In the course of the long and agonizing day, Washington consistently apologized to those trying to ease his suffering for the trouble he was causing them. He apologized to Tobias Lear, who was helping move him to different positions in his endless quest for oxygen, and worried that the effort would fatigue Lear. He even asked his personal body servant, Christopher Sheels, who had been standing by the bed throughout the day, to sit down. It was the last request Washington made of his personal servant, and it was one that Christopher was probably happy to oblige. We do know that he sat down, but sadly, unlike the other three people gathered immediately around Washington's deathbed, we have no idea of what Christopher was thinking as he watched his master's final struggle. (Nor do we know what the Master of Mount Vernon thought about Christopher. It is perhaps significant that even after learning of Christopher's plan to run away, George Washington still kept him as his personal servant.) How many powerful leaders, in the midst of an excruciating terminal illness, would either notice or be concerned with the fact that a personal servant had been standing on his feet for most of the day? Such actions speak volumes about Washington's character.

Equally as striking as his concern for those around him was George Washington's remarkable ability to remain "awesomely organized" to the end. Order for Washington was always like a salve. Drs. Craik and Dick reported, "During the short period of his illness, he economized his time, in the arrangement of such few concerns as required his attention." His ability to do this while suffering from acute epiglottitis is truly remarkable. If ever a man strove to control and master the environment he found himself in, that man was George Washington. Since at least 1775 George Washington's overriding concern had always been "Amor Patriae," but he devoted as much time as possible to his personal interests. Washington firmly believed that all men, himself included, were driven by both interest and honor, and while the latter was always the more important to him, Washington was not an altruist unconcerned with his own interests. The result of his drive and ability had been the amassing of a considerable personal fortune, making Washington one of the richest men in America: "What he had acquired with ambition and had protected with zeal, he would distribute with infinite care."

The end result of his concern was a remarkable and revealing final will and testament full of detailed instructions, which Washington spent many "leisure hours" composing during the summer of 1799. As he contemplated his death, his "greatest anxiety" was to leave all his own affairs and those of others for whom he was responsible "in such a clear, and distinct form . . . that no reproach may attach itself to me, when I have taken my departure for the land of Spirits." (This is yet one more example of Washington worrying about how he would be judged.) Late in the afternoon of December 14th, Washington knew his departure was at hand, and he had Martha go to his study and retrieve two wills from his desk. When she returned with the wills in hand, the General indicated which was the operative one and requested she burn the other, which she did.

Having taken care of his will, Washington then proceeded to make his longest recorded speech of this sad day. Speaking with great difficulty he ordered Lear to: "Arrange & record all my late Military letters & papers—arrange my accounts & settle my books, as you know more about them than anyone else, and let Mr Rawlins finish recording my other letters, which he has begun." It is not coincidental that George Washington's longest speech, when verbal communication was so very difficult, involved concern with his personal papers. From an early date, Washington was fascinated with the record of his existence. In Professor William Abbot's words, Washington had an "uncommon awareness of self . . . what he decided and what he did, and how others perceived his decisions and deeds always mattered." His intense interest in his personal papers had been a long-standing concern.

When it seemed early in the war that Lord Dunmore might move against Mount Vernon and perhaps seize Mrs. Washington, the General wrote his manager, Lund Washington, to provide safety "for her and *my papers*" (emphasis added). In late 1776, when the patriot cause looked particularly bleak, he ordered Lund to "have my papers in such a situation as to remove at a short notice in case an Enemy's Fleet should come up the River." At Washington's urging, Congress provided money to have General Washington's correspondence, orders, and instructions from the war properly arranged and copied into bound volumes. (This was a major undertaking and will ultimately fill approximately forty volumes of the new edition of George Washington's papers. He described these papers as "of immense value to me.") Sometime in the 1780s, Washington decided it was equally important to organize his papers from the French and Indian War. As Professor Abbot explains, "finding them marred by awkward constructions, faulty grammar, and misspellings, the hero of the Revolution proceeded to correct what the young Washington had written more than a quarter of a century before." It too was a large undertaking. Finally, at the end of his presidency, Washington had his secretaries take from his files material that should remain for President Adams, but he shipped the remainder to Mount Vernon. There he hoped to construct what would have been in effect the first presidential library in order to house all his papers, both of a public and a private nature. This extreme interest and concern for his papers was closely connected to George Washington's desire for fame and secular immortality, which were such driving forces in his life.

Freeman's biography of Washington emphasized another aspect of his character: "The same self-discipline served Washington as patient that had served him as a planter, as Commander-in-chief, as President. Duty . . . was his governing principle. . . . Today, this 14th of December 1799, he responded as if clearly it was his duty not to deny the doctors and others their valiant efforts to restore him, unavailing though he believed them to be." Throughout the entire ordeal, the General displayed remarkable fortitude and patience. Grace in the presence of mortal danger comprised a key part of Washington's code of honor, and the ultimate test of honor was courage in the face of one's own death. This was a rare strength, and he once again lived up to his creed. There is an old Spanish proverb: "It is one thing to talk about the bull in the ring. It is another thing to be in the ring *with* the bull." Washington was able to face the bull in the ring.

George Washington's courage in the face of death is indisputable. The source of that courage is more controversial. To better understand it, a brief look at the death of Virginia's other great popular figure of the eighteenth century, Patrick Henry, can be instructive. Patrick Henry, suffering from severe intestinal blockage, met his death in June of 1799 with the courage of a convinced Christian. More than a decade earlier he had written his sister on the death of her husband, "This is one of those trying scenes, in which the Christian is eminently superior to all others and finds a refuge which no misfortune can take away." Facing his own imminent demise, Henry used his courage in the face of death as further proof of the truth of the Christian religion. His wife recounted his death scene in a letter to their daughter, "He met death with firmness and in full confidence that through the merits of a bleeding saviour that his sins would be pardoned."

Although the records of George Washington's final hours are much more comprehensive than those for Henry, they leave a very different picture. Washington "died like a Roman Stoic, not a Christian saint." While no one can know what Washington was thinking on this subject on December 14th, the complete lack of religious context is striking. As expanded upon in the previous chapter (where his religious views are examined in depth), George Washington did not draw his courage from a Christian concept of redemption and the hope of eternal bliss through the sacrifice of Christ. Rather, Washington drew his strength from a stoical courage, a powerful desire to play his last role on earth's stage in a praiseworthy fashion, and confidence in his virtue and effort to live by the highest ideals. Deeds were always more important than faith to Washington. When a favorite niece died, he wrote somewhat paradoxically, "She is now no more! but she must be happy, because her virtue has a claim to it." Washington hoped the same could be said of him. As he expressed it to Bryan Fairfax, he had "always walked on a straight line, and endeavoured as far as human frailties, and perhaps strong passions, would enable him, to discharge the relative duties to his Maker and fellow men, without seeking any indirect or left handed attempts to acquire popularity." Finally, and not to be discounted, Washington was strengthened by his trust in a rather vaguely defined but all-powerful and benign Providence who ultimately controlled human destiny.

Certainly, he would need all of his resources to bear his final ordeal. He expressed both the difficulty of the ordeal and his confidence by informing Dr. Craik, "I die hard, but I am not afraid to go." In view of the virtual torture that he was enduring, it is not surprising that eventually Washington, who appeared to realize relatively early on that the disease would prove fatal, sought to convince his physicians to stop their ministrations. He pleaded, "Let me go off quietly." Even though they were "without a ray of hope," and despite Washington's heartfelt plea, the physicians found it next to impossible not to try something else to save his precious life. Dr. Dick, who had opposed the final bleeding of Washington, proposed a radical course of action. He wanted to perform a tracheotomy, essentially making a hole in the trachea below the obstruction in order to ease Washington's breathing. Many have expressed their regret that the other physicians overruled him, arguing that it would have saved Washington's life. Over time, Dick became increasingly convinced that the operation should have been performed and particularly singled out Dr. Brown for criticism, although he noted the advanced age and timidity of both of the other physicians. Dick declared, "I shall never cease to regret that the operation was not performed."

No doubt, creating an airway for the General was the number one priority, but one must seriously question the likelihood of its success in this case. In 1799, even elective tracheotomy, let alone emergency tracheotomy, was a near-mythical surgical procedure long footnoted but rarely performed (and almost never in the United States). A workable procedure had been described in surgical detail only the year before. Dr. Dick had never performed such an operation on a live patient, although he apparently had recently attempted one on a five-year-old girl just as she died. His efforts to resuscitate her were unavailing. In Washington's case, Dr. Dick would have had to perform the procedure under difficult conditions with poor lighting on a conscious patient in extremis, and on one who had already lost five pints of blood. Because of the airway swelling, forcing Washington to lie down would have caused the hugely enlarged epiglottis to fall back and might have obstructed his trachea completely. Secondly, any attempt to give pain relief with laudanum, a derivative of opium that is administered orally and had to be swallowed, might have suppressed his respiration, thus speeding up his demise. Attempting to perform a tracheotomy on an awake, semi-sitting patient without local anesthesia would have been extremely difficult to accomplish even in the best of hands.

Adding to the difficulties, the danger of excessive bleeding from cutting a major blood vessel was significant, and there was a lesser possibility of cutting into the esophagus behind the trachea or puncturing a lung. Finally, the chance of the airway collapsing was high since Dr. Dick almost certainly had no tracheotomy tube-like device to keep the opening working. In short, there was a very high probability that the operation would have proved fatal, and one can imagine the uproar if the beloved Washington had died as a result of his own physicians slitting his throat. Also not to be discounted, the evidence clearly indicates that Washington himself was ready "to go," and would not have favored such a heroic measure, a point likely influencing Dr. Craik's final decision. Thus Dr. Dick's radical proposal was consequently rejected, but as late as eight o'clock the doctors still felt compelled to act, and, among other steps, they applied additional blisters to Washington's legs. In Dr. Dick's bitter words, the physicians were acting as a drowning man does who feels impelled "to grasp at a straw." It was to be their final treatment. Washington's agonizing struggle was nearing an end.

As the microbial storm raged unabated throughout his body, it became increasingly clear that this was one storm that even the heroic George Washington could not weather, although his bodily strength probably prolonged his dying. With the end approaching, Washington, always desirous of being in control, feared that he might be buried alive. (Ironically, he was in fact slowly suffocating, the very thing which would happen to persons put in a coffin before they were actually dead.) The idea of being buried alive was a more realistic concern then than it would be today, and for whatever reason, the issue was obviously of the utmost importance to Washington. After several unsuccessful efforts, he at last managed to convey his final request to the faithful Lear. He was not to be buried until he had been dead for at least two days. When Lear, choked up with emotion, simply nodded, Washington pressed him, "Do you understand me?" Lear said that he did, and then Washington uttered his last recorded words, "Tis well."

The losing struggle for oxygen and the corresponding build-up of carbon dioxide ultimately overwhelmed the great general. As Washington lapsed into unconsciousness, he closed his eyes, his hand that had been taking his pulse fell to his side (yet another measurement), his countenance changed and Washington then "expired without a struggle or a sigh." "The great body, which had endured so much, the great mind, so steady in its operation, so sure in its conclusions, was all stilled. Here was no more than an empty vessel, drained for the subsistence of a nation." Thomas Jefferson, quoting David's response to Saul's tragic death as recorded in the Bible, expressed it well: "verily a great man hath fallen this day in Israel." So he had.

George Washington died as he lived. He completed his race with his precious honor intact. The Resolution adopted by the United States Senate got it right: "The scene is closed—and we are no longer anxious lest misfortune should sully his glory; he has traveled on to the end of his journey, and carried with him an increasing weight of honor: he has deposited it safely where misfortune can not tarnish it; where malice can not blast it." John Marshall wrote the day after his burial, "Our Washington is no more! the Hero, the Sage, and the Patriot of America—the man on whom in times of danger every eye was turned, and all hopes were placed—lives now only in his own great actions and in the hearts of an affectionate and afflicted people." If ever a man deserved secular immortality and eternal remembrance from a grateful nation, that man was George Washington.

Epilogue

The Measure of the Man

> It is not my intention to exaggerate. I wish only to
> express the impression General Washington has left
> on my mind, the idea of a perfect whole.—*Marquis de
> Chastellux*

GEORGE WASHINGTON WAS DEAD. ONLY THE OUTER SHELL OF THE
great man remained, and that shell had to be prepared for burial. As
part of that necessary ceremony, Dr. Elisha Dick carefully noted the
measurements of the fallen hero so that the correct size coffin could
be built.

$6'3^1/_2''$ length exact
$1'9''$ across shoulders exact
$2'9''$ across elbows exact

Measuring the outer, physical attributes of the man was a relatively
simple task. Measuring the inner quality and character of the man is
a much more difficult task, and one that can never be punctuated with
the word, "exact." How does one measure and understand such a complex and remarkable man?

Washington had his share of those dichotomies in his composition that make analyzing human personality both so fascinating and
so frustrating. He combined a towering ambition and desire for fame
with an intense fear of failure. His ambition drew him relentlessly to
the centers of power and influence. His fear of failing and damaging
his reputation caused him to have an unquenchable desire for approbation and to be inordinately sensitive to criticism. (Washington's desire

for "approbation" can be illustrated by the fact he used the word over six hundred times in the Fitzpatrick edition of his papers.) He feared words of criticism in a way he never feared enemy bullets. Whether this endless quest for approval was rooted in his relationship with his demanding and apparently never satisfied mother is, of course, a debatable point, but his desire for approval from his countrymen is not.

Always aware of his "defective education" and that many men possessed "much abler heads" than his own, he combined this insight with the recognition that at the core of his being he was in fact a remarkable and exceptional man. When one looks for examples of consistency between his public and private careers, one notes his tendency to see himself as the person best qualified to carry out a required course of action.

George Washington was a man of intense passion with a potential for violent outbursts. One contemporary noted, "Intimates say that he is by nature a man of fierce and irritable disposition." The great artist, Gilbert Stuart, after carefully studying the physiognomy of his famous subject, found "features in his face totally different from what I had observed in any other human being. The sockets of the eyes, for instance, were larger than what I had ever met before, and the upper part of the nose broader. . . . All his features were indicative of the strongest passions. . . . Had he been born in the forests . . . he would have been the fiercest man among the savage tribes." Yet, Washington presented to the world the face of a cool, aloof, and distant man. His ability to control his passions and utilize his towering ambitions and abilities for positive rather than negative results is the key to his greatness. As Ellis summarizes: "The passions that stirred Washington's soul required the creation of equally massive control mechanisms that ultimately served the nation so well. . . . The psychological struggle for self-control prepared Washington to perform the crowning political achievement of his career, withdrawal from power. What we might call Washington's internal muscularity is, of course impossible to see, but it was just as impressive as his marvelous physique."

One of the most common words used to describe George Washington is "selfless." While hinting at an important truth, the word is the wrong one to use to describe Washington, who in many ways is the opposite of the selfless altruist. His surviving correspondence makes crystal clear that he had "an unabashed concern for his own economic interest." It is difficult to underestimate what Edmund Morgan described as Washington's "constant, wary, and often cold eye on making a profit." Something of a perfectionist and possessing an almost obsessive need to be in control, George Washington was a very difficult man for whom to work. While fair and honest in his business dealings, he was extremely demanding and exact, figuring what was due him to the penny or the ounce. He was rarely satisfied with his workers, and this was as true for his white workers as it was for his black slaves. His statement concerning his slaves' labor, "I expect to reap the benefit of the labour myself," could properly be applied to white workers as well. His near harangues to his overseers and managers are a case in point. A river of sarcasm runs through Washington's correspondence as time and time again people failed to live up to his high and exacting standards.

Most people are familiar with the first part of Henry Lee's eulogy—"First in war, first in peace, and first in the hearts of his countrymen," but the second half is just as important—"he was second to none in the humble and endearing scenes of private life." To live freely and autonomously at Mount Vernon was *one* of George Washington's central desires. (He would say it was *the* central desire: "I have no wish which aspires beyond the humble and happy lot of living and dying a private citizen on my farm.") Mount Vernon was his hobby as well as his home. It symbolized his origins, achievements, and aspirations. Washington identified Mount Vernon with his freedom and autonomy, away from public cares and responsibilities. It was a source of his serenity and the safe harbor he turned toward in the midst of difficult moments in his public life.

One is struck by how often he wrote about Mount Vernon, even in the midst of the war and the problems of his presidency, including detailed instructions about its upkeep and improvement. Writing to his manager in the darkest days of 1776, the harried General bemoaned the sorry state of his army and confided that the "game" might "be pretty well up." Then, in almost the next sentence, he declared, "If you can get some Holly Trees to plant upon the Circular Banks in a manner, or rather thicker than I did a year or two ago I should be glad of it." If all could not be as he wished with the army, then at least he would have it so at his distant, beloved home. He received a pleasure from farming and cultivating Mount Vernon in various ways that is hard to overestimate. His longing to live freely under his own vine and fig tree was not simply posturing. It expressed a key part of his very essence.

That is why the story of George Washington contains an element of sadness. If ultimately Washington's desire for love trumped his desire for power, it also trumped his desire for autonomy. Increasingly, he sacrificed his autonomy and responded to the call of disinterested service on behalf of his country and their citizens. He became the epitome of the "servant leader." It is "a grim thing to be plunged into an endless sequence of war, controversy and crisis, walking the knife edge of catastrophe." While he longed for retirement and personal ease, the call of duty—and the winning of public esteem for answering it—had to be heeded. In Richard Norton Smith's analogy, "Like Faust, forced to pay the price of his ambitions, George Washington discovered that the fame and veneration pursued over a lifetime could only be had at enormous cost." In enabling other men to pursue happiness according to their individual preference, Washington had to deny himself the same pleasure. In that sense, he sacrificed himself for a greater cause. (Only in that sense is the word "selfless" appropriate.)

One thing that George Washington desired more than autonomy at Mount Vernon was what an admirer called "Honest Fame." Washington desperately wanted to enter the Temple of Fame, but he wanted to enter it only through the Doors of Honor. This emphasis on disinterested service (the trick of character that welds ego to larger purpose) and on integrity to principles was the way Washington navigated the tensions between his self-interest and the interest of others. He sought to transform any self-aggrandizing impulses into public service. Ultimately, it appears Washington resolved a potential conflict by convincing himself and his countrymen that he was acting purely out of the interest of his country. Time and time again he announced to the world that his driving motive was that of disinterested service. By making such explicit proclamations, Washington set high standards that made it easier for him to guard against slipping into self-aggrandizement. Thus, for example, as he prepared to enter New

York City for his inauguration as the nation's first president, he wrote the governor, "I can assure you, with the utmost sincerity, that no reception can be so congenial to my feelings as a quiet entry devoid of ceremony."

Washington must have known such a request would not be followed. Inevitably, his entry into the city drew huge throngs, all eager to catch a glimpse of their hero and participate in a historic moment. He made the same type of heartfelt, but clearly unrealistic, request when he drew up his final will and testament: "It is my express desire that my corpse be interred in a private manner, without parade or funeral oration." Why would such a realistic man make such an unrealistic request? As he had numerous times before, he needed to prove to the world—and to himself—that he had acted only for the good of the country, and now that his service to his country was over, he would emphasize his victory over any lusting for fame and glory by specifically requesting that he be buried in a purely private ceremony. The request would comport with the world's image of him and his image of himself. Yet Washington almost certainly knew that this was one request that would not and could not be honored.

Some critics may say that George Washington's inordinate love of fame was his greatest moral weakness, but what is truly impressive is the manner in which he channeled his great ambition in a positive way. Washington was not "disinterested" and "selfless," but neither was he narrowly "selfish." He had a deep and healthy self-love that found fulfillment in striving to always comport himself in an honorable way that would bring lasting benefits to others. It would entail great personal sacrifice, but there would be much to savor in such a course, standing unmoved and unbowed throughout the travails connected to his life of public service. Words from Addison's *Cato* seem applicable:

> Thou has seen Mount Atlas:
> While storms and tempests thunder on its brows,
> And oceans break their billows at its feet,
> It stands unmoved, and glories in its height.
> Such is that haughty man [Cato, or in this case, Washington];
>   his towering soul,

Midst all the shocks and injuries of fortune,
Rises superior . . .

In the end, given the difficult choices he found himself facing, Washington concluded that only a life of continued public service was truly worthy of him and his talents.

A French admirer, the Marquis de Chastellux, recorded his impression of the American commander. He was struck by "the perfect harmony which reigns between the physical and moral qualities which compose his personality. . . . It is not my intention to exaggerate. I wish only to express the impression General Washington has left on my mind, the idea of a *perfect whole*" (emphasis added). A "perfect whole" doesn't mean a man without any flaws or shortcomings. This work has pointed out many. But when we view George Washington as a total entity, the image of a perfect whole rings true. It focuses our attention on the remarkable balance of powerful forces within Washington—in effect, one man's separation of powers. Here was a rare man who combined personal charisma and leadership skills in such a way to be potentially, in Abigail Adams's words, "a very dangerous" man. And yet, because George Washington was "one of the best intentioned men in the world," he used his remarkable gifts in the "glorious cause" of expanding liberty and republican values, not only for his generation of Americans but for "millions unborn" around the globe. Unlike most of the powerful leaders of his time (and since), George Washington realized that the true glory of a leader must ultimately "depend on the prosperity and happiness of his People." In the final analysis, character is the decisive factor in the life of an individual, and it was the greatness of Washington's character that so distinguishes him as America's "matchless man." To paraphrase the equally immortal William Shakespeare, "Take his character all together, and we shall not look upon his like again."

Notes on Sources

Abbreviations

PAH	*The Papers of Alexander Hamilton*
MVLA	Mount Vernon Ladies' Association

The abbreviations for the University of Virginia's edition (1983–) of the *Papers of George Washington* (*PGW*) are as follows:

PGWCL	Colonial Series (1744–1775)
PGWRV	Revolutionary War Series (1775–1783)
PGWCF	Confederation Series (1784–1788)
PGWP	Presidential Series (1788–1797)
PGWRT	Retirement Series (1797–1799)

Preface

ix   *"I fancy the skill"*: George Washington (GW) to Jonathan Boucher, 21 May 1772, *PGWCL* 9:49.

x   *"No great man in history"*: Noemie Emery, *George Washington: A Biography* (New York, 1976), 13–14.
"the most ambitious": Joseph Ellis, *His Excellency* (New York, 2004), xiv.

xi   *"that is the striking thing"*: Interview with the Objectivist Center: http://www.objectivistcenter/articles/interview_american-enlightenment-other-side.asp
As Don Higginbotham: This point is from Edward Lengel, *General George Washington: A Military Life* (New York, 2005), 370.
"Historians try mightily": William Safire, *Scandalmonger: A Novel* (San Diego, 2000), 445.

1. His First Proving Ground

The most valuable single source was the first six volumes of the Colonial Series of the magisterial new edition of the *Papers of George Washington* (University of Virginia Press, 1983–), especially the correspondence between George Washington and Governor Dinwiddie. The single best treatment of the French and Indian War is *Crucible of War* by Fred Anderson (New York, 2001). Chapter 5 is particularly helpful in understanding the Jumonville Affair and the surrender of Fort Necessity. Two recent books were also very useful. *George Washington Remembers* (Oxford, 2004) contains an annotated edition of George Washington's "Remarks" on the war, which he prepared for his aide, David Humphreys, along with three fine essays by Don Higginbotham, Rosemarie Zagarri, and Fred Anderson. I drew particularly on Anderson's essay in discussing the war's impact on Washington. Also very helpful in that regard is the first chapter of *His Excellency* (New York, 2004) by Joseph Ellis, which promises to be the most significant study of Washington in many years. I drew very heavily on Guthrie Sayen's excellent and underutilized unpublished dissertation, "'A Compleat Gentleman': The Making of George Washington, 1732–1775" (Ph.D. dissertation, University of Connecticut, 1988), for Washington's relationship with both Generals Loudoun and Forbes. Ed Lengel's new work, *General George Washington: A Military Life* (New York, 2005), was very helpful. Paul Longmore's *The Invention of George Washington* (California, 1988) is full of good insights. Two older but complete and interesting treatments of this period are Douglas Southall Freeman's *George Washington*, 7 vols. (New York, 1948–1957), especially volume 2, and James Flexner's lively *George Washington and the Forge of Experience* (Boston, 1965). Thomas Lewis's *For King and Country* (New York, 1993) takes a different interpretation than I do, but it is also a lively read with much on Native Americans, including narratives of their atrocities. John Ferling's *First of Men* (Knoxville, 1988) is rather unsympathetic to Washington, but is well worth reading for his treatment of Washington and the French and Indian War.

1   *"If it be a sin to covet honor"*: William Shakespeare, *Henry V*, act 4, scene 3.
     "born with his clothes on, and his hair powdered": Thomas Woodson, ed., *The Centenary Edition of the Works of Nathaniel Hawthorne* (Columbus, Ohio, 1980) 14:281.
     "I can't tell a lie": Mason Locke Weems, *The Life of Washington*, ed. Peter Onuf (New York, 1996), 10.

2   *"Never did nature"*: Thomas Jefferson (TJ) to Dr. Walter Jones, 2 January 1814, in Merrill Peterson, ed., *Thomas Jefferson: Writings* (New York, 1984), 1318.
     "every hour mispent": GW to George Steptoe Washington, 5 December 1790, *PGWP* 7:32.
     "Throughout his life, the ambition": Paul Longmore, *The Invention of George Washington* (California, 1988), 1.
     "You are to require of Them": The British warning to the French is quoted in *PGWCL* 1:57.

3 *"My inclinations are strongly bent to arms"*: GW to William Fitzhugh, 15 November 1754, *PGWCL* 1:226.

"They told me": George Washington's *Journal*, quoted in Dorothy Twohig, ed., *George Washington Diaries: An Abridgement* (Charlottesville, 1999), 23.

5 *"We daily Experience"*: GW to Robert Dinwiddie, 9 March 1754, *PGWCL* 1:73–74.

"manage a number of selfwill'd": GW to Robert Dinwiddie, 20 March 1754, *PGWCL* 1:78.

6 *a warrant for his arrest*: Lewis, *For King and Country*, 133.

"being too ambitious": Quoted in Longmore, *Invention*, 24.

7 *Anderson asserts that the massacre of the wounded*: Fred Anderson, *Crucible of War* (New York, 2001), 55–59.

"There were 5, or 6 other Indian": GW to Robert Dinwiddie, 3 June 1754, *PGWCL* 1:124. I want to acknowledge my debt to Ed Lengel for pointing this out.

"I heard Bulletts whistle": GW to John Augustine Washington, 31 May 1754, *PGWCL* 1:118.

"If the whole Detach[ment]t of the French": GW to Robert Dinwiddie, 3 June 1754, *PGWCL* 1:124.

8 *"There is nothing more unworthy"*: Most of this is quoted in Ellis, *Excellency*, 17–18.

"the most infamous": Quoted in Flexner, *Forge of Experience*, 107.

"That we were wilfully": GW to unknown recipient, ca. 1757, *PGWCL* 1:169–70.

"detachment to reconnoitre": GW's "Remarks," in Fred Anderson, ed., *George Washington Remembers* (Oxford, 2004), 17.

"It was a madly ambitious plan": Anderson, *Crucible of War*, 88.

9 *"Who is there"*: GW to Sally Cary Fairfax, 25 September 1758, *PGWCL* 6:42.

10 *"Death was levelling"*: GW to John Augustine Washington, 18 July 1755, *PGWCL* 1:343.

"He seemed in the grip": John Ferling, *First of Men* (Knoxville, 1988), 58.

"There is something unlikable": Marcus Cunliffe, *Man and Monument* (Mount Vernon, 1998), 40.

11 *"His ingratitude and his treachery"*: Guthrie Sayen, "'A Compleat Gentleman': The Making of George Washington, 1732–1775" (Ph.D. dissertation, University of Connecticut, 1988), 6.

"This Proceeding, I am affraid": Robert Dinwiddie to GW, 10 December 1756, *PGWCL* 4:51.

"imbibed prejudices": GW to Robert Dinwiddie, 19 December 1756, *PGWCL* 4:64–65.

12 *"He condemned local authorities"*: Sayen, "A Compleat Gentleman," 63.

"Altho' I have not the Honour": GW to John Campbell, Earl of Loudoun, 10 January 1757, *PGWCL* 4:89.

12   *The Earl "dismissed George Washington"*: Flexner, *Forge of Experience*, 175.
13   *"I wish I was sent immediately home"*: GW to John Robinson, 1 September
      1758, *PGWCL* 5:433.
      "By a very unguarded letter": John Forbes to Henry Bouquet, 9 August 1758,
      Alfred Procter James, ed., *Writings of General John Forbes Relating to His
      Service in North America*, 170–71, quoted in *PGWCL* 5:377 n.2.
      "no ways like a Soldier": John Forbes to Henry Bouquet, 4 September
      1758, Sylvester K. Stevens et al., eds., *The Papers of Henry Bouquet*, 5 vols.
      (Harrisburg, Pa., 1951–), 2:477–78, quoted in *PGWCL*, 6:3 n.2.
      "and his own great merit": Quoted in Ellis, *Excellency*, 5.
14   *Robert Orme: "My dear friend"*: Orme to GW, 10 November 1755, *PGWCL*
      2:165.
      Robert Munford: "our colonel": Quoted in Flexner, *Forge of Experience*, 159.
      William Ramsay: "Your disinterestedness": Quoted in Freeman, *George
      Washington*, 2:212.
      Governor Robert Dinwiddie: "He is a person much beloved": Dinwiddie to James
      Abercromby, 28 May 1756, Dinwiddie Papers, Virginia Historical Society,
      Richmond, quoted in *PGWCL* 3:181 n.12.
      Governor William Shirley: "No provisional officer": Quoted in Don Higginbotham,
      "Young Washington: Ambition, Accomplishment, and Acclaim," in Anderson,
      GW Remembers, 80.
      Rev. Samuel Davies: "uncommon bravery, conduct, and knowledge": Ibid., 84
      John Robinson: "I have never heard": Robinson to GW, 16 November 1756,
      PGWCL 4:28–29.
      George William Fairfax: "[I] beg that you'l freely": Fairfax to GW, 9 May
      1756, *PGWCL* 3:108.
15   *"heroick Virtue"*: Lengel, *General George Washington*, 62.
      "his faithful services": Freeman, *George Washington*, 3:6.
      "Sit down, Mr. Washington": Lewis, *For King including Country*, 273.
      Excerpts from the tribute: Address from the Officers of the Virginia Regiment,
      December 1758, *PGWCL* 6:179.
      George Mercer penned a detailed physical description: Quoted in Flexner, *Forge
      of Experience*, 191–92.
16   *"His stature was exactly what one would wish"*: TJ to Dr. Walter Jones, 2
      January 1814, in Peterson, *Jefferson: Writings*, 1318.
      "A deportment so firm": Monroe, quoted in David McCullough, *1776* (New
      York, 2005), 247.
      Patronage was the basic: Gordon Wood, *The Americanization of Benjamin
      Franklin* (New York, 2004), 26.
17   *"Live in perfect harmony"*: GW to John Augustine Washington, 28 May
      1755, *PGWCL* 1:289.
      "I have now a good oppertunity": GW to John Augustine Washington, 14
      May 1755, *PGWCL* 1:278.
      "powerful Virginia elders": Freeman, *George Washington*, 2:384.
      "By combining an acute sense": Longmore, *Invention*, 52.

17 "*I have been posted*": GW to Richard Washington, 15 April 1757, *PGWCL* 4:132.

"*Desolation and murder still increase*": GW to Robert Dinwiddie, 27 April 1756, *PGWCL* 3:59.

18 "*I cannot conceive the best white men*": GW to Henry Bouquet, 16 July 1758, *PGWCL* 5:292.

"*No troops in the universe*": GW to John Robinson, 25 October 1757, *PGWCL* 5:33.

"*the most insolent*": GW to Robert Dinwiddie, 24 May 1757, *PGWCL* 4:163.

"*plunder, kill*": GW to John Robinson, 9 November 1756, *PGWCL* 4:12.

19 "*prowl about like Wolves*": GW to Robert Dinwiddie, 7 April 1756, *PGWCL* 2:333.

"*The timidity of the inhabitants*": GW to John Robinson, 16 April 1756, *PGWCL* 3:6.

"*You may, with almost equal success*": GW to John Augustine Washington, 28 May 1755, *PGWCL* 1:289.

"*In all things I meet with*": GW to Robert Dinwiddie, 11 October 1755, *PGWCL* 2:102.

"*I am very sorry*": GW to Denis McCarty, 22 November 1755, *PGWCL* 2:176.

20 "*They are obstinate*": GW to Robert Dinwiddie, 9 November 1756, *PGWCL* 4:2.

"*the first in arms, of any Troops*": and "*If it shou'd be said the Troops of Virginia*": GW to Robert Dinwiddie, 10 March 1757, *PGWCL* 4:112–13.

"*acquired these skills*": Anderson, *Crucible*, 290.

21 "*One has to be impressed*": Higginbotham, "Young Washington," in Anderson, *GW Remembers*, 80.

"*a connection between . . . the interior regions*": Ellis, *Excellency*, 7.

"*Instead of going to college*": Ibid., 12–13.

22 "*in as much jeopardy*": GW's "Remarks" in Anderson, *GW Remembers*, 23.

"*The shocking Scenes*": Ibid., 20.

"*The supplicating tears*": GW to Robert Dinwiddie, 22 April 1756, *PGWCL* 3:34, 33.

23 "*That appearance of Glory*": GW to John Robinson, 1 September 1758, *PGWCL* 5:432.

"*I am now I beleive fixd at this Seat with an agreable Consort*": GW to Richard Washington, 20 September 1759, *PGWCL* 6:359.

2. Taking Command

There are of course many excellent sources on George Washington and the coming of the war. Two of the best are Paul Longmore's *Invention of George Washington* (California, 1988) and Guthrie Sayen's dissertation, "'A Compleat Gentleman': The Making of George Washington, 1732–1775" (University of Connecticut, 1988). His letters to Bryan Fairfax are the best statement of Washington's philosophy for resisting British actions. They are compiled in Donald Sweig, editor, *Fairfax Friendship* (Fairfax, 1982). The most recent treatment, with numerous insightful comments, is chapter 2 of Joseph Ellis's study *His Excellency* (New York, 2004). Noemie Emery's *George Washington: A Biography* (New York, 1976) is little known but very interesting and readable, with a strong dose of psychohistory. An early study emphasizing that Washington was more involved on the road to revolution than traditionally believed is Curtis P. Nettels, *George Washington and American Independence* (Boston, 1951).

25   *"There is a tide in the affairs":* William Shakespeare, *Julius Caesar,* act 4, scene 2, lines 269–76.

26   *"Good Breeding," wrote John Locke:* Quoted in Sayen, "A Compleat Gentleman," 20. I want to particularly acknowledge my major debt to Sayen's work, which informs the next couple of pages.

27   *as Paul Longmore effectively demonstrates:* Longmore, *Invention,* chapter 6, is excellent on this point.

28   *"I hope, and indeed make no doubt":* GW to Van Swearingen, 15 May 1761, *PGWCL* 7:43.

       "code of noblesse oblige": Douglas Southall Freeman, *George Washington* (New York, 1948), 3:185.

29   *"He was excessively":* Ellis, *Excellency,* 46.

       "the cream of the crop": Quoted in James Flexner, *George Washington and the Forge of Experience* (Boston, 1965), 300.

       "If it had not been for my unremitting attention": GW to Charles Mynn Thurston, 13 March 1773, *PGWCL* 9:198.

30   *As Linda Colley has argued:* Colley develops the theme of British nationalism in detail in her book, *Britons: Forging a Nation* (New Haven, Conn., and London, 1992).

       "The English now": Gordon Wood, *The Americanization of Benjamin Franklin* (New York, 2004), 113.

       "We cant conceive": GW to Robert Dinwiddie, 10 March 1757, *PGWCL* 4:113.

31   *"I conceive the services":* GW to Thomas Lewis, 17 February 1774, *PGWCL* 9:483.

32   *"I can never look":* GW to William Crawford, 17 September 1767, *PGWCL* 8:28.

33   *"Events were swirling":* John Ferling, *First of Men* (Knoxville, 1988), 85.

       "At a time when our lordly Masters": GW to George Mason, 5 April 1769, *PGWCL* 8:178.

34   *"Washington was putting":* Willard Sterne Randall, *George Washington: A Life* (New York, 1997), 236.

       "I never forgot your declaration": Arthur Lee to GW, 15 June 1777, *PGWRV* 10:43–44.

       "Does it not appear": GW to Bryan Fairfax, 4 July 1774, *PGWCL* 10:109–10.

35   *"Shall we supinely sit":* GW to Bryan Fairfax, 20 July 1774, *PGWCL* 10:130–31.

35　*"An Innate Spirit of freedom"*: GW to Bryan Fairfax, 24 August 1774, *PGWCL* 10:155.

　　"are every day receiving fresh proofs": GW to Robert Mackenzie, 9 October 1774, *PGWCL* 10:171.

　　"I am as well satisfied . . . more blood will be spilt": Ibid., 172.

36　*"Unhappy it is though to reflect"*: GW to George William Fairfax, 31 May 1775, *PGWCL* 10:368.

　　"devote my Life and Fortune": GW to John Augustine Washington, 25 March 1775, *PGWCL* 10:308.

38　*"He has so much martial dignity"*: Benjamin Rush to Thomas Rushton, 29 October 1775, *Letters of Benjamin Rush*, ed. L. H. Butterfield, 2 vols. (Princeton, N.J., 1951), 1:92.

　　"The more I am acquainted": Quoted in Sayen, "A Compleat Gentleman," 204.

　　"no harum Starum ranting fellow": Ibid.

　　"He is a complete gentleman": Ibid., 205.

　　As Guthrie Sayen explains: Ibid., 205–6.

39　he agreeably blended the gentleman and the soldier: Abigail Adams quoted in Longmore, *Invention*, 182.

　　"The Master of Mount Vernon" Don Higginbotham, *George Washington: Uniting a Nation* (Lanham, Md., 2002), 6.

　　"he removes all jealousies": Quoted in Emery, *Washington*, 179.

　　"I have used every endeavor": GW to Martha Washington, 18 June 1775, *PGWRV* 1:3.

40　*"My inclinations"*: GW to William Fitzhugh, 15 November 1754, *PGWCL* 1:226.

　　"be distinguished": GW to Thomas Gage, 12 April 1758, *PGWCL* 5:126.

　　"Who is there": GW to Sally Cary Fairfax, 25 September 1758, *PGWCL* 6:142.

　　wearing a brand-new uniform: On new uniform, see editorial note, *PGWCL* 10:174, where Lund Washington paid for "GW Regimentals" in November 1774.

41　If we look at his subsequent life: I wish to credit John Riley for this observation.

　　"His claim that he had no interest": Ellis, *Excellency*, 70–71.

42　As Longmore observes, he carefully regarded appearances: Longmore, *Invention*, 32.

43　*"I date my fall and the ruin"*: Quoted in James Flexner, *George Washington in the American Revolution* (Boston, 1967), 9.

3. "A Kind of Inevitable Necessity"

There are a number of excellent studies on George Washington's presidency which informed this chapter. Perhaps most valuable was chapter 6 of Joseph Ellis's book *His Excellency* (New York, 2004). Others were Richard Norton Smith's *Patriarch: George Washington and the New American Nation* (New York, 1993); James MacGregor Burns and Susan Dunn's *George Washington: President of the United States of America, 1789–1797* (New York, 2004); Jack D. Warren's *The Presidency of George Washington* (Mount Vernon, 2001); and Glenn A. Phelps's *George Washington and American Constitutionalism* (Kansas, 1993). Frank T. Reuter's *Trials and Triumphs: George Washington's Foreign Policy* (Fort Worth, 1983) is very helpful on its subject matter. Paul M. Zall, editor, *Washington on Washington* (Kentucky, 2003) presents a nice compilation of quotes illustrating Washington's perspective. Helpful articles included Seymour Martin Lipset, "George Washington and the Founding of Democracy," in *Journal of Democracy* 9:4 (1998), 24–38, and Todd Estes, "The Art of Presidential Leadership: George Washington and the Jay Treaty," in *The Virginia Magazine of History and Biography* 109:2 (2001), 127–58.

45 *"Necessity so bowed":* William Shakespeare, Henry IV, second part, act 3, scene 1.

   "Throughout all [this country]": The chaplain was Abbé Claude Robin. Quoted in Gilbert Chinard, *George Washington as the French Knew Him* (Princeton, 1940), 69.

   "Oh, Washington": Quoted in Gordon S. Wood, "The Greatness of George Washington," *Virginia Quarterly Review* 68 (Spring 1992), 190.

   "the best and greatest man": Quoted in Ellis, *Excellency,* 147.

46 *"Other men might want":* Douglas Southall Freeman, *George Washington* (New York, 1948), 5:500.

   King George III declared: Quoted in Gordon S. Wood, *The Radicalism of the American Revolution* (New York: Vintage Books, 1993), 206.

   the greatest exit in American history: Ellis, *Excellency,* 146–47.

   "Washington was not naïve": Wood, *Radicalism of the American Revolution,* 206.

47 *"At this auspicious period":* GW, Circular Letter to the States, 8 June 1783, in John C. Fitzpatrick, ed., *Writings of George Washington,* 39 vols. (Washington, D.C., 1931–39), 26:485.

   "Their local views": Glenn A. Phelps, *George Washington and American Constitutionalism* (Kansas, 1993), 57.

   "a secret and powerful influence": James McHenry to GW, 29 March 1789, *PGWP* 1:461.

   "Be assured": Quoted in James Flexner, *George Washington and the New Nation* (Boston, 1969), 139.

48 *"Energy in the executive":* The quote is from *Federalist Paper No. 70,* written by Alexander Hamilton.

   "Entre nous": The delegate was Pierce Butler from Maryland. See Flexner, *GW and the New Nation,* 134.

   "Your cool steady Temper": Gouverneur Morris to GW, 30 October 1787, *PGWCF* 5:400.

49 *"the ten thousand embarrassments":* GW to Samuel Vaughan, 21 March 1789, *PGWP* 1:424.

   "The great Searcher": GW to William Gordon, 23 December 1788, *PGWP* 1:200.

49 *"a kind of inevitable necessity"*: GW to Gouverneur Morris, 28 November 1788, *PGWP* 1:136.

"my refusal might induce": GW to Benjamin Lincoln, 26 October 1788, *PGWP* 1:71.

50 *"sacrifice of inclination to the opinion of duty"*: From Washington's Farewell Address.

"Like you, my dear Sir": GW to Lafayette, 19 March 1791, Fitzpatrick, *Writings* 31:249.

"with a mind oppressed": GW *Diaries*, 16 April 1789. Quoted in Dorothy Twohig, ed., *George Washington Diaries: An Abridgement* (Charlottesville, 1999), 338.

"My movements": GW to Henry Knox, 1 April 1789, *PGWP* 2:2.

"You are now a King": James McHenry to GW, 29 March 1789, *PGWP* 1:461.

"central figure in an extended rite": This point is taken from Stanley Elkins and Eric McKitrick, *The Age of Federalism* (New York, 1993), 45.

"The whole city": Quoted in *PGWP* 2:114.

"achievement must be recovered": Ellis, *Excellency*, 188.

51 *"to bind America together." The Unifier*: Don Higginbotham, *George Washington: Uniting a Nation* (Lanham, Md., 2002), 2.

"Many things which appear": GW, *Queries on a Line of Conduct to be Pursued by the President*, 10 May 1789, Fitzpatrick, *Writings*, 30:321.

"My political conduct": GW to Bushrod Washington, 27 July 1789, *PGWP* 3:334.

52 *Joanne Freeman*: The last section of this paragraph is taken almost verbatim from Joanne Freeman, *Affairs of Honor* (New Haven, 2001), 45–46.

"modest dignity which excited involuntary respect": James Madison as quoted in Stuart Leibiger, *Founding Friendship: George Washington, James Madison, and the Creation of the American Republic* (Charlottesville, 1999), 225.

Americans got charisma: Flexner, *GW and the New Nation*, 423.

sat for innumerable portraits: This point is developed in Higginbotham, *Uniting*, 60.

53 *the embodiment of the new nation*: Smith, *Patriarch*, 87, which informs several points in the paragraph.

"genius": Edmund Morgan's little volume, *The Genius of George Washington* (New York, 1977) is rightly viewed as a classic.

54 *"No man, I believe"*: Quoted in Flexner, *GW and the New Nation*, 223.

"The establishment of our new Governmant": GW to Catharine Macauley Graham, 9 January 1790, *PGWP* 4:552.

the national government, in the Revolutionary decade: Bernard Bailyn, *To Begin the World Anew* (New York, 2003), 132.

What was politically essential: Ellis, *Excellency*, 190. Much of this paragraph comes from Ellis.

"a kind of Fabian presidency": Ibid., 214.

55 *"What strikes us as a poignant failure"*: Ibid., 202.

55 *"Our public credit stands"*: GW to David Humphreys, 20 July 1791, *PGWP* 8:359.

56 *"implied that there was"*: Phelps, *American Constitutionalism*, 81.

"It will be our prudence": GW to James McHenry, 13 December 1798, *PGWRT* 3:253. While this quote is from a later date, I believe it accurately summarizes GW's view of the crisis while he was president.

58 *Jay's appointment was criticized:* Quotes from Walter Stahr, *John Jay* (New York and London, 2005), 319.

"No nation is to be trusted": GW to Henry Laurens, 14 November 1778, Fitzpatrick, *Writings*, 13:256.

59 *"There can be no greater error"*: GW Farewell Address, 19 September 1796. The Farewell Address is reprinted in Matthew Spalding, *A Sacred Union of Citizens* (Lanham, Md., 1996), 175ff. The book contains much valuable information on this historic document.

"May it please": Quoted in Stahr, *John Jay*, 336.

"Damn John Jay": Quoted in Ron Chernow, *Alexander Hamilton* (New York, 2004), 486.

"At present the cry": GW to Alexander Hamilton, 29 July 1795, Fitzpatrick, *Writings*, 34:262.

60 *"the public mind in a higher degree"*: GW to Thomas Pinckney, 22 May 1796, Fitzpatrick, *Writings*, 35:62.

"the sacred fire of liberty": GW, First Inaugural Address, 30 April 1789, *PGWP* 2:175.

"For sure I am": GW to Gouverneur Morris, 22 December 1795, Fitzpatrick, *Writings*, 34:401.

"Men in responsible situations": GW to Duc de la Rochefoucauld, 8 August 1796, Fitzpatrick, *Writings*, 35:167.

"While I feel the most lively gratitude": GW to Boston Selectmen, 28 July 1795, Fitzpatrick, *Writings*, 34:253.

61 *"Next to a conscientious"*: GW to Henry Knox, 20 September 1795, Fitzpatrick, *Writings*, 34:310.

GW *"acted boldly and forthrightly"*: Estes, "The Art of Presidential Leadership," 127.

"The President will not see the country wronged": Citizen quoted ibid., 146.

"No sooner did General Washington": Benjamin Rush to John Adams, 13 June 1811, *Letters of Benjamin Rush*, ed. L. H. Butterfield, 2 vols. (Princeton, N.J., 1951), 2:1084.

"The name of the President": Quoted in Leibiger, *Founding Friendship*, 203.

62 *"Brilliantly fusing constitutionality"*: Estes, "The Art of Presidential Leadership," 152.

63 *"The Nation, which indulges"*: GW Farewell Address, 19 September 1796. Quoted in Spalding, *A Sacred Union of Citizens*, 175ff.

"The Unity of Government": Ibid.

"these national exhortations": Ellis, *Excellency*, 236.

64 *After the inauguration, Washington went back:* This paragraph is essentially

taken in total from an editorial by historian and author, Thomas Fleming, celebrating President's Day in 2004.

64   *"The world will be puzzled"*: Quoted in James Flexner, *George Washington, Anguish and Farewell* (Boston, 1969), 4:324.

   "If ever there was a period": Quoted in Richard N. Rosenfeld, *American Aurora* (New York, 1997), 31. The last half of the quote is from Barry Schwartz, *George Washington, The Making of an American Symbol* (New York, 1987), 68.

66   *"destiny of the republican model"*: GW, First Inaugural Address, 30 April 1789, *PGWP* 2:175.

4. "A Votary to Love"

There were a number of very useful sources which I consulted in preparing this chapter. The best presentation of the view I considered but ultimately rejected is Don Higginbotham's "George Washington and Three Women," in Tamara Harvey and Gregg O'Brien, *George Washington's South* (Gainesville, Florida, 2004), 121–42. Bernard Knollenberg, *George Washington: The Virginia Period, 1732–1775* (Durham, 1964), is good on the history of the letter. While emphasizing different aspects of the story, I found the following works most helpful: Wilson Miles Cary, *Sally Cary: A Long Hidden Romance of Washington's Life* (New York, 1916); Rupert Hughes, *George Washington: The Human Being and the Hero, 1732–1762* (New York, 1926), 398–419; John Alden, *George Washington: A Biography* (Baton Rouge, 1984), 73–80; William Rasmussen and Robert Tilton, *George Washington: The Man behind the Myth* (Charlottesville, 1999); James Flexner, *George Washington and the Forge of Experience* (Boston, 1965), 196–205; and Noemie Emery, *George Washington: A Biography* (New York, 1976), 126–37.

67   *"Tis true, I profess myself"*: GW to Sally Cary Fairfax, 12 September 1758, *PGWCL* 6:11.

   New York Herald: Bernard Knollenberg, *George Washington: The Virginia Period, 1732–1775* (Durham, 1964), 59–61.

   "If it still exists": Nathaniel Wright Stephenson, "The Romantics and George Washington," *American Historical Review*, January, 1934, 275.

68   *"the surviving letters are ambiguous."*: Richard Brookhiser, *Founding Father: Rediscovering George Washington* (New York, 1996), 7.

   "We know that in September 1758": Higginbotham, "Three Women," 127–28.

   "If GW were so completely": John C. Fitzpatrick, *George Washington Himself* (Indianapolis, 1933), 110–11.

   "Historians try mightily": William Safire, *Scandalmonger: A Novel* (San Diego, 2000), 445.

69   *"Dear Madam"*: GW to Sally Cary Fairfax, 12 September 1758, *PGWCL* 6:10–12.

70   *"peppered their letters"*: Peter Gay, quoted in Higginbotham, "Three Women," 128, from which this paragraph is drawn.

   "can be downright impudent": Martha Dangerfield Bland to Frances Bland Randolph, 12 April 1777, Proceedings of the New Jersey Historical Society, July, 1933, 152.

70 *"if you will come and dine"*: GW to Annis Boudinot Stockton, 2 September 1783, John C. Fitzpatrick, ed., *Writings of George Washington*, 39 vols. (Washington, D.C., 1931–39), 27:127–28.

71 *"Once the woman"*: Ibid., 128.

"a lesson in the School for Scandal": GW to Eliza Powel, 30 July 1787, *PGWCF* 5:280.

"I have a heart": GW to Lafayette, 30 September 1779, Fitzpatrick, *Writings*, 16:375.

"The first [letter] Mrs. Fairfax undertakes": George William Fairfax to GW, 1 September 1758, *PGWCL* 5:436.

72 *"absurdities of misinterpretation"*: Douglas Southall Freeman, *George Washington* (New York, 1948), 2:338 n.75.

"Misfortunes never come singly": Quoted in Rasmussen and Tilton, *Man behind the Myth*, 24.

73 *The inventory of items for sale:* Ibid., 26.

"In all he did, young Washington": Paul Longmore, *The Invention of George Washington* (California, 1988), 16.

"Although he had given": Flexner, *Forge of Experience*, 77.

"make me happier": GW to Sally Cary Fairfax, 7 June 1755, *PGWCL* 1:308.

"He undoubtedly learned": Higginbotham, "Three Women," 131.

74 *"Washington was almost twenty-seven"*: John Alden, *George Washington: A Biography* (Baton Rouge, 1984), 73.

"his austerity in the arms": John Kirkpatrick to GW, 23 August 1758, *PGWCL* 5:414.

"A great Imperfection": George Mercer to GW, 17 August 1757, *PGWCL* 4:371.

"I imagine you By this": William La Péronie to GW, 5 September 1754, *PGWCL* 1:203. I want to thank Guthrie Sayen for comment on Nell.

75 *"To asswage her Melancholy"*: Gouverneur Morris to GW, 12 November 1788, *PGWP* 1:104.

"At present, tho' young": GW to William Fitzhugh Jr., 15 May 1786, *PGWCF* 4:52.

"I feel myself much": GW to Richard Sprigg, 28 June 1786, *PGWCF* 4:134.

to Royal Gift's credit: Frank Grizzard, *George Washington: A Biographical Companion* (Santa Barbara, 2002), 153.

"I am glad to hear": GW to William Gordon, 20 December 1784, *PGWCF* 2:197.

76 *"I beg that you'll freely"*: George William Fairfax to GW, 9 May 1756, *PGWCL* 3:108.

"quivering white rabbit,": Flexner, *Forge of Experience*, 202.

77 *to ask for her help in procuring medicines:* GW to Sally Cary Fairfax, 15 November 1757, *PGWCL* 5:56.

"if you will not come": Sally Cary Fairfax to GW, 26 July 1755, *PGWCL* 1:346.

78 *"In the composition"*: GW to Eleanor Parke Custis, 16 January 1795, Fitzpatrick, *Writings*, 34:92.

"A hint here": Ibid., 91.

"Experience will convince you": GW to Elizabeth Parke Custis, 14 September 1794, Ibid., 33:501.

his close friend, Captain Robert Stewart: The editors of the *George Washington Papers* make this point in their editorial notes. See *PGWCL* 6:13.

79 *"George Washington was going to marry"*: Freeman, *George Washington*, 2:338 n.75.

"When I viewed them": GW to George William Fairfax, 27 February 1785, *PGWCF* 2:386–87.

80 *"produced many tears"*: George William Fairfax to GW, 23 June 1785, *PGWCF* 3:78.

Lawrence Washington accused the Reverend Charles Green: Peter R. Henriques, "Major Lawrence Washington Versus the Reverend Charles Green: A Case Study of the Squire and the Parson," *Virginia Magazine of History and Biography* 100 (1992), 233–64.

"another sex-scandal": Higginbotham, "Three Women," 131.

"Dear Madam: Do we still misunderstand": GW to Sally Cary Fairfax, 25 September 1758, *PGWCL* 6:41.

81 *"sent Washington a coded message"*: Willard Sterne Randall, *George Washington: A Life* (New York, 1997), 181.

82 *Sally's handsome mahogany double chest of drawers:* A good description of the items for sale is in Rasmussen and Tilton, *Man behind the Myth*, 26.

"It has been suggested": Higginbotham, "Three Women," 128.

"without choking up": Thomas Lewis, *For King and Country* (New York, 1993), 25.

83 *"nor all of them together"*: GW to Sally Cary Fairfax, 16 May 1798, *PGWRT* 2:272.

"Surely it was no small": Flexner, *Forge of Experience*, 203–4.

"George William was not just another husband": Emery, *Washington*, 133.

84 *"In the end, however much"*: Alden, *George Washington*, 80.

"His letter, however confusing": Hughes, *Human Being and Hero*, 410.

5. From an "Agreable Consort" to "My Dear Patsy"

At the time of writing this chapter, the published sources on Martha Washington are generally disappointing. Most early biographies of Martha are more hagiography than biography. I found Helen Bryan's *Martha Washington: First Lady of Liberty* (New York, 2002) to lack a good grasp of both her subject and eighteenth-century Virginia. Much better, and very helpful to me in writing this chapter, is the little biography of Martha written by Ellen McCallister Clark and published by the Mount Vernon Ladies' Association in 2002. Coming out just as I finished my chapter, Patricia Brady's new biography, *Martha Washington: An American Life* (New York, 2005), promises to be the most important study to date. Martha's scanty collection of papers are gathered together in one volume, *Worthy Partner*, edited by Joseph Fields (Westport, Connecticut, 1994), although Martha often copied letters written by either her husband or Tobias Lear. Her numerous letters to her niece, Fanny Bassett, are the most revealing. Sections of the major George Washington biographies by Douglas Southall Freeman and James Flexner both contain interesting material on the subject. The most valuable cache of information, however, is contained in an unpublished collection of material on Martha Washington compiled by and housed in the library of the Mount Vernon Ladies' Association (MVLA). Research historian Mary Thompson is a fount of knowledge on the subject.

85   *"I have always considered marriage"*: GW to Burwell Bassett, 23 May 1785, *PGWCF* 3:10.

     "What would you have been": Quoted in Helen Bryan, *Martha Washington: First Lady of Liberty* (New York, 2002), 2.

86   *some deep secret*: Martha's burning of the letters is the backdrop for the best historical novel on GW: William Martin, *Citizen Washington* (New York, 1999).

     "the world has no business knowing": GW to Sally Cary Fairfax, 12 September 1758, *PGWCL* 6:11.

87   *The Custis estate*: The information about the estate of Martha Custis is drawn from Guthrie Sayen, "'A Compleat Gentleman': The Making of George Washington, 1732–1775" (Ph.D. dissertation, University of Connecticut, 1988), 142.

88   *"small with lively eyes"*: Julian Niemcewicz, a Polish nobleman who visited Mount Vernon. This is one of the various quotes about Martha Washington collected by researchers at Mount Vernon, and is in the library of the Mount Vernon Ladies' Association, Mount Vernon, Virginia.

     "retains strong remains": Benjamin Latrobe, ibid.

     "has the remains": William Thornton, ibid.

     "buxom, yet small and delicate": Don Higginbotham, "George Washington and Three Women," in Tamara Harvey and Gregg O'Brien, *George Washington's South* (Gainesville, Florida, 2004), 133.

89   *"raised emotional support"*: Patricia Brady, *Martha Washington: An American Life* (New York, 2005), 35.

     "everything that is benevolent and good": Tobias Lear. Collection of quotes about Martha Washington, MVLA.

     "create love and esteem": Abigail Adams in Stewart Mitchell, ed., *New Letters of Abigail Adams, 1788–1801* (Boston, 1947), 15.

     "appeared to me": Collection of quotes about Martha Washington, MVLA.

     "like two cats": William North to Ben Walker, 9 March 1784. Copy at MVLA.

     "This comes at last": John Power to Daniel Parke Custis, n.d. (probably 1749). Quoted in Mary V. Thompson, "'An Agreable Consort for Life': The Wedding of George and Martha Washington," *Historic Alexandria Quarterly*, Fall, 2001, 3.

90   *"I am now I beleive fixd"*: GW to Richard Washington, 20 September 1759, *PGWCL* 6:359.

90 *"My Dearest":* This is a compilation of two letters: GW to Martha Washington, 18 June 1775, *PGWRV* 1:3–5, and GW to Martha Washington, 23 June 1775, *PGWRV* 1:27.

91 *"I shall hope that my Friends":* GW to John Augustine Washington, 20 June 1775, *PGWRV* 1:20.

"Washington, age 43": Higginbotham, "Three Women," 133.

"the great perambulator": Quoted in Higginbotham, ed., *George Washington Reconsidered* (Charlottesville, 2001), 153.

92 *"I know you will feel":* GW to Martha Washington, 18 June 1775, *PGWRV* 1:4.

"his own Peace, & the happiness of another": GW to Benedict Calvert, 3 April 1773, *PGWCL* 9:209.

"the benevolence of her heart": Mercy Otis Warren to Abigail Adams, 17 April 1776, L. H. Butterfield, ed., *Adams Family Correspondence* (Cambridge, 1963), 1:385.

93 *"now one bone, and one flesh":* GW to William Gordon, 6 December 1785, *PGWCF* 3:436.

"sweets of Matrimony": GW to Elizabeth Parke Custis, 10 February 1796, John C. Fitzpatrick, ed., *Writings of George Washington,* 39 vols. (Washington, D.C., 1931–39), 34:458.

"greatest blessings": GW to Fitzhugh, 19 June 1793, ibid., 32:504.

94 *"Do not then in your contemplation":* GW to Elizabeth Parke Custis, 14 September 1794, ibid., 33:501.

"In my estimation": GW to Armand, 10 August 1786, *PGWCF* 4:203–4.

"So your day": GW to Chastelux, 25 April–1 May 1788, *PGWCF* 6:228.

"His Worthy Lady": Martha Dangerfield Bland to Frances Bland Randolph, 12 April 1777. Quoted in Peter R. Henriques, "The Amiable Washington," *Northern Virginia Heritage,* February, 1979, 1:8.

"Mrs. Washington is excessive fond": Nathanael Greene to Catharine Greene, 8 April 1777, Richard K. Showman, ed., *The Papers of General Nathanael Greene* (Chapel Hill, N.C., 1980) 2:54.

Martha loved the General *"madly.":* Lafayette to Adrienne de Noailles de Lafayette, 6 January 1778, Stanley D. Idzerda, ed., *Lafayette in the Age of the American Revolution: Selected Letters and Papers, 1776–1790* (Ithaca, 1977) 1:225.

95 *"my dearly beloved wife":* George Washington's will, with excellent editorial notes, is published in *PGWRT* 4:479–92.

"By her actions as First Lady": The Internet site for this quote is http://www.historywise.com/KoTrain/Courses/GW/GW_The_First_Lady.htm

96 *"There was never married people":* The interesting, unpublished journal of Elizabeth Washington of Hayfield is in the library of the MVLA.

"I think the bride fitted": Mary Higgins Clark, *Mount Vernon Love Story* (New York, 1968, 2002), 128. While this quote is insightful, the novel as a whole does not have a good grasp of its subject matter and must be used with caution.

97   *"The pore General"*: Martha Washington to Burwell Bassett, 18 July 1780, Joseph E. Fields, ed., *Worthy Partner: The Papers of Martha Washington* (Westport, Conn., 1994), 183.

    "spirit enough to laugh": "A Diplomat's Wife in Philadelphia: Letters of Henrietta Liston, 1796–1800," ed. Bradford Perkins, *William and Mary Quarterly*, October 1954, 613.

    he might play the fool: In GW's words, "While I retain the faculty of reasoning, I shall never marry a girl." GW to George Augustine Washington, 25 October 1786, *PGWCF* 4:308. The latest treatment of the ultimately unanswerable question of why GW fathered no children is by John K. Amory in *Fertility and Sterility* 81:3 (March 2004), 495–99.

    "it makes me miserable": Martha Washington to Fanny Bassett Washington, 25 February 1788, Fields, *Worthy Partner*, 206.

    "Mrs. W's happiness is bound up in the boy": Lear quoting George Washington. Quoted in Miriam Bourne, *First Family: George Washington and His Intimate Relations* (New York, 1982), 137. Lear's letter is at MVLA.

98   *"could not rest satisfied"*: GW to Jonathan Boucher, 20 April 1771, *PGWCL* 8:448.

    "As his Guardian": GW to Benedict Calvert, 3 April 1773, *PGWCL* 9:209.

    "At length, I have yielded": GW to Myles Cooper, 15 December 1773, *PGWCL* 9:406–7.

99   *"She rose from Dinner"*: GW to Burwell Bassett, 20 June 1773, *PGWCL* 9:243.

    "Went with Mrs. Washington": Donald Jackson, ed., *George Washington Diaries* (Charlottesville, 1978), 3:188–93.

100   *"treated more like a child"*: GW to James McHenry, 1 September 1796, Fitzpatrick, *Writings*, 35:201–2. This paragraph is informed by Henry Wiencek, *Imperfect God: George Washington, His Slaves, and the Creation of America* (New York, 2003), especially p. 329.

    "my love": One of only two known surviving notes from Martha to her husband, it reads in its entirety, "My love the sliver cup I mentioned in my letter by the last post—Wt 113 ouz." *PGWRV* 11:203 note.

    "I am certain, adduce arguments": GW to Charles Thomson, 22 January 1784, *PGWCF* 1:71.

    "we should have been left to grow old": Martha Washington to Mercy Otis Warren, 26 December 1789, Fields, *Worthy Partner*, 223. Quoted in Cokie Roberts, *Founding Mothers* (New York, 2004), 237.

    "I have been so long accustomed": Martha Washington to Janet Livingston Montgomery, 29 January 1791, Fields, *Worthy Partner*, 230. Quoted in Roberts, *Founding Mothers*, 241.

101   *"Her manners are modest"*: Abigail Adams in Mitchell, *New Letters of Abigail Adams*, 13. Quoted in *PGWP* 2:206.

    "I live a very dull life": Martha Washington to her sister. Quoted in editorial notes, *PGWP* 2:206.

101 *"Betsy" Hamilton, wife of the secretary of the treasury:* Quoted in Ron Chernow, *Alexander Hamilton* (New York, 2004), 335.
Under false pretenses: GW to Tobias Lear, 12 April 1791, *PGWP* 8:85. This is one of the most disturbing letters to survive from GW's hand.

102 *"Love is a mighty pretty thing":* GW to Elizabeth Parke Custis, 14 September 1794, Fitzpatrick, *Writings*, 33:501.
"the love Letters of a Lady addressed to you": Elizabeth Willing Powel to GW, 11–13 March 1797, *PGWRT* 1:28–29.
"more fraught with expressions of friendship": GW to Elizabeth Willing Powel, 26 March 1797, *PGWRT* 1:52.

103 *By the early hours of Saturday morning:* The account of Martha and GW's death is a summary of the longer treatment of the subject in my book. Peter R. Henriques, *He Died as He Lived: The Death of George Washington* (Mount Vernon, 2000).
"She reminded me": Pierre Du Ponceau, quoted in the *Pennsylvania Magazine of History and Biography* (July, 1939), 312–13.

104 *"Tis well":* Tobias Lear, "The Last Illness and Death of General Washington," quoted in Henriques, *He Died as He Lived*, 74. The reference to "rejoicing" is not in that account but from a letter, Tobias Lear to Mary S. Lear, 16 December 1799. Copy at MVLA.
"Sorrow had turned": Brady, *Martha Washington*, 221.
"She met death": Thomas Law to John Law, 23 May 1802. Quoted in Ellen McCallister [Clark], "This Melancholy Scene," *Annual Report 1981* (Mount Vernon Ladies' Association), 15.
"I thought she well deserved": Pierre Du Ponceau. Quoted in the *Pennsylvania Magazine of History and Biography* (July, 1939), 313.
"The first of men": The quote is from Eliza Parke Custis Law. "Self-Portrait: Eliza Custis, 1808," *Virginia Magazine of History and Biography* (April, 1945), 91.
"The worthy partner": *Alexandria Advertiser and Commercial Intelligencer* 5 May, 1802.

6. Reluctant Enemies

The literature on Jefferson is almost overwhelming. I found a few sources particularly helpful for this chapter: Andrew Burstein, *The Inner Jefferson: Portrait of a Grieving Optimist* (Charlottesville, 1995); Dumas Malone, *Jefferson the Virginian* (Boston, 1948) and *Jefferson and the Rights of Man* (Boston, 1951); and Joseph J. Ellis, *American Sphinx: The Character of Thomas Jefferson* (New York, 1997). Also very helpful was Ellis's *Founding Brothers: The Revolutionary Generation* (New York, 2000), chapter 4, and his Washington biography, *His Excellency* (New York, 2004). Don Higginbotham wrote a very helpful article, "Virginia's Trinity of Immortals: Washington, Jefferson and Henry, and the Story of Their Fractured Relationships," *Journal of the Early Republic* 23:4 (Winter, 2003). Richard Norton Smith's study *Patriarch: George Washington and the New American Nation* (New

York, 1993), had some good insights as did Noemie Emery's *George Washington: A Biography* (New York, 1976). Joanne Freeman's interesting study *Affairs of Honor* (New Haven, 2001) had a brief but penetrating analysis on how Jefferson rationalized his opposition to the president. Henry Lee's scathing and hard to find work *Observations on the Writings of Thomas Jefferson* (1832) portrays the third president in a very negative light, and one can understand why Jefferson supporters apparently sought to buy up all extant copies. MVLA owns a copy, as does the University of Virginia.

105 *[Thomas Jefferson] "is a man of whom":* GW to Lafayette, 10 May 1786, *PGWCF* 4:44.

106 *he articulated the basic American ideology:* Part of this paragraph draws heavily on the insights of Gordon Wood.

   At first glance . . . one is struck: Some of the examples cited are from Robert Dalzell, "Constructing Independence: Monticello, Mount Vernon, and the Men Who Built Them," *Eighteenth-Century Studies* 26:4, 174.

   In his Notes on the State of Virginia: Noble Cunningham, *In Pursuit of Reason: The Life of Thomas Jefferson* (Baton Rouge, 1987), 78.

107 *A Summary View:* GW Cash Accounts, PGWCL 10:139.

   "Where is . . . Jefferson?": GW to Benjamin Harrison, 18–30 December 1778, John C. Fitzpatrick, ed., *Writings of George Washington*, 39 vols. (Washington, D.C., 1931–39), 13:467.

   the recently captured Sir Henry Hamilton: This is drawn from Malone, *Jefferson the Virginian*, 308–12.

108 *"affecting scene" of Washington's resignation:* Ibid., 407.

   "of discernment and liberality": GW to Thomas Jefferson, 29 March 1784, *PGWCF* 1:238.

   "fullest latitude of a friend": GW to Thomas Jefferson, 8 April 1784, *PGWCF* 1:275.

   "matters of difficulty to you": GW to Thomas Jefferson, 25 February 1785, *PGWCF* 2:381.

   "It was not just Jefferson's": Andrew Burstein, *The Inner Jefferson: Portrait of a Grieving Optimist* (Charlottesville, 1995), 221.

109 *"I consider the Office of Secretary":* GW to Thomas Jefferson, 21 January 1790, *PGWP* 5:30.

   "You are to marshal": Thomas Jefferson to GW, 15 December 1789, *PGWP* 4:412–13.

   no need to correct the error: James Roger Sharp, *American Politics in the Early Republic: The New Nation in Crisis* (New Haven, Conn., 1993), 27.

110 *"My Dear Sir" for those closest:* Stuart Leibiger, *Founding Friendship: George Washington, James Madison, and the Creation of the American Republic* (Charlottesville, 1999), 2–3.

   "The natural progress": Thomas Jefferson to Edward Carrington, 1788, Paul Leicester Ford, ed., *Writings of Thomas Jefferson*, 10 vols. (New York, 1892–99), 2:404.

110 *"in the natural integrity"*: Thomas Jefferson to John Melish, 1813, ibid., 9:376.

"change the form of our government": Thomas Jefferson to GW, 14 November 1786, *PGWCF* 4:365.

111 *"against an innocent institution"*: GW to William Barton, 7 September 1788, *PGWCF* 6:502.

"was a rock-ribbed realist": Ellis, *Founding Brothers*, 131.

"With devious brilliance": Douglas Adair, *Fame and the Founding Fathers: Essays by Douglas Adair*, ed. Trevor Colbourn (Indianapolis, 1998, originally published 1974), 195.

"The instruments of government": Robert F. Dalzell and Lee Baldwin Dalzell, *George Washington's Mount Vernon: At Home in Revolutionary America* (New York, 1998), 206.

112 *"change from the present"*: Thomas Jefferson to GW, 23 May 1792, *PGWP* 10:410.

"was not only a monarchist": Quoted in Joel Achenbach, *The Grand Idea: George Washington's Potomac and the Race to the West* (New York, 2004), 173.

"to Jefferson's utter astonishment": Freeman, *Affairs of Honor*, 76.

"in attracting Freneau to Philadelphia": Cunningham, *In Pursuit of Reason*, 171.

113 *"little short of being a fiend"*: Higginbotham, "Virginia's Trinity," 539.

"that internal dissentions": GW to Thomas Jefferson, 23 August 1792, *PGWP* 11:30. The final sentence has been changed from its original sequence.

"North and South will hang together": Thomas Jefferson to GW, May 1792, Ford, ed., *Writings of Jefferson*, 6:4.

114 *"shreds of stuff from Aesop's fables."*: Quoted in Ellis, *American Sphinx*, 154.

"Washington spoke in the name": Dumas Malone, *Jefferson and the Ordeal of Liberty* (Boston, 1958), 262.

"The great champion": Smith, *Patriarch*, 225–26.

115 *"As Jefferson saw it"*: Ellis, *American Sphinx*, 159.

If the President was not moved: Burstein, *Inner Jefferson*, 217.

"His memory was already sensibly": Anas of Thomas Jefferson, Ford, *Writings of Jefferson*, 1:168.

"In his private correspondence": Ellis, *Founding Brothers*, 141.

"He appears to have an invincible Diffidence": Eliza Powel to Martha Washington, 7 December 1796, Joseph E. Fields, ed., *Worthy Partner: The Papers of Martha Washington* (Westport, Conn., 1994), 294.

116 *No doubt, it was psychologically easier*: Leibiger, *Founding Friendship*, 194. While the point was made by Leibiger concerning James Madison, it is equally applicable to Jefferson.

"Washington's blindness": Freeman, *Affairs of Honor*, 76.

Washington was "deceived" *but . . . not* "depraved": Jefferson used these words in a later letter. Jefferson to Walter Jones, 2 January 1814, Ford, *Writings of Jefferson*, 9:448–49.

117 *"My Dear Friend"*: Thomas Jefferson to Philip Mazzei, 24 April 1796, Julian

P. Boyd, ed., *The Papers of Thomas Jefferson*, 29 vols. (Princeton, 1950–), 29:82. Various versions, with useful editorial notes, are in 29:73–89.

117   *"[Shall I] set up my judgment"*: GW "Proposed Address to Congress," April 1789, Fitzpatrick, *Writings*, 30:299.
"I do it on the presumption": GW to Gouverneur Morris, 28 January 1792, *PGWP* 9:516.

118   *"he has set me down"*: GW to Henry Lee, 26 August 1794, Fitzpatrick, *Writings*, 33:479. Fitzpatrick includes the pertinent sections of Lee's letter to GW in the same entry.
"I had never discovered": GW to Thomas Jefferson, 6 July 1796, ibid., 35:119.
"Washington's response": Ellis, *Excellency*, 232.

119   *"a perfect Slave"*: George Washington to Joseph Reed, 29 July 1779, Fitzpatrick, *Writings*, 16:9.
"The Funeral of George Washington": Smith, *Patriarch*, 174. Jefferson's quote is on the same page.

120   *"embroil me with one"*: Thomas Jefferson to James Madison, 3 August 1797, James M. Smith, ed., *The Republic of Letters: The Correspondence between Jefferson and Madison, 1776–1826*, 3 vols. (New York, 1995), 985.
"O what a tangled web": Henry Lee, *Observations on the Writings of Thomas Jefferson* (2d ed., Philadelphia, 1839), 89. GW's response to Randolph is on page 88.
"Think for me": Thomas Jefferson to James Madison, 3 August 1797, Smith, *The Republic of Letters*, 986. Also Boyd, *Jefferson Papers*, 29:240.

121   *"one of the most artful"*: John Nicholas to GW, 22 February 1798, *PGWRT* 2:101.
"Nothing short of the Evidence": GW to John Nicholas, 8 March 1798, *PGWRT* 2:128.
"Monroe's book is considered masterly": Thomas Jefferson to James Madison, 3 January 1798. Quoted in *PGWRT* 2:138.

122   *"GW's remarks"*: *PGWRT* 2:170.
"If he [i.e., Nicholas] could prove": GW to Bushrod Washington, 12 August 1798, *PGWRT* 2:514–15.
Martha Washington's response to Jefferson's election: Quoted in the *Life Journals and Correspondence of the Rev. Manasseh Cutler*, 2:56ff. The quote is included with the collection of quotes about Martha Washington at MVLA.
the worst day of her life: John Cotton Smith, *The Correspondence and Miscellanies* . . . (New York, 1847), 224–25. Quoted in Higginbotham, "Virginia's Trinity," 541.
a generally favorable summary of Washington's character: The assessment is in Jefferson to Walter Jones, 2 January 1814, Ford, *Writings of Jefferson*, 9:448–49.

123   *"I never saw him afterwards"*: Ibid., 451.
By "Samsons" and "Solomons": Thomas Jefferson to Martin Van Buren, 29 June 1824. Quoted in Boyd, *Jefferson Papers*, 29:77–78.

123 *"Party animosities"*: Thomas Jefferson to Angelica Schuyler Church, 11 January 1792, Ford, *Writings of Jefferson*, 6:116.
"I think he feels": Thomas Jefferson to James Madison, June 1793, ibid., 6:293.

7. The Great Collaboration

When I retired from George Mason University in 2003, I little expected any of my future research would focus on Alexander Hamilton. Indeed, I disposed of or gave away my notes on the subject. As luck would have it, shortly after disposing of my material, I attended an excellent symposium on Hamilton sponsored by the New-York Historical Society in conjunction with the bicentennial celebration of the famous duel between Hamilton and Aaron Burr (which occurred on July 11, 1804). The symposium whetted my appetite to refocus on him and his relationship with George Washington. (Happily, one of my best students, Mark Radeline, kept the paper and notes he had written for me in a senior seminar, so I didn't have to start from scratch.)

While I consulted a great many different sources for this chapter, I would like to specifically acknowledge my special debt to Ron Chernow and Richard Brookhiser. The entire chapter is informed by Ron Chernow's best-selling biography, *Alexander Hamilton* (New York, 2004). Ron also read an early draft of this chapter and made helpful suggestions. In addition to his study of George Washington, Rick Brookhiser (who also read a draft of the chapter) has written *Alexander Hamilton: American* (New York, 1999). Most helpful to me, however, were various interviews and talks he gave that are on the Internet. In these, he pointed out aspects of their relationship which I had not previously thought about. On Hamilton, in addition to the Chernow biography, I found the following insightful and interesting: Jacob E. Cooke, *Alexander Hamilton* (New York, 1982); John C. Miller, *Alexander Hamilton: Portrait in Paradox* (New York, 1959); and Stephen Knott, *Alexander Hamilton and the Persistence of Myth* (Lawrence, Kansas, 2002). Both Christine Patrick, associate editor of the Washington Papers, and Joseph Ellis read earlier drafts of the chapter and made constructive suggestions for improving it.

125 *"In every relation"*: GW to Alexander Hamilton (AH), 2 February 1795, John C. Fitzpatrick, ed., *Writings of George Washington*, 39 vols. (Washington, D.C., 1931–39), 34:110.
stigmatized childhood: By far the most detailed and thorough examination of Hamilton's youth is in the first two chapters of Chernow, *Hamilton*.
the dark side of the American picture: Joseph Charles, *The Origins of the American Party System* (New York, 1961), is one example of portraying a Machiavellian Hamilton controlling a rather dimwitted Washington.

126 *"a bastard brat"*: Quoted in, among other places, Stephen Knott, *Alexander Hamilton and the Persistence of Myth* (Lawrence, Kansas, 2002), 11.
"a superabundance of secretions": Quoted in, among other places, John C. Miller, *Alexander Hamilton: Portrait in Paradox* (New York, 1959), 523.
"shock jock" radio shows: I am indebted to Rick Brookhiser for this analogy.

126   *"I have read his heart"*: Quoted in Jacob E. Cooke, *Alexander Hamilton* (New York, 1982), 266 n.44.

      "the great collaboration": The book is Adrienne Koch, *Jefferson and Madison: The Great Collaboration* (New York, 1950).

      if you want to see Alexander Hamilton's memorial: George Will, quoted in preface of Knott, *Hamilton and the Persistence of Myth.*

127   *"Hamilton's reach of thought"*: Quoted in Chernow, *Hamilton,* 189–90.

      "really a colossus": TJ to James Madison. Ibid., 496.

      "The real debt Hamilton": Richard B. Morris, *Seven Who Shaped Our Destiny* (New York, 1976), 223.

      "not the Roman Cato": Quoted in Chernow, *Hamilton,* 308.

      "affairs of honor": Joanne Freeman, *Affairs of Honor* (New Haven, 2001), 167.

128   *"For all his superlative"*: Chernow, *Hamilton,* 5.

      A born fighter: Freeman, *Affairs of Honor,* 161.

      "principal & most confidential aid": GW to John Adams, 25 September 1798, *PGWRT* 3:41.

      "persons that can think for me": GW to Joseph Reed, 23 January 1776, *PGWRV* 3:173.

      "able to project himself": Chernow, *Hamilton,* 89.

      General Horatio Gates: Hamilton's difficult dealings with Gates are recounted in Chernow, *Hamilton,* 100–106.

129   *"Every part of this"*: AH to GW, 12 November 1777, *PGWRV* 12:225.

      abandoned by his birth father: This point is taken from Cooke, *Alexander Hamilton,* 27.

130   *"I hate Congress"*: AH to John Laurens, 12 September 1780, Harold C. Syrett, ed., *The Papers of Alexander Hamilton (PAH),* 27 vols. (New York, 1961–87), 2:428.

      "three fourths of them": AH to John Laurens, 8 January 1780, *PAH* 2:255.

      as sociologist Barry Schwartz demonstrates: Barry Schwartz, *George Washington: The Making of an American Symbol* (New York, 1987), 88.

      "Being brilliant and coldly": Chernow *Hamilton,* 89.

      "I explained to you": AH to GW, 22 November 1780, *PAH* 2:509.

131   *stern, obstinate, and insensitive:* This point is taken from Miller, *Portrait in Paradox,* 71.

      "Some people are only": AH to Eliza Schuyler, 2 October 1780, *PAH* 2:448.

132   *"You have kept me waiting"*: AH to Philip Schuyler, 18 February 1781, *PAH* 2:564.

      "For the past three years": AH to Philip Schuyler, 18 February 1781, *PAH* 2:566.

      "The Great Man": AH to James McHenry, 18 February 1781, *PAH* 2:569.

133   *George Washington saw much of himself:* I am indebted to Dorothy Twohig for this insight.

      "is more firmly engaged": GW to John Sullivan, 4 February 1781, Fitzpatrick, *Writings,* 21:181.

134   *"I know the General's"*: Lafayette to AH, 28 November 1780, *PAH* 2:517.

      the General was a "very honest" man: James Madison's notes of a discussion with AH on 13 February 1783. *PAH* 3:264.

134 *"I never saw the general":* AH to Elias Boudinot, 5 July 1778, *PAH* 1:512.
Almost in the manner of a recalcitrant son: This point is taken from Cooke, *Hamilton*, 28.

135 *"By dint of his youth":* Chernow, *Hamilton*, 157.
he and Washington did not discuss: GW wrote to AH on 3 July 1787, "Not having compared ideas with you, Sir, I cannot judge how far our sentiments agreed." *PGWCF* 5:245.
Hamilton was surprisingly blunt: AH to GW, 13 August 1788, *PGWCF* 6:444.
"I trust that the greatest": AH to GW, 9 September 1792, *PGWP* 11:92.

136 *"me and my administration":* AH to Edward Carrington, 26 May 1792, *PAH* 11:429.
"a messenger from the future": Chernow, *Hamilton*, 6, 4.

137 *"surveyed the political landscape":* James Roger Sharp, *American Politics in the Early Republic: The New Nation in Crisis* (New Haven, Conn., 1993), 49.
As Jefferson and Madison saw it: These points are drawn from an unpublished talk by Eugene R. Sheridan, "Thomas Jefferson and the American Presidency," in the possession of the author.
"change . . . the present republican form": Thomas Jefferson to GW, 23 May 1792, *PGWP* 10:410.
"I assure you on my private faith": AH to Edward Carrington, 26 May 1792, *PAH* 11:443–44.
"Hamilton promoted": Chernow, *Hamilton*, 628.

138 *"beclouded by the slanders":* Thomas Jefferson to GW, 9 September 1792, *PGWP* 11:104.
"At bottom, Thomas Jefferson": Knott, *Hamilton and the Persistence of Myth*, 11.
"as to the idea of transforming": TJ Memo, 1 October 1792, Julian P. Boyd, ed., *The Papers of Thomas Jefferson*, 29 vols. (Princeton, 1950–), 24:435.

139 *"gained incomparable power":* Chernow, *Hamilton*, 290.
"the motives which": GW to James Madison, 3 December 1784, *PGWCF* 2:166.
It is now clear: Eugene Sheridan, "Thomas Jefferson and the Giles Resolution," *William and Mary Quarterly*, 3rd ser., 49:3, July, 1992, 589–608.

140 *"It shall never be said":* AH to GW, 29 July–1 August 1798, *PGWRT* 2:467.
"You remember the saying": Miller, *Portrait in Paradox*, 244.
"There must be some": AH to Robert Troup, 13 April 1795, *PAH* 18:329.
"You will ask why": AH to Angelica Church, Quoted in Chernow, *Hamilton*, 457.
"modest and sage": Letter From Alexander Hamilton, Concerning the Public Conduct & Character of John Adams, Esq. President of the United States, 24 October 1800, *PAH* 25:214.
"Washington's Farewell Address": Richard Norton Smith, *Patriarch: George Washington and the New American Nation* (New York, 1993), 280. Chapter 4 of Joseph Ellis's *Founding Brothers: The Revolutionary Generation* (New York, 2000) has an excellent discussion of this topic.
the Maria Reynolds scandal: This fascinating chapter of Hamilton's life is

sympathetically but not uncritically presented in Chernow, *Hamilton*, especially chapters 21 and 30.

141   *"as a token of my sincere regard"*: GW to AH, 21 August 1797, *PGWRT* 1:313. I am indebted to Rick Brookhiser for the insight about how this incident reflects GW's tact and sensitivity.

    "The token of your regard": AH to GW, 28 August 1797, *PGWRT* 1:322.

142   *"I would wish you to believe"*: GW to AH, 27 May 1798, *PGWRT* 2:297. Another example of their friendship: GW to AH, 8 October 1797, *PGWRT* 1:388.

    whom Washington declared that he "loved.": GW to Henry Knox, 2 March 1797, Fitzpatrick, *Writings*, 35:409.

143   *"as a proof of my frankness"*: GW to AH, 9 August 1798, *PGWRT* 2:500.

    "My friend McHenry": AH to GW, 29 July–1 August 1798, *PGWRT* 2:467.

    Joseph Ellis argues: Joseph J. Ellis, *His Excellency* (New York, 2004), 250–52.

    "Tis only for me": General Orders, December 1799, *PAH* 24:112.

    "the numerous and distinguished": AH to Martha Washington, 12 January 1800, *PAH* 24:184.

    "Perhaps no friend": AH to Charles C. Pinckney, 22 December 1799, *PAH* 24:116.

    "I have been much indebted": AH to Tobias Lear, 2 January 1800, *PAH* 24:155. AH used the same word "aegis" in a letter to Martha Washington, 12 January 1800, *PAH* 24:184.

    Critics have interpreted the term "aegis": Joseph Charles is a good example of historians who have done this.

144   *the many confidential letters:* AH to Tobias Lear, 2 January 1800, *PAH* 24:155. AH wrote to GW on 16 February 1799 and made reference to using codes. *PGWRT* 3:383.

    "many which every public and private": Tobias Lear to AH, 16 January 1800, *PAH* 24:198.

    Hamilton never visited Mount Vernon: For GW's invitation, see *PGWP* 11:39. On AH not venturing far, see Chernow, *Hamilton*, 332.

    his eulogist, Gouverneur Morris: Morris *Diary*, 13 July 1800, quoted in *PAH* 26:324 n. 3.

8. "The Only Unavoidable Subject of Regret"

Happily, over the past several years, the controversial and very complicated subject of George Washington and slavery is finally receiving scholarly attention of a high order. In my judgment, the most perceptive scholar on the subject of George Washington and slavery is Philip Morgan. The best single treatment is his article "'To Get Quit of Negroes': George Washington and Slavery," which is available on the Internet and is scheduled to be published in the December 2005 issue of the *Journal of American Studies*. Other valuable published work by Professor Morgan includes his award-winning *Slave Counterpoint: Black Culture in the Eighteenth-Century Chesapeake and Low Country* (Chapel Hill, N.C., 1998) and his chapter with Michael Nicholls, "Slave Flight: Mount Vernon, Virginia, and the Wider Atlantic World," in Tamara Harvey and Greg O'Brien, editors, *George Washington's South* (Gainesville, Florida, 2004), 197–222. Joseph Ellis's treatment of Washington and slavery in *His Excellency* (New York, 2004), especially pages 257–64, is brief but helpful. A good, solid, moderate treatment is found in Kenneth Morgan, "George Washington and the Problem of Slavery," *Journal of American Studies* 34 (2000), 279–301. Another good brief treatment is the entry on the subject in Frank Grizzard Jr., *George Washington: A Biographical Companion* (Santa Barbara, 2002), 282–86. Henry Wiencek's *Imperfect God: George Washington, His Slaves, and the Creation of America* (New York, 2003) is the most comprehensive treatment in print with much helpful information, although in my judgment, Wiencek engages in unwarranted speculation and confuses readers by commenting that Washington had an "epiphany" on the slavery question, by overemphasizing the differences between Washington and his wife on slavery, and by giving the question of his fathering the slave child (West Ford) more attention than it deserves. The best treatment of George Washington and the political implications of slavery is Dorothy Twohig, "'That Species of Property': Washington's Role in the Controversy over Slavery," in Don Higginbotham, editor, *George Washington Reconsidered* (Charlottesville, 2001), 114–38. On slavery and Washington's will, see John P. Riley, "Written with My Own Hand: George Washington's Last Will and Testament," *Virginia Cavalcade* 48 (Autumn 1999), 168–77. Another fine scholar on the subject is Jean B. Lee, whose article, "Mount Vernon Plantation: A Model for the Republic," is in Philip Schwarz, editor, *Slavery at the Home of George Washington* (Mount Vernon, 2001). An insightful article by Norma Granley, "'A Certain Species of Property Which I Possess . . .': George Washington as a Slaveholder," *Northern Virginia Heritage*, 7:2 (June, 1985), 3–10, deserves a wider readership than it received. Mary Thompson, the research historian at Mount Vernon and a fount of knowledge on this topic, has compiled a great deal of valuable information. Some of her work is published, but much is still in unpublished form at the library of the MVLA. The library has also compiled a valuable collection of material, "Transcripts Relating to General Washington's Slaves."

145 *"shall frankly declare"*: GW to Alexander Spotswood, 23 November 1794, John C. Fitzpatrick, ed., *Writings of George Washington*, 39 vols. (Washington, D.C., 1931–39), 34:47.

"ecstasy of sanctimony": Philip Roth, *The Human Stain* (New York, 2001), 2.

"Ages to come": Edward Rushton to GW, July 1796. Quoted in Twohig, "That Species of Property," 115. A copy of the very long diatribe is at the Papers of George Washington at the University of Virginia.

146 *"if any slave shall happen"*: Walter W. Hening, ed., *The Statutes at Large: Being a Collection of All the Laws of Virginia* (Richmond, Virginia, 1819–1823), 4:130.

147 *"Slaves were part"*: Philip Morgan, "'To Get Quit of Negroes': George Washington and Slavery." Copy in possession of the author and also available on the Internet.

He purchased 13: Ibid.

147   *"Sir: With this letter"*: GW to Joseph Thompson, 2 July 1766, *PGWCL* 7:453–54.

An uneasy mixture of commercial: Kenneth Morgan, "George Washington and the Problem of Slavery," *Journal of American Studies* 34 (2000), 282.

"all of them to be strait limbed": GW to Daniel Adams, 20 July 1772, *PGWCL* 9:70.

"He was not moved": John Ferling, *First of Men* (Knoxville, 1988), 68.

148   *"be at their work"*: Philip Morgan, *Slave Counterpoint: Black Culture in the Eighteenth-Century Chesapeake and Low Country* (Chapel Hill, N.C., 1998), 191.

"that every laborer": GW to John Fairfax, 1 January 1789, *PGWP* 1:223.

"It has always been my aim": GW to James Anderson, 20 February 1797, "Transcripts Relating to General Washington's Slaves," MVLA.

"they [the slaves] have a just claim": GW to Lund Washington, 10 December 1776, *PGWRV* 7:290.

"If you can eat with one hand": Quoted in Mary Thompson, "I Never See That Man Laugh to Show His Teeth: Relationship between Blacks and Whites at George Washington's Mount Vernon," unpublished paper, MVLA.

"every thing that is proper": GW to Anthony Whitting, 5 May 1793, Fitzpatrick, *Writings*, 32:442–43.

"I wish you would": GW to Anthony Whitting, 16 December 1792, ibid., 32:263.

149   *he did a time and motion study*: Morgan, "To Get Quit of Negroes."

"Lost labour": GW to John Fairfax, 1 January 1789, *PGWP* 1:223.

"There are few Negroes": GW to Lawrence Lewis, 14 August 1797, Fitzpatrick, *Writings*, 36:11.

"I expect to reap": GW to the overseers at Mount Vernon, 14 July 1793, Fitzpatrick, *Writings*, 33:11.

"in pursuits of other objects": Quoted in Jean B. Lee, "Mount Vernon Plantation: A Model for the Republic" in Philip Schwarz, ed., *Slavery at the Home of George Washington* (Mount Vernon, 2001), 32.

the slaves would get two glasses: Gerald Mullin, *Flight and Rebellion* (New York and London, 1975), 62.

Everything not nailed down: This point and quote are taken from Lee, "Mount Vernon Plantation," 32.

Washington tried hard to thwart: Most of this paragraph is a close paraphrase of Lee, "Mount Vernon Plantation," 33, with the exception of the quote about the dogs.

150   *"if any Negro [still] presumes"*: GW to Anthony Whitting, 16 December 1792, Fitzpatrick, *Writings*, 32:264.

testimony of Henrietta Liston: "Lady Henrietta Liston's Journal of Washington's 'Resignation,' Retirement and Death," *Pennsylvania Magazine of History and Biography* 95:4 (October 1971), 515.

"as differently as if he had been quite another man": Quoted in Ken Morgan, "George Washington and the Problem of Slavery," 287.

150 *"if the Negros will not"*: GW to Anthony Whitting, 20 January 1793, Fitzpatrick, *Writings*, 32:307.

"give him a good whipping.": Ferling, *First of Men*, 478.

"Your treatment of Charlotte": GW to Anthony Whitting, 20 January 1793, Fitzpatrick, *Writings*, 32:307.

"Let Abram get his deserts": GW to William Pearce, 30 March 1794, ibid., 33:309.

151 *"I will ship him off"*: GW to Anthony Whitting, 3 March 1793, ibid., 32:365–66.

had his manager tell Muclus: GW to Anthony Whitting, 19 May 1793, ibid., 32:463.

"that what has been done": GW to Anthony Whitting, 23 December 1792, ibid., 32:277.

"Harsh treatment will not do": GW to William Pearce, 11 January 1795, ibid., 34:85.

"for one can not call them": Julian Niemcewicz, *Under Their Vine and Fig Tree: Travels through America* (Elizabeth, N.J., 1965 [1805]), 100.

"might not be thought good enough": GW to Arthur Young, 12 December 1793, Fitzpatrick, *Writings*, 33:177–78.

"swarm with pickaninnies": Louis-Philippe, *King of France, 1830–1848. Diary of My Travels in America.* Quoted in Mary Thompson, "The Lives of Enslaved Workers on George Washington's Outlying Farms." Copy at MVLA.

petitioning their master: Ferling, *First of Men*, 479.

152 *"slaves were well fed"*: Quoted in Ken Morgan, "George Washington and the Problem of Slavery," 285.

"warmly lodged chiefly": Philip Morgan, *Slave Counterpoint*, 118.

Julian Niemcewicz noted: Niemcewicz, *Under Their Vine and Fig Tree*, 100–101.

Washington recognized that slaves: This point is taken from Grizzard, *George Washington*, 284.

"To disperse families": GW to Robert Lewis, 17 August 1790, *PGWRT* 4:256.

"to hurt the feelings of those unhappy": GW to John Francis Mercer, 24 November 1786, *PGWCF* 4:394.

153 *"he seems to a great deal disconcerted"*: James Flexner, *George Washington: Anguish and Farewell* (Boston, 1969), 443.

Sambo's small boat: Story is in "Mount Vernon Reminiscences," *Alexandria Gazette*, 18 & 22 January 1876. Copy at MVLA in file on GW and slavery.

154 *"In the most explicit language"*: GW to Anthony Whitting, 28 April 1793, Fitzpatrick, *Writings*, 32:437–38.

"I never wish my people": Quoted in Ferling, *First of Men*, 477.

"It is foremost in my thoughts": GW to Anthony Whitting, 14 October 1792, Fitzpatrick, *Writings*, 32:184.

"Taken together, the archaeological evidence": Dennis Pogue, "The Archaeology of Plantation Life," *Virginia Cavalcade* 41:2 (Autumn, 1991), 76.

154 *"his most unusual purchase was their teeth!"*: Wiencek, *Imperfect God*, 112. Also Philip Morgan, "To Get Quit of Negroes."

155 *"Blacks were ignorant and shiftless . . . deceitful & impudent huzzy"*: Ferling, *First of Men*, 477.
     Of his black carpenters: GW to William Pearce, 22 February 1794, Fitzpatrick, *Writings*, 33:275.
     "at work with the gardener": GW to Anthony Whitting, 30 December 1792, *ibid.*, 32:279.
     "I know of no black person": GW to William Pearce, 25 October 1795, ibid., 34:343.
     "I know not the Negro": GW to Anthony Whitting, 5 May 1793, ibid., 32:144.
     "engrained sense of racial superiority": Ken Morgan, "George Washington and the Problem of Slavery," 283.
     "a parcel of Barbarian's": Quoted in Warren Hofstra, "A Parcel of Barbarian's and an Uncooth Set of People" in Warren Hofstra, ed., *George Washington and the Virginia Backcountry* (Madison, 1998), 88.

156 *"finding it troublesome to instruct"*: GW to William Pearce, 25 January 1795, Fitzpatrick, *Writings*, 34:104.
     "too much upon a level with Negroes": GW to William Pearce, 18 December 1793, ibid., 33:194.
     "but it deserves consideration": GW to Arthur Young, 12 December 1793, ibid., 33:181.
     "as separate, and as distinct as possible": GW to William Pearce, 16 November 1794, ibid., 34:25.
     "a receptacle for stolen produce": See GW to William Pearce, 30 November 1794, ibid., 34:48–80 and GW to William Pearce, 16 November 1794, ibid., 34:24.
     "This may seem a contradiction": John Bernard, *Retrospections of America, 1797–1811* (reprinted New York, 1969) 90–91. Quoted in Fritz Hirschfeld, *George Washington and Slavery: A Documentary Portrayal* (Columbia, Mo., 1997), 73.

157 *"as tame and abject slaves"*: GW to Bryan Fairfax, 24 August 1774, *PGWCL* 10:155.
     "tended to regard the condition": Joseph J. Ellis, *Founding Brothers: The Revolutionary Generation* (New York, 2000), 158.
     Washington had a more optimistic view: Philip Morgan, "To Get Quit of Negroes."
     "trusty old negro Jack.": GW to William Pearce, 25 October 1794, Fitzpatrick, *Writings*, 34:343.

158 *Davy "carries on his business"*: GW to William Pearce, 18 December 1793, ibid., 33:194.
     At one time, Washington even seriously considered: Philip Morgan, *Slave Counterpoint*, 173.
     "I am a good deal in want of": GW to Tench Tilghman, 24 March 1784, *PGWCF* 1:232.

158 *"be happy to see a person"*: GW to Phillis Wheatley, 28 February 1776, *PGWRV* 3:387.

"*I can only say*": GW to Robert Morris, 12 April 1786, *PGWCF* 4:16.

"*It [is] among my first wishes*": GW to John Francis Mercer, 9 September 1786, *PGWCF* 4:243.

"*I wish from my soul*": GW to Lawrence Lewis, 4 August 1797, *PGWRT* 1:288.

"*I shall be happily mistaken*": Fitzpatrick, *Writings*, 34:47–48.

"*No man desires more heartily*": Bernard, *Retrospections*, 91. Quoted in Hirschfeld, *Washington and Slavery*, 73.

159 *would cast his lot with the North:* Jefferson's memo on Washington's comment is in Julian P. Boyd, ed., *The Papers of Thomas Jefferson*, 29 vols. (Princeton, 1950–) 28:568.

"*to liberate a certain specie of property*": GW to Tobias Lear, 6 May 1794, Fitzpatrick, *Writings*, 33:358.

"*The unfortunate condition*": Quoted in David Humphreys, "Life of General Washington," ed. Rosemary Zagarri (Athens, Ga., 1991), 78.

"*shrank in repugnance from*": Wiencek, *Imperfect God*, 135.

"*tortuously gradual*": Philip Morgan, "To Get Quit of Negroes."

"*Morgan and I tend*": Ellis, *Excellency*, 311.

160 "*I wish to have it accomplished*": GW to Tobias Lear, 12 April 1791, Fitzpatrick, *Writings*, 37: 573–74.

"*But when slaves [who] are happy and contented*": GW to Robert Morris, 12 April 1786, *PGWCF* 4:16.

claim freedom under Pennsylvania law: Flexner, *Anguish and Farewell,* 4:432–34.

161 "*Renting out four fifths of Mount Vernon*": Robert F. Dalzell and Lee Baldwin Dalzell, *George Washington's Mount Vernon: At Home in Revolutionary America* (New York, 1998), 212.

"*I possess very repugnantly*": GW to Tobias Lear, 6 May 1794, Fitzpatrick, *Writings,* 33:358.

"*Time, patience, and education*": Quoted in Ken Morgan, "Washington and the Problem of Slavery," 293.

"*the only true policy is justice*": Edward Rushton to GW, 20 February 1797. Copy at the *PGW* at the University of Virginia.

"*politically shackled*": Roger Wilkins, *Jefferson's Pillow: The Founding Fathers and the Dilemma of Black Patriotism* (Boston, 2001), 122.

162 "*shall frankly declare*": GW to Alexander Spotswood, 23 November 1794, Fitzpatrick, *Writings,* 34:47.

"*at length been put to sleep*": GW to David Stuart, 28 March 1790, *PGWP* 5:224.

163 "*the last and greatest*": Garry Wills, *Cincinnatus: George Washington and the Enlightenment* (New York, 1984), 235.

he freed all of his personal slaves: For the terms regarding the freeing of his slaves, see *PGWRT* 4:480–81 and notes.

164 "*she did not feel as tho her Life were safe*": Abigail Adams to her sister, Mary, 21 December 1800. Copy in file on early descriptions of Mount Vernon, MVLA. Letter is quoted in full in Hirschfeld, *Washington and Slavery,* 214.

164   *For those who are tempted to criticize:* I wish to credit John Riley for this observation.

     "George Washington's lifelong commitment": Hirschfeld, *Washington and Slavery*, 237.

     "Surely I cannot on the one hand": Wilkins, *Jefferson's Pillow*, 144.

165   *There has never been a credible tale:* Richard Brookhiser, *Founding Father: Rediscovering George Washington* (New York, 1996), 181.

9. A Few Simple Beliefs

There has been a great deal of material produced on the subject of George Washington and religion, but much of it is so slanted and biased as to significantly limit its value. The best book on the subject is Paul F. Boller Jr., *George Washington and Religion* (Dallas, 1963). Mary Thompson, the research historian at Mount Vernon, is working on a book on this subject and has gathered a great deal of material on the subject which she graciously made available to me. She would put more emphasis on the "religious side" of Washington than I did in my assessment, but her help has been very valuable. A recent doctoral dissertation by Gregg Frazer, "The Political Theology of the American Founding" (Claremont University, 2004), is of particular interest in that it is written by a scholar who, while an evangelical Christian himself, makes a strong case that George Washington was not one. I have dealt in part with the topic earlier in my essay "The Final Struggle between George Washington and the Grim King: Washington's Attitude toward Death and Afterlife," *Virginia Magazine of History and Biography*, Winter, 1999 (reprinted in Don Higginbotham, editor, *George Washington Reconsidered* [Charlottesville, 2001]). A small volume, *The Ways of Providence: Religion and George Washington* (Buena Vista, Virginia, 2005) by Frank E. Grizzard Jr., was published too late for use, but is a good brief treatment with many helpful documents. The main works that I consulted which stressed the Christian beliefs of the first president were William J. Johnson, *George Washington the Christian* (1919, reprinted by the Christian Liberty Press, Arlington Heights, Illinois, n.d.); Paul Buffington, *The Soul of George Washington* (Philadelphia, 1936); E. C. McQuire, *The Religious Opinions and Character of George Washington* (New York, 1836); and George Washington Nordham, *George Washington's Religious Faith* (Chicago, 1986). The best accounts of Washington as a "Freethinker" are Franklin Steiner, "The Religious Beliefs of Our Presidents: From Washington to F.D.R.," and John Remsburg, "Six Historic Americans," both available on the Internet.

167   *"In religion my tenets":* GW to Dr. James Anderson, 24 December 1795, John C. Fitzpatrick, ed., *Writings of George Washington*, 39 vols. (Washington, D.C., 1931–39), 34:407.

     "Washington has been": Richard Brookhiser, *Founding Father: Rediscovering George Washington* (New York, 1996), 144.

     "an infidel": John Remsburg, *Six Historic Americans*, chapter 3. This article is readily accessible on the Web at www.infidels.org

168   *"George Washington came to a living faith":* A copy of Dr. Kennedy's remark-

able sermon is at the library of MVLA in a file, "George Washington and Religion."

168 *"That President George Washington"*: Timothy LaHaye, *Faith of the Founding Fathers* (1990), 113. One of the most extreme statements is in Verna Hall, *The Christian History of the American Revolution: George Washington and the Character and Influence of One Man* (San Francisco, 1999): "If one is not himself knowledgeable of the admonitions in the Bible, the fruits of the Spirit and the fruits of the flesh, he cannot fully comprehend the Christian life of George Washington. . . . If one would truly know George Washington, one must be a Bible-believing scholar such as he" (page 153).

"A prodigious amount of nonsense": Marcus Cunliffe quoted in *William and Mary Quarterly*, 3rd ser., 20:4, October, 1963, 614–15.

"possesses the two great": Edward Thornton to Sir James Burgess, 2 April 1792, quoted in *William and Mary Quarterly*, 3rd ser., 21:1, January 1961, 102.

"gift of silence": John Adams quoted in Joseph J. Ellis, *His Excellency* (New York, 2004), 194.

"Most people say too much": "Lady Henrietta Liston's Journal of Washington's 'Resignation,' Retirement and Death," *Pennsylvania Magazine of History and Biography* 95:4 (October 1971), 514.

169 *"unusual but uniform"*: Quoted in Boller, *GW and Religion*, 67.

"When it came to religion": Ibid.

"neither religiously fervent": This quote is from Paul Longmore, *The Invention of George Washington* (California, 1988), 169.

"his ways are wise": GW to Henry Knox, 8 September 1791, Fitzpatrick, *Writings*, 31:360.

170 A handy list of the various names for Providence are listed in Johnson, *George Washington the Christian*, 288–91.

"warm deist": Edwin S. Gaustad, *Sworn upon the Altar of God: A Religious Biography of Thomas Jefferson* (Grand Rapids, Mich., 1996), 143.

"agent for this ultimate power": I took this point from William Rasmussen and Robert Tilton, *George Washington: The Man behind the Myth* (Charlottesville, 1999), 153.

"that Providence": GW to Martha Washington, 18 June 1775, *PGWRV* 1:4.

"No matter how violent": Fred Anderson, ed., *George Washington Remembers* (Oxford, 2004), 129.

"as visibly the finger": GW to Lafayette, 28 May 1788, *PGWCF* 6:299.

"The hand of Providence": GW to Thomas Nelson, 20 August 1778, Fitzpatrick, *Writings*, 12:343. Brookhiser gives a number of other examples on page 146 of *Founding Father*.

171 *"To have viewed"*: GW to Lafayette, 10 May 1786, *PGWCF* 4:41.

"can only form": GW to John Robinson, 1 September 1758, *PGWCL* 5:432.

"without perplexing ourselves": GW to David Humphreys, 23 March 1793, Fitzpatrick, *Writings*, 32:398.

"I will not lament": GW to Joseph Reed, 26 February 1776, *PGWRV* 3:373.

171   *"He that gave"*: GW to Archibald Cary, 15 June 1782, Fitzpatrick, *Writings*, 24:346.
       "The will of Heaven": GW to George Augustine Washington, 27 January 1793, ibid., 32:315–16.

172   *"There is a Destiny"*: GW to Sally Cary Fairfax, 25 September 1758, *PGWCL* 6:42.
       "Nothing, however": GW to Benjamin Lincoln, 28 August 1788, *PGWCF* 6:483.
       "Unanimity in our": GW to Thomas Nelson, 15 March 1779, Fitzpatrick, *Writings*, 14:246.
       "the Womb of Fate": GW to Robert Howe, 24 September 1781, ibid., 23:132.

173   *"How little"*: James Flexner, *George Washington: Anguish and Farewell* (Boston, 1969), 4:490.
       Fanny Wright: The story is recounted in the historical novel, *Jackson* (1997) by Max Byrd, 342.
       "I should have thought": Nelly Custis Lewis to Jared Sparks, 26 February 1833. Quoted in Johnson, *Washington the Christian*, 244–45.
       "To say that he was not a Christian": Jared Sparks, *Life of George Washington* (Boston, 1843), 520.
       his pew at Christ Church: Rasmussen and Tilton, *Man behind the Myth*, 152.

174   *"practice of Christianity was limited"*: Barry Schwartz, *George Washington: The Making of an American Symbol* (New York, 1987), 175.
       "It is almost inconceivable": Gregg Frazer, "The Political Theology of the American Founding" (Ph.D. dissertation, Claremont University, 2004), 165.

175   *"You would do well"*: GW to Delaware Indian Chiefs, 12 May 1779, Fitzpatrick, *Writings*, 15:55.
       "the warmth of the faith": Douglas Southall Freeman, *George Washington* (New York, 1948), 5:493.
       "Washington's Prayer": GW's Circular Letter to the States, 8 June 1783, Fitzpatrick, *Writings*, 26:496.
       "Divine Author of our blessed Religion": While it is logical to assume it does refer to Christ, it is worth noting that Thomas Jefferson wrote about a plan to change the wording of the Preamble to the Virginia Statute for Religious Freedom. "Where the preamble declares that coercion is a departure from the plan of the holy author of our religion, an amendment was proposed, by inserting the word 'Jesus Christ,' the holy author of our religion. This insertion was rejected by a great majority." Thomas Jefferson, *Autobiography*, 1821. Additionally, the quote is from the Old Testament prophet Micah.
       Church attendance: Mary Thompson of Mount Vernon has compiled a detailed list of George Washington's church attendance. It averages no more than once a month. MVLA.
       "when you ought to have": GW to Burwell Bassett, 28 August 1762, *PGWCL* 7:147.

176   *"Why would one"*: Frazer, "Political Theology," 167.

176 *Both by inclination and principle:* This point is from Garry Wills, *Cincinnatus: George Washington and the Enlightenment* (New York, 1984), 23.

Washington praying on his knees: The problems with this story are well documented in Rupert Hughes, George *Washington: The Savior of the States, 1777–1781* (New York, 1930), 270–98. Samuel Eliot Morison noted in his "The Young Man Washington" (in James Morton Smith, ed., *George Washington: A Profile* [New York, 1969]) that the pious fable "is so little in accord with Washington's character, habits and gentlemanly reticence as to be considered untrue per se."

"All the legends": Boller, *GW and Religion*, 14.

"She never received": Benjamin Chase, "Interview with Ona Judge [Stains]," *The Liberator*, 1 January 1846. John Blassingame, ed., *Slave Testimony* (Baton Rouge, 1977), 246–48. Copy at MVLA.

177 *"in his many letters":* Moncure Conway, quoted in Rupert Hughes, *George Washington: The Human Being and the Hero, 1732–1762* (New York, 1926), 555.

Reverend Dr. Bird Wilson: Hughes, *Savior of the States*, 286.

Bishop William White: Ibid., 287.

"communicate with the Devil": Lafayette to GW, 14 May 1784, *PGWCF* 1:380.

"Being no bigot myself": GW to Lafayette, 15 August 1787, *PGWCF* 5:295.

178 *"I am about to change":* Tobias Lear to Alexander Hamilton, 16 January 1800, *PAH*, 24:198.

"dreary mansions of my fathers": GW to Lafayette, 8 December 1784, *PGWCF* 2:175.

"just bid an eternal farewell": GW to Henry Knox, 27 April 1787, *PGWCF* 5:157.

179 *"I took a final leave of my Mother":* GW to Betty Washington Lewis, 13 September 1789, *PGWP* 4:32.

"I often asked myself": GW to Lafayette, 8 December 1784, *PGWCF* 2:175.

"How was it possible": Quoted in Boller, *GW and Religion*, 89.

"he had frequently disapproved": Thomas Law to Edward Law, 15 December 1799. Copy at the *PGW* at the University of Virginia.

"remember you are a Christian": John Parke Custis to Martha Washington, 5 July 1773, in Joseph E. Fields, ed., *Worthy Partner: The Papers of Martha Washington* (Westport, Conn., 1994), 152–53.

180 *"who hold the keys":* GW to Lafayette, 28 May 1788, *PGWCF* 6:297–98.

"Indeed, my dear General": David Humphreys to GW, 17 July 1785, *PGWCF* 3:131.

Washington Prayer Book. W. Herbert Burk, ed., *Washington's Prayers* (Norristown, Pa., 1907). The original copy is housed at the library of Bard College, which graciously made a typescript copy available to me. A good summary of the case against the Prayer Book's being in George Washington's hand is in Hughes, *Human Being and Hero*, 552–59, which also includes an illustration comparing the handwriting in the Prayer Book with known examples of Washington's handwriting. (Additional illustrations can be found in Frank E. Grizzard's new little book, *The Ways of Providence*, 53–55.) My own examination supports Hughes's and Grizzard's conclusion.

"Even a cursory comparison": Quoted in Grizzard, *Ways of Providence*, 51.

181 *Washington tried to live by three books:* This point is from Henry Wiencek, *Imperfect God: George Washington, His Slaves, and the Creation of America* (New York, 2003), 35.

"The man of religion": Carl Richard, *The Founders and the Classics: Greece, Rome, and the American Enlightenment* (Cambridge, 1995), 185.

Washington "was just": Freeman, *Washington*, 5:500.

182 *Providence is "inscrutable"*: I want to acknowledge my debt to Phil Chase of the *Papers of George Washington* for the point about the impossibility of receiving revealed truth through ministers, etc.

"care to perform the parts": GW to David Humphreys, 23 March 1793, Fitzpatrick, *Writings*, 32:398.

"with the internal consciousness": GW to Chastellux, 18 August 1786, *PGWCF* 4:219.

"found no better guide": GW to Henry Knox, 20 September 1795, Fitzpatrick, *Writings*, 34:310.

"truth thro' any channel": GW to Boston Selectmen, 28 July 1795, ibid., 34:253.

"the importance of religious faith": This point is from James Hutson, *Religion and the Founding of the American Republic* (Washington, D.C., 1998), 80.

"Religion and morality": GW's Farewell Address, 19 September, 1796. The Farewell Address is reprinted in Matthew Spalding, *A Sacred Union of Citizens* (Lanham, Md., 1996), 175ff.

183 *"conventional enough to satisfy most religionists"*: Boller, *GW and Religion*, 64.

"Dr. Rush tells me": Paul L. Ford, ed., *The Works of Thomas Jefferson* (New York, 1904), 1:352. Quoted in Franklin Steiner, *The Religious Beliefs of Our Presidents* (1936). Steiner's article on Washington is readily available on the Web. Also quoted in Boller, *GW and Religion*, 80.

"an unbeliever": Quoted in unpublished talk by Mary Thompson, "Seriously and with Reverence: Religious Practices in George Washington's Family." Copy at MVLA.

184 *"Religious controversies"*: GW to Edward Newenham, 22 June 1792, Fitzpatrick, *Writings*, 32:73.

"Of all the animosities": GW to Edward Newenham, 20 October 1792, ibid., 32:190.

"No man's sentiment": George Washington to George Mason, 3 October 1785, *PGWCF* 3:292. Paul Boller praises Washington's fight against bigotry, particularly in his article, "George Washington and Religious Liberty," *William and Mary Quarterly*, 3rd ser., 16:4 (October, 1960), 486–506.

"If I could have entertained": GW to the General Committee Representing the United Baptist Churches of Virginia, ca. 10 May 1789, Fitzpatrick, *Writings*, 30:321.

"evangelicals would whip": Quoted in Joseph Ellis, *Passionate Sage: The Character and Legacy of John Adams* (New York, 1993), 123.

185 *"While we are contending"*: GW to Benedict Arnold, 14 September 1775, *PGWRV* 1:456.

"We have abundant reason": GW to the Members of the New Church in Baltimore, 27 January 1793, *PGWP* 12:52–53.

"All possess alike liberty": GW To the Hebrew Congregation, 18 August 1790, *PGWP* 6:285. The special emphasis on the "vine and fig tree" is from Brookhiser, *Founding Father*, 147.

"Theistic rationalism": Frazer, "Political Theology," 2.

10. He Died as He Lived

The indispensable primary sources on this subject are Tobias Lear's narrative accounts (a journal account and a diary account) of the death of George Washington, conveniently reprinted with editorial comment in *PGWRT* 4:542–55. How much credence to give Lear's accounts is of course a major consideration. Clearly, he sanitizes Washington's death and downplays some horrific aspects of it. Nevertheless, I believe they have the ring of truth about them, even if they are incomplete and perhaps incorrect in some details. There is a tremendous vividness to a deathbed scene such as Lear witnessed. He wrote about it immediately after the fact, including a private letter to his mother, which he told her not to make public. His account was later supported by Dr. James Craik. It does not seem implausible to me that Washington, who had demonstrated remarkable courage throughout his life and knew this was his final act, would have done everything he possibly could, consistent with human reaction to pain and difficulty in breathing, to end his life in a praiseworthy fashion. I have previously published material on this subject, which forms the basis of this chapter. These works include *The Death of George Washington: He Died as He Lived* (Mount Vernon, 2000) and "The Final Struggle between George Washington and the Grim King: Washington's Attitude toward Death and Afterlife," *Virginia Magazine of History and Biography* (Winter, 1999), reprinted in Don Higginbotham, editor, *George Washington Reconsidered* (Charlottesville, 2001). A fine short account is White McKenzie Wallenborn, "George Washington's Terminal Illness," copy in file at the *Papers of George Washington* at the University of Virginia and also available on their Web site (http://gwpapers.virginia.edu). A great deal of primary material and other helpful information is included in a large information file on George Washington's death compiled by the library of the Mount Vernon Ladies' Association. Dr. David Morens graciously made his large library of material on this subject available to me.

187 *"When the summons comes"*: GW to Burgess Ball, 22 September 1799, *PGWRT* 4:318.

"Who is there that does": GW to Sally Cary Fairfax, 25 September 1758, *PGWCL* 6:42.

"Who, that hath worth": Quoted in Garry Wills, *Cincinnatus: George Washington and the Enlightenment* (New York, 1984), 174.

"How beautiful is death": Joseph Addison, *Cato*, act 4, scene 1.

188 *"The contempt of death"*: Quoted in Samuel Eliot Morison, "The Young Man

Washington," in James Morton Smith, ed., *George Washington: A Profile* (New York, 1969), 46.

188   *"Will you realize"*: Epictetus, *Book 3*. Quoted in Thomas Wolfe, *A Man in Full* (New York, 1998), 475.

"Cowards die many": William Shakespeare, *Julius Caesar*, act 2, scene 2.

"I heard Bulletts": GW to John Augustine Washington, 31 May 1754, *PGWCL* 1:118.

"He would not say so if he had been used": Editorial note, *PGWCL* 1:119.

"to blow out my brains": GW to Robert Dinwiddie, 11 October 1755, *PGWCL* 2:102.

"die by inches": GW to Robert Dinwiddie, 22 April 1756, *PGWCL* 3:33.

"I [have]... the resolution to Face": GW to Robert Dinwiddie, 29 May 1754, *PGWCL* 1:107.

189   *"cool like a bishop"*: This quote was made about Washington in a different context but seems appropriately descriptive for his conduct at Yorktown. Paul Longmore, *The Invention of George Washington* (California, 1988), 138.

"He was incapable of fear": Thomas Jefferson to Walter Jones, 2 January 1814, in Merrill Peterson, ed., *Thomas Jefferson: Writings* (New York, 1984), 1318.

"There is a streak": Noemie Emery, *George Washington: A Biography* (New York, 1976), 378–79.

"I know it is very doubtful": David Humphreys to Martha Washington, 5 July 1800, Joseph E. Fields, ed., *Worthy Partner: The Papers of Martha Washington* (Westport, Conn., 1994), 389.

"Do not flatter me": Rev. John McVickar, "A Domestic Narrative of the Life of Samuel Bard." Quoted in Nordham, *Washington's Relgious Faith*, 28–29.

"seemed less concerned": Martha Washington to Mercy Otis Warren, 12 June 1790, Fields, *Worthy Partner*, 226.

"But to one, who engages": GW to Lafayette, 28 July 1791, *PGWP* 8:377.

"The want of regular exercise": GW to James Craik, 8 September 1789, *PGWP* 4:1.

190   *"entered into an engagement"*: Martha Washington to Elizabeth Powel, 18 December 1797, Fields, *Worthy Partner*, 310.

191   *"It is the duty"*: I wish to credit Frank Grizzard for sharing this quotation with me.

"All must die": GW to Israel Putnam, 19 October 1777, John C. Fitzpatrick, ed., *Writings of George Washington*, 39 vols. (Washington, D.C., 1931–39), 9:401.

"There is a time": GW to James Anderson, 10 December 1799, *PGWRT* 4:466.

"Altho' Bishop": GW to William Pearce, 25 January 1795, Fitzpatrick, *Writings*, 34:103.

"It is happy for old Betty": GW to William Pearce, 1 February 1795, ibid., 34:109.

"Having, through life": GW to Landon Carter, 5 October 1798, *PGWRT* 3:79.

191 *"I was the* first*":* GW to Burgess Ball, 22 September 1799, *PGWRT* 4:318.

192 *"the weather was very":* Tobias Lear to Mary Stillson Lear, 16 December 1799. Copy in information file on GW's death, MVLA.

"Alas! He relied": Thomas Law to Edward Law, 15 December 1799. Copy at the *PGW* office at the University of Virginia.

"Mer. 28 at night": This point is made by Joel Achenbach, *The Grand Idea: George Washington's Potomac and the Race to the West* (New York, 2004), 209.

193 *"he expired without":* Tobias Lear, *Journal Account of the Death of George Washington,* quoted in *PGWRT* 4:545.

"It is a pleasing": Levin Powell to Col. Charles Simms, 18 December 1799, Mount Vernon Condolence Book I, MVLA.

"closes his eyes": Mason Locke Weems, *The Life of Washington,* ed. Peter Onuf (New York, 1996), 135.

"The Beautiful Death": *Alexandria Gazette,* December, 1931. Copy in information file on GW's death, MVLA.

"It is hard to find": George Washington Nordham, "200 Years at Rest: Revisiting the Death of George Washington," *GW Magazine* (George Washington University), Fall, 1999, 19.

"a great thing from him": Bryan Fairfax to Earl of Buchan, 28 January 1800. Copy in information file on GW's death, MVLA.

"who, if his body": Quoted in Willard Sterne Randall, *George Washington: A Life* (New York, 1997), 44.

194 *"A textbook case":* Drooling was not explicitly mentioned but had to have occurred since GW was unable to swallow his saliva and mucus. The three best studies on this subject are White McKenzie Wallenborn, "George Washington's Terminal Illness," copy in file at *PGW;* Heinz H. E. Scheidemandel, M.D., "Did George Washington Die of Quinsy?" *Archives of Otolaryngology* 102 (September, 1976), copy in information file on Washington's death, MVLA; and David Morens, "Death of a President," *New England Journal of Medicine* 341:24 (December, 1999).

195 *"The habits of intimacy":* GW to James McHenry, 3 July 1789, Fitzpatrick, *Writings,* 30:351.

"A mixture of Molasses": Lear, *Journal Account, PGWRT* 4:543.

196 *The theory behind phlebotomy:* Peter Stavrakis, "Heroic medicine, bloodletting, and the sad fate of George Washington," *Maryland Medical Journal* 46:10 (Nov./Dec., 1997), 539.

"copious discharge of the bowels": Quoted in Henriques, *He Died as He Lived,* 35.

"blood and stench and sweat": Richard Norton Smith, *Patriarch: George Washington and the New American Nation* (New York, 1993), 353.

"Speaking which was painful": The account of Drs. Craik and Dick was published in the *Times and Alexandria Advertiser,* 19 December 1799. Copy in information file on GW's death, MVLA.

"Lear later informed Alexander Hamilton": Tobias Lear to Alexander Hamilton, 16 January 1800, *PAH* 24:199.

197 *"He died as he lived"*: Tobias Lear to William Augustine Washington, 15 December 1799. Quoted in Worthington Chauncey Ford, ed., *The Writings of Washington* (14 vols.; New York and London, 1889–93), 14:257.
"George Washington was one of the few": Quoted in Smith, *Patriarch*, 359.
"Don't be afraid.": Lear, *Journal Account*, *PGWRT* 4:543.
We do know that he sat down.: Lear, *Diary Account*, *PGWRT* 4:551.

198 *what Christopher was thinking*: For more on Christopher and GW, see Peter R. Henriques, *The Death of George Washington*, 39–40.
"awesomely organized": Smith, *Patriarch*, 354.
"During the short period": Drs. Craik and Dick's account. Copy in information file on GW's death, MVLA.
"What he had acquired": Douglas Southall Freeman, *George Washington* (New York, 1948), 7:583–84.
"in such a clear": GW to James McHenry, 25 March 1799, *PGWRT* 3:439.

199 *"Arrange & record"*: Lear, *Journal Account*, *PGWRT* 4:545.
"uncommon awareness of self": W. W. Abbot, "An Uncommon Awareness of Self: The Papers of George Washington," *Prologue* 21 (1989), 7. This fine article is also in Higginbotham, *George Washington Reconsidered* and on the Web site maintained by *PGW*, http://gwpapers.virginia.edu
"for her and my papers.": GW to Lund Washington, 20 August 1775, *PGWRV* 1:355.
"have my papers": GW to Lund Washington, 10–17 December 1776, *PGWRV* 7:291.
"At Washington's urging": This is examined in an editorial note in *PGWRT* 4:500.
"immense value to me": GW to Bezaleel Howe, 9 November 1783, Fitzpatrick, *Writings*, 27:238. Quoted in Stanley Weintraub, *General Washington's Christmas Farewell* (New York, 2003), 20.
"finding them marred": Abbot, "An Uncommon Awareness of Self," 15.

200 *"The same self-discipline"*: Freeman, *George Washington*, 7:624.
"This is one of those trying scenes": Patrick Henry to Anne Henry Christian, 15 May 1786. Quoted in William Wirt Henry, *Patrick Henry: Life, Correspondence and Speeches* (New York, 1969) 2:286–87.
"He met death": Dorothy Dandridge Henry to Elizabeth Henry Aylett, no date. At the Patrick Henry Memorial Association, Brookneal, Virginia.
"died like a Roman": Joseph J. Ellis, *His Excellency* (New York, 2004), 269.

201 *"She is now no more"*: GW to Tobias Lear, 30 March 1796, Fitzpatrick, *Writings*, 35:6.
"always walked": GW to Bryan Fairfax, 20 January 1799, *PGWRT* 3:325.
"I die hard": Lear, *Journal Account*, *PGWRT* 4:550.
"Let me go off quietly.": Morens, "Death of a President." Benjamin Rush, on information probably received from Dick, asserted the president's chief concern during the ordeal had not been survival, but rather that his physicians "enable him to die easy."
"without a ray of hope": Quoted in Henriques, *He Died as He Lived*, 46.

202 *"I shall never cease"*: Elisha Dick, "Facts and Observations Relative to the Disease of Cynanche Trachealis, or Croup," *Philadelphia Medical and Physical Journal*, 1809 (May, supplement 3), 253. Copy at MVLA.

Dr. Dick had never: Ibid., 246.

203 *"to grasp at a straw."*: Ibid., 253.

As the microbial storm raged: I wish to credit Joel Achenbach for this analogy.

He was not to be buried: In Lear's slightly later "diary" account he says "three days" which was more customary. Washington most likely said "two days" for that is what Lear wrote the day following his death and repeated to his mother on the 16th. Additionally, Thomas Law, writing on the day after GW's death, used "two days" as well, obviously repeating what Lear told him.

"tis well.": Lear, *Journal Account, PGWRT* 4:551.

"The great body": William Martin, *Citizen Washington* (New York, 1999), 574. This historical novel is the best of its genre on the life of Washington.

"verily a great man": Thomas Jefferson to Walter Jones, 2 January 1814. Paul Leicester Ford, ed., *Writings of Thomas Jefferson*, 10 vols. (New York, 1892–99), 9:451.

"The scene is closed": Quoted in Richard Brookhiser, *Founding Father: Rediscovering George Washington* (New York, 1996), 199, who also points out the Senate got it right.

204 *"Our Washington is no more!"*: John Marshall, 19 December 1799. Most of quote is in Brookhiser, *Founding Father*, 199.

Epilogue

A great many scholars have attempted to sum up George Washington's character. One of the most interesting and perceptive is the concluding chapter of Douglas Southall Freeman's fifth volume on Washington, "By Taking Heed Thereto" (New York, 1948). James Flexner attempts a similar task in his chapter, "Cincinnatus Assayed," in his *George Washington in the American Revolution* (Boston, 1967), as does John Ferling in his chapter "The Character of George Washington" in his study, *First of Men* (Knoxville, 1988). A particularly perceptive summary is the final chapter of Joseph Ellis's biography, *His Excellency* (New York, 2004). I briefly attempted such a summary in my book *The Death of George Washington: He Died as He Lived* (Mount Vernon, 2000, 52–54), and in my short biography for the National Park Service (*George Washington* [2002], 62–64), parts of which are incorporated in this chapter. Noemie Emery's book *Washington: A Biography* (New York, 1976), 376–81, has several keen insights.

205 *"It is not my intention to exaggerate"*: Quoted in Gilbert Chinard, *George Washington as the French Knew Him* (New York, 1940), 62–63.

measurements of the fallen hero: Information file on GW's death, MVLA.

206 *When one looks for examples*: William Rasmussen and Robert Tilton, *George Washington: The Man behind the Myth* (Charlottesville, 1999), xiii.

"Intimates say that he is": Isaac Weld, *Travels through the States of North America*, 2nd ed., 1:106. Copy at MLVA.

206   *"features in his face"*: Weld, *Travels*, 1:93.

     "The passions that stirred": Ellis, *Excellency*, 273–74.

207   *"an unabashed concern"*: Edmund S. Morgan, *The Meaning of Independence* (New York, 1976), 30.

     "constant, wary": Edmund S. Morgan, "The Aloof American," in Don Higginbotham, ed., *George Washington Reconsidered* (Charlottesville, 2001), 289.

     "I expect to reap": GW to the overseers at Mount Vernon, 14 July 1793, John C. Fitzpatrick, ed., *Writings of George Washington*, 39 vols. (Washington, D.C., 1931–39), 33:11.

     "First in war": Quoted in Patricia Brady, *Martha Washington: An American Life* (New York, 2005), 222.

     "I have no wish": GW to Charles Pettit, 16 August 1788, *PGWCF* 6:448.

     "If you can get some Holly Trees": GW to Lund Washington, 10–17 December 1776, *PGWRV* 7:289–91.

208   *his distant, beloved home:* This observation is from David McCullough, *1776* (New York, 2005), 228. He gives a different but similar example to illustrate the point.

     "a grim thing to be plunged": Marcus Cunliffe, *Man and Monument* (Mount Vernon, 1998), 145.

     "Like Faust": Richard Norton Smith, *Patriarch: George Washington and the New American Nation* (New York, 1993), 250.

209   *"I can assure you"*: GW to George Clinton, 25 March 1789, *PGWP* 1:444.

     "It is my express desire": GW's "Final Will and Testament," *PGWRT* 4:491.

     He had a deep and healthy self-love: The next several sentences follow very closely the points made in Peter McNamara, *Noblest Minds* (Lanham, Md., 1999), 70.

     "Thou hast seen Mount Atlas": Addison, *Cato*, act 2, scene 4.

210   *"a very dangerous man"*: Abigail Adams observed that GW "has so happy a faculty of appearing to accommodate and yet carrying his point that if he was not really one of the best intentioned men in the world, he might be a very dangerous one." Quoted in Phyllis Lee Levin, *Abigail Adams: A Biography* (New York, 1987), 261.

     "depend on the prosperity": GW to Lafayette, 19 June 1788, *PGWCF* 6:337.

     "Take his character": See William Shakespeare, *Hamlet*, act 1, scene 2, lines 187–88.

Index